RAINER MARIA RILKE'S
'GEDICHTE AN DIE NACHT'
AN ESSAY IN INTERPRETATION

RAINER MARIA RILKE'S
'GEDICHTE AN DIE NACHT'

AN ESSAY IN INTERPRETATION

ANTHONY STEPHENS

Senior Lecturer in German, University of Sydney

CAMBRIDGE
AT THE UNIVERSITY PRESS

1972

Published by the Syndics of the Cambridge University Press
Bentley House, 200 Euston Road, London NW1 2DB
American Branch: 32 East 57th Street, New York, N.Y.10022
© Cambridge University Press 1972

Library of Congress Catalogue Card Number: 72–178284

ISBN: 0 521 08388 5

Printed in Great Britain
at the University Printing House, Cambridge
(Brooke Crutchley, University Printer)

Uns aber, wo wir Eines meinen, ganz,
ist schon des andern Aufwand fühlbar.

CONTENTS

PREFACE

This study is based on a doctoral thesis submitted in the University of Sydney in August 1968. I wish to thank Professor R. B. Farrell for his great help and encouragement, Professors Ulrich Fülleborn and E. L. Stahl for their valuable suggestions and criticisms and my wife for her help and patience. The study is published with the generous assistance of the Australian Academy of the Humanities.

ANTHONY STEPHENS

ABBREVIATIONS

In the text the following abbreviations will be used for Rilke's works and letters:

SW I, SW II, etc.	*Rainer Maria Rilke. Sämtliche Werke*, 6 vols., ed. Ernst Zinn, Wiesbaden/Frankfurt am Main 1955–1966.
AB I, AB II	*Briefe*, 2 vols. ed. K. Altheim, Wiesbaden 1950.
B. 1902–06, etc.	*Briefe aus den Jahren 1902–1904 etc.*, ed. Ruth Sieber-Rilke and C. Sieber, Leipzig 1930–1937.
BM	*Briefe aus Muzot*, ed. Ruth Sieber-Rilke and Carl Sieber, Leipzig 1937.
BLA-S	*R. M. Rilke, Lou Andreas-Salomé – Briefwechsel*, ed. E. Pfeiffer, 1 vol. Zürich/Wiesbaden 1951.
TF	*Tagebücher aus der Frühzeit*, ed. Ruth Sieber-Rilke and C. Sieber, Leipzig 1942.
BT, 1899–1902	*Briefe und Tagebücher aus der Frühzeit*, Leipzig 1931.

not appear at all with the result that the conflicts and uncertainties in Rilke's poetic thought are very much played down. The method I have chosen is to put the interpretation first and to develop the theories afterwards. So the first part of the study consists of a thematic analysis of the *Gedichte an die Nacht*, undertaken with as few preconceptions as possible. Thus the interpretation of *Die spanische Trilogie*, with which the study begins, leaves a number of questions open which can only be answered later. When dealing with Rilke's poetry, the use of parallel quotations and fragmentary poems is often the only way of establishing the meaning of a given text with any certainty, but throughout the thematic analysis I have tried to preserve a maximum of differentiation and to refrain from premature syntheses, tempting as these may be for the sake of the neatness of the argument.

In the second part of the study there is not so much concentration on the period 1913–14, but rather the results of the first part are given wider application. In the period of the *Gedichte an die Nacht* the meaning of night often comes close to that of the angel in the Elegies, while at other times it has a quite different content or function, and the genesis of this ambivalence can be found in other poems from the period of the *Stunden-Buch* onward. In this way questions arise whose relevance is not confined to the period of the *Gedichte an die Nacht* and these are answered by a theory of Rilke's work which shows the necessity of the incomplete and sometimes contradictory nature of his poetic thought. This involves a discussion of the concepts of 'Gegenständlichkeit' and transcendence in their application to Rilke's poetry.

Considering the amount that has been written on Rilke's poetry, the debt of such a study as the present one to previous secondary literature must necessarily be large. I wish to acknowledge at the outset my debt to Professor Ulrich Fülleborn's book *Das Strukturproblem der späten Lyrik Rilkes*. It provided the stimulus for the study of the *Gedichte an die Nacht* and had a considerable influence on the method pursued here. At the same time, I disagree with Professor Fülleborn on a number of points, particularly on questions of attitude and evaluation. Fülleborn takes Rilke to task for what he terms 'die Unverbindlichkeit' of the poetry and for the speculative quality of much of its content. In this way he arrives at conclusions which I do not share, as I think that the speculative quality of Rilke's poetry can be seen as something entirely positive. Another debt which I would like to acknowledge is to Frau Käte Hamburger's essay on Rilke in her recent book *Philosophie der Dichter*. Other critics, whose work I have found very helpful, are E. C. Mason, H.-E. Holthusen, E. L. Stahl and F. W. Wodtke.

A major point of difference with Fülleborn's work – and indeed with many critics since Fritz Kaufmann's *Sprache als Schöpfung* (1934) and E. C. Mason's *Lebenshaltung und Symbolik* (1939) – is the question of how much importance is to be given to the theme of Rilke's own artistic vocation in his poems. Fülleborn tends to follow Mason in seeing it as a common denominator to which virtually all other themes can be reduced. It is with the exclusiveness of this attitude that I disagree. The theme of Rilke's 'Künstlersehnsucht' is an integral part of his work and it is quite ilegtimate to discover it in poems where it is not one of the explicit themes; but to say that it is the only 'real' meaning of poems which have every appearance of being about something else is surely open to question. As it has been amply shown how this line of interpretation may be applied, very little space is devoted to it here. The aim has been rather to see how else one might interpret the poems and thus offer other possibilities of understanding.

Nevertheless, where many of the familiar Rilkean 'doctrines' are concerned, my attitude is as sceptical as that of Mason or Fülleborn. Rilke's poetry has suffered at the hands of critics who, for reasons of their own, have treated it as divine revelation, as a panacea for the ills of modern man and, above all, as if it were pure philosophy. In present day Germany, Rilke seems well on the way to becoming an untouchable; one is told by serious scholars that his work is 'suspekt'. But it is not Rilke's work which is suspect, but what has been made of it, and the predictable reaction of a generation who saw the vogue for Rilke arise and

I-2

decline is now firmly entrenched. That Rilke, particularly in his letters, did nothing to stop the formation of exaggerated views of his work and that parts of it invite one to treat them like philosophical doctrines, is quite undeniable. On the other hand, his poetic thought is, by a number of criteria, unsatisfactory as philosophy. In Rilke's case one is, as Frau Hamburger says, dealing with the case of 'eine Lyrik *statt* einer Philosophie' and this distinction is very important for the present study.[2] Often it is where the work leaves most to be desired, if one demands philosophical consistency from it, that it is most interesting as poetry. The question of the responsibilities which poetry may incur – whether it must also be a valid religious or social document and be committed to propagating doctrines or attitudes – is answered differently by each phase of each cultural tradition and I see no point in being dogmatic here.

Another point of controversy in Rilke-criticism is the question of what is 'subjective' and what is 'objective' in his poetry. Particularly in the hands of German critics, these two adjectives can acquire such a weight of emotive connotations that Rilke is condemned when something appears to be 'subjektiv', or still worse 'subjektiv-unverbindlich', and rewarded with approbation when the critic finds something he can call 'objektiv' in the work.[3] That the word 'objektiv' usually conceals more emotional prejudices than one finds in a straight-out piece of personal evaluation, has resulted in a fair amount of confusion in Rilke-criticism. While the problem of the subjectivity of experience occurs as a theme in Rilke's work from about 1903 onwards, it is very doubtful whether the poetry itself has any objectivity, other than the very relative sort imparted to it by its place in a given literary tradition. In the present study, Rilke's poetry has none of the metaphysical connotations of 'absolute Dichtung' or 'Seinsdichtung'.[4]

The poems will be interpreted largely with the aim of showing the nature and transformations of 'das lyrische Ich'. Here the emphasis will lie mainly on themes and structure. There is much to be said for approaching Rilke purely from his language and

4

poetic techniques and this has been done in a number of valuable studies.[5] However, I doubt whether it is wise to approach the later Rilke from the point of view of form alone before the content has been thoroughly understood, and the position of the *Gedichte an die Nacht* in the period of composition of the Elegies makes their themes the most immediately interesting aspect. The night has a relatively minor place in the thematic field of the Elegies, but in 1913 Rilke completes the development of this motif in ways which point back to the period of *Malte Laurids Brigge* and *Das Stunden-Buch* and which are closely related to his treatment of the angel.

The period in Rilke's life is one of crisis. His journey through Spain in late 1912 had at first seemed to offer him the necessary confidence and inspiration to complete the Elegies. However, for reasons which remain obscure, there was a sudden reversal and in the poems which he writes in Ronda in January 1913 his disorientation and despair show through clearly. The same is true of his letters of the period and in the year which follows he writes a number of confessional poems, to be found in the 'Entwürfe' in the second volume of the *Sämtliche Werke*, which are as desolate as anything in *Malte Laurids Brigge*. Most of the *Gedichte an die Nacht* are written in Paris, but the city itself does not figure in the poems. Rather, it becomes a place of isolation, a kind of no-man's-land in which the relation of self to world is explored without the rich allusiveness and décor of the Elegies and Sonnets. There is the 'Ich', the night, the angel, the 'Geliebte' and very little else. *Die große Nacht* does invoke specific surroundings, but from its original title *Nacht in der Fremde* and from its similarity with the first poem of *Die spanische Trilogie* it seems likely that this too was a memory of Spain. The period of the *Gedichte an die Nacht* ends with Rilke's meeting with Magda von Hattingberg early in 1914. In the poems to Benvenuta he consciously renounces what he has been trying to do in the poetry of the year before, but the essay *Puppen* written earlier in February 1914 draws the negative conclusions of the *Gedichte an die Nacht* most compellingly. In June of the same year Rilke writes the poem *Wendung*, which it has been fashionable in Rilke-criticism to see as a genuinely new beginning. However I tend to agree with Fülleborn and Frau Hamburger that it is not, but rather, like the poems and letters to Benvenuta or the attempt to write 'aus dem gemeinsamen Herzen' in the *Fünf Gesänge* of August 1914, a false alarm whose significance one can easily exaggerate.[6] To direct one's love inwards towards 'die geschautere Welt', towards images from one's own experience, is only a further step from loving 'die Dinge' themselves in preference to people and this is already formulated in the *Schmargendorfer Tagebuch* of 1899.[7] In fact, I doubt whether the accusation in the poem: 'daß es der Liebe nicht habe' fairly applies to Rilke's attitude to his own store of accumulated images at all. The third poem of *Die spanische Trilogie*, written some eighteen months before, is 'Herz-Werk' in the sense of *Wendung* if anything is, and in the poem *Vor Weihnachten 1914* of a few months later the very possessiveness and aggression which he criticises in the first stanza of *Wendung* is there once again:

> ...O daß
> du immer wieder wehren mußt: genug,
> statt *mehr*! zu rufen, statt Bezug
> in dich zu reißen, wie der Abgrund Bäche?
> Schwächliches Herz. Was soll ein Herz aus Schwäche?
> Heißt Herz-sein nicht Bewältigung?
> Daß aus dem Tier-Kreis mir mit einem Sprung
> der Steinbock auf mein Herzgebirge spränge?   (SW ii, 98)

Rilke was quite right to accuse himself of a failure in love, but this failure was not in his attitude to his own 'inneres Mädchen' but elsewhere, and the poem *Wendung* is a simplification of problems which are better seen in the diversity of the thematic field of the *Gedichte an die Nacht*.

Of necessity a new work on Rilke's must be to some extent criticism of criticism. I have not tried to take account of every mention of every poem, but have included in the text and notes discussions of the work of such critics as Else Buddeberg, O. F. Bollnow, E. C. Mason, August Stahl, F. W. Wodtke, especially where these are representative of certain directions in Rilke-criticism. August Stahl's study of Rilke's imagery appeared when this study was already complete and the field of investigation occasionally coincides. But Stahl's method tends to be descriptive rather than analytical and the aims of the two studies are not very similar. The discussion of the modes of transcendence in Part 2 raises the question of the relation of poetry to philosophy. This has already been treated in E. Heftrich's book *Die Philosophie und Rilke*, although Heftrich's allegiance to Heidegger and his tendency to paraphrase rather than criticise very much limit the usefulness of the study. The view I have taken on general issues is similar to that of the American critic Walther Kaufmann in his essay *Philosophy versus Poetry*.[8] As far as transcendence is concerned, there is a problem of definition and a problem of interpretation and much controversy about Rilke's poetry has resulted from a confusion of the two. Which of the possible definitions of transcendence a critic espouses when dealing with Rilke, will obviously determine his critique or evaluation of Rilke's achievement, and such evaluations have a tendency to interpose between the interpreter and the poem. What is for one critic 'echte Transzendenz' is for another merely a pose or an attempt to counterfeit religion. The fabric of interpretation is often tailored to clothe such attitudes, which may never be made explicit and which may lead to disagreements about the meaning of the poetry that are in fact disagreements about the meaning of a philosophical term. The modes of experience in Rilke's poetry which may in one sense or another be called transcendence are treated in Chapter 7. But since the word must be used in the earlier parts of the study, it is perhaps as well to indicate one, necessarily somewhat arbitrary, understanding of it which will be adhered to. A transcendent entity will be defined by its similarity with the angel of the first two Duino Elegies; that is: by having both splendour and otherness and by being, initially at any rate, beyond the reach of human empathy. The act of transcendence will therefore be the attempt to go beyond the limits of finite existence, as they appear in a given context, and achieve an emotional rapport with such an entity. Obviously, in a successful act of transcendence the otherness of the intentional object will disappear. This is one of the paradoxes surrounding the concept and will be treated further in the final chapter. This definition is admittedly rather narrow and does not cover all the instances in Rilke's work; but as it is used essentially as an instrument of interpretation and not offered as a philosophical proposition, its narrowness may have distinct advantages.

PART I

INTERPRETATION OF THE 'GEDICHTE AN DIE NACHT'

1. 'DIE SPANISCHE TRILOGIE'

Although the three parts of the trilogy are not specifically addressed to the night, they were included in the collection presented to Rudolf Kassner as *Gedichte an die Nacht*, and are chronologically the first of the poems to be written. They were composed in Ronda between the sixth and fourteenth of January 1913.[1] Their importance for an understanding of the whole of the *Gedichte an die Nacht* lies in the fact that they contain many of the themes of the later poems in an extremely condensed form. Since for this reason *Die spanische Trilogie* may serve as an example of the problems of interpretation offered by the collection as a whole, and since a preliminary examination of its themes may well render the themes of the other poems more accessible, this chapter will be concerned with analysing it in detail.

Interpretations of the first poem of the trilogy, notably those of Fülleborn and Käte Hamburger, concur in equating the 'Ding' of which the poem speaks with the kind of poetry which Rilke wanted to write at the time.[2] If we concede at the outset that such a view is tenable, there still remains a great deal to be said about the poem. For there are many aspects which have not been treated at all closely, in particular the situation from which the poem speaks and the possibility of conflicts within the 'Ich' of the poem, which may make the interpretation of the 'Ding' as 'Kunst-Ding' somewhat questionable.

The first poem of the trilogy has the form of a prayer, is cast in a single sentence without a finite principal verb and an effect of increasing intensity is created by the repetition of the three elements: 'Herr', 'mir' and 'das/ein Ding zu machen'. The first six lines present the image of a nocturnal landscape:

Aus dieser Wolke, siehe: die den Stern
so wild verdeckt, der eben war – (und mir),
aus diesem Bergland drüben, das jetzt Nacht,
Nachtwinde hat für eine Zeit – (und mir),
aus diesem Fluß im Talgrund, der den Schein
zerrissner Himmels-Lichtung fängt – (und mir); (SW II, 43f.)

There are clear formal parallels between the three two-line groups. Each begins by pointing to some element of the landscape: 'Aus dieser Wolke, siehe:...aus diesem Bergland drüben ...aus diesem Fluß im Talgrund...', and the use of the demonstratives makes each of these very immediate. Then to each of these three nouns is attached a relative clause, the first two expressing not merely a visual but also a temporal relation between the elements of the scene. This indicates that the observing consciousness is not wholly absorbed in the visual immediacy of the situation, but is aware that it exists only 'für eine Zeit'. The third relative clause however:

> ...der den Schein
> zerrissner Himmels-Lichtung fängt...

does state a purely visual relationship, but one in which the visual elements of the first four lines are in effect brought together in a form of synthesis. The 'Schein/zerrissner Himmels-Lichtung' proceeds from the image of the cloud:

> ...die den Stern
> so wild verdeckt, der eben war –

in that the clouds blowing across the sky make the 'Himmels-Lichtung' ragged, the vehemence of 'so wild verdeckt' being echoed in the word 'zerrissner'. The second relative clause:

> ...das jetzt Nacht
> Nachtwinde hat für eine Zeit –

emphasises the presence of the night and the wind, and provides a direct continuity to the third relative clause. Hence there is a remarkable degree of organisation in the way the scene is presented. The poem establishes first a night-sky with clouds blowing over it, then mountains which 'have' both night and night-wind and thirdly what is in effect the meeting of earth and heavens in the reflection in the river, thus creating a certain harmony and completeness in what the poet perceives. At the same time, this configuration is not seen as something immutable, but as existing precisely 'für eine Zeit', that is to say: against the background of the poet's continuing consciousness.

Now the question of the reiterated '– (und mir)'. After each element of the configuration the self of the poem is introduced as an eventual ingredient of the 'einzig Ding'. But it is significant that whereas the other elements are related to one another in the way shown above, the 'mir' is kept apart, is bracketed, and in line 7 appears almost in opposition to the word 'alledem'. From this we may conclude that while the consciousness perceives, virtually creates an order in what it sees, it is at the same time in some way excluded from this order. In terms of syntax everything in the first six lines is ultimately governed by the preposition 'aus', so that it is left to the lines:

> aus mir und alledem ein einzig Ding
> zu machen, Herr...

to complete the sense of the opening lines. And yet in these lines we already have the persona of the poem both as an organising consciousness and as 'mir', one of the elements of which the 'Ding' is to be composed.

On the one hand there are the various elements of the landscape grouped together in the word 'alledem' and on the other the poet's self. The prayer is directed towards the removal of this separateness, towards the combination of the self with what it perceives in some kind of unity. How this is to come about is not immediately clear. 'Ein einzig Ding/zu machen' may indeed be seen as the task the poet sets himself, that is: the creation of a kind of poetry in which the self and the external world form a unity. But let us examine the rest of the poem.

> ...aus mir und dem Gefühl,
> mit dem die Herde eingekehrt im Pferch
> das große dunkle Nichtmehrsein der Welt
> ausatmend hinnimmt –

Here the poet is aware of the 'Gefühl', but this awareness is not enough to make a final unity of the feeling and the self. The phrase 'das große dunkle Nichtmehrsein der Welt' offers some difficulty. If it is understood as just another way of saying 'Nacht', then there is the problem that the night as presented in the first six lines does not appear as an entity but rather as a quality of the landscape ('...das jetzt Nacht,/Nachtwinde hat für eine Zeit...'). 'Nichtmehrsein der Welt' suggests at once the negation of 'Welt', in the sense of a system of relationships prevailing in the daytime and an actual and powerful presence – one such as we will encounter in some of the later *Gedichte an die Nacht*. Here it remains undefined. It is, however, interesting that the night of the first six lines is an immediate visual phenomenon, whereas 'das große dunkle Nichtmehrsein' does not evoke a direct response in the poet. The response he registers, the 'Gefühl', is that of the herd and between this feeling and what is represented by the word 'mir' there is precisely that lack of empathy which the eventual creation of the 'Ding' would remedy. One could conjecture that an integration of *feeling* between the self and its surroundings might result in, or indeed take the form of an encounter with the night, not merely as a visual pheno-menon but also as an entity possessing power and attributes of its own.

> ...mir und jedem Licht
> im Finstersein der vielen Häuser, Herr:
> ein Ding zu machen; aus den Fremden, denn
> nicht Einen kenn ich, Herr, und mir, und mir
> *ein* Ding zu machen...

Rilke continues to enumerate elements of his environment which are ultimately to be included in the 'Ding' and always with the repetition of 'mir'. The increased fervency, one might say anxiety of tone, is unmistakable and it is significant that this intensification coincides with the introduction of the word 'fremd'. The protest against this separation, this estrangement of the self from its surroundings becomes more audible. It becomes apparent that behind the desire '*ein* Ding zu machen' stands the need to overcome this feeling of privation, of exclusion which emerges more and more strongly as the poem progresses. As evidence for this there is the fact that after line 6 there is no longer the same tendency to perceive ordered relationships among the various external phenomena – what now predominates is their strangeness. It seems in fact that the more elements for inclusion in the 'Ding' the poet enumerates the more the balance between the observing consciousness and that aspect of the self denoted by 'mir' becomes precarious:

> aus vielen Ungenaun und immer mir,
> aus nichts als mir und dem was ich nicht kenn,
> das Ding zu machen...

If we ask what is comprised in the words: 'und dem was ich nicht kenn', the answer comes close to being: everything. When speaking of the strangers, the old men and the children, Rilke insists: 'nicht Einen kenn ich', and the three things which combine to communicate the feeling of exclusion are the repetition of 'fremd' in its various forms, of the phrase 'nicht kennen', and the increased insistence on 'mir': 'und mir und mir', 'und immer mir', 'aus nichts als mir'. The duality of the poet's self which we have observed above devolves into that of a 'wissen von' and a 'nicht kennen' which amounts to desperation. In this sense the poet knows of the feeling with which the herd accepts 'das große dunkle Nichtmehrsein der Welt', but the further stage: 'aus mir und dem Gefühl...ein Ding zu machen' remains to be achieved. So that when the growing fervency of the prayer reaches its climax in the thrice repeated 'Herr Herr Herr' the situation has become simplified to:

> nichts als mir und dem was ich nicht kenn,

to the bare need of the self to be in some way integrated with its environment.

In a letter to Lou Andreas-Salomé, written from Ronda a few weeks before the *Die spanische Trilogie* was composed, we find a somewhat similar situation described:

Wenn ich am Morgen aufwache, so liegt vor meinem offenen Fenster im reinen Raum, ausgeruht, das Gebirg, wie stell ich's nur an, daß mich das nicht innen bewegt...und jetzt sitz ich da und schau und schau bis mir die Augen wehtun, und zeigs mir und sag mirs vor als sollt ich's auswendig lernen und hab's doch nicht und bin so recht einer, dem's nicht gedeiht. (B. 1907–14, 265)

We must seek clarification of the words with which this quotation ends, and it is best to be found in earlier sections of the same letter. In speaking of his response to the landscape of Toledo:

dem wirklich unendlich Erwarteten und doch alle Erwartung
unendlich Übertreffenden athemlos ausgesetzt. . .

Rilke says he felt himself to be 'auf dem Wege zu einer weiteren
Beteiligung am endgültig Daseienden'. It is precisely the lack
of such a 'Beteiligung' that lies behind the words:

. . . und jetzt sitz ich da und schau und schau. . .

and which is expressed in the estrangement, in the 'nicht kennen',
and in the desperate insistence 'und mir und mir' of the first
poem of *Die spanische Trilogie*. And one may also infer that a
'Beteiligung' of this kind is implicit in the concept: 'das Ding
zu machen', which, by being presented in constant opposition
to the estrangement and exclusion, emerges as being tantamount
to a redemption of the self from this state.

Rilke speaks of 'being on the way to a further participation
in ultimately valid existence'. Undoubtedly 'aus mir und alledem
ein Ding zu machen' involves a communication of the self with
its environment, which the intense exercise of the visual sense is
powerless to bring about. It seems, then, that such a participation
would *presuppose* a different state of the self, one may say a
more unified one, than that revealed in the first poem of the
trilogy. In the same letter Rilke quotes the following sentence
from Angela da Foligno:

Quand tous les sages du monde et tous les saints du paradis m'accableraient de
leurs consolations et de leurs promesses, et Dieu lui-même de ses dons, s'il ne
me changeait pas moi-même, s'il ne commençait pas au fond de moi-même une
nouvelle opération, au lieu de me faire du bien, les sages, les saints et Dieu
exaspéreraient au delà de toute expression ma fureur, ma tristesse, ma douleur
et mon aveuglement. (B. 1907–14, 263)

and it is precisely the phrase 'nouvelle opération', meaning a
radical change within the self, which Rilke uses to describe what
has been lacking in his encounter with the Spanish landscape:

. . . kannst Du sehen, daß ich das, was vielleicht bestimmt war, *la nouvelle opération*
zu wirken, nicht bestand. . .

We are then justified in saying that the two concepts: 'das
Ding zu machen' in the poem and 'la nouvelle opération' in the

letters are very closely related to each other. 'La nouvelle opération' is envisaged as something which would change the 'Fremdheit' and 'Nicht-kennen' into a participation in ultimately valid existence and as something to be produced by some outside stimulus or agency. In the letter it seems to be some numinous quality in the landscape – and it may well be because the intervention of some such numinous agency is required that the poem is cast in the form of the prayer.

As we have seen, the phrase 'das Ding zu machen' has been understood to mean 'das Gedicht zu machen', an interpretation which one may certainly justify from Rilke's use of the words 'Ding' and 'Kunst-Ding' in the time of his encounter with Rodin and the composition of the *Neue Gedichte*. And indeed, if we compare some of Rilke's statements of this time with the description of the 'Ding' given in the last three lines of the poem under discussion, there is some similarity in the claims made:

Das Ding ist bestimmt, das Kunst-Ding muß noch bestimmter sein; von allem Zufall fortgenommen, jeder Unklarheit entrückt, der Zeit enthoben und dem Raum gegeben, ist es dauernd geworden, fähig zur Ewigkeit. (BLA-S, 84)

and he says further of Rodin's 'Kunst-Dinge':

...ihre allseitige Loslösung vom Ungewissen, ihr Vollendet- und Gutsein, ihre Unabhängigkeit; sie stehen nicht mehr auf der Erde, sie kreisen um sie.

The image at the end of the poem is not quite identical:

das welthaft-irdisch wie ein Meteor
in seiner Schwere nur die Summe Flugs
zusammennimmt, nichts wiegend als die Ankunft.

Yet in both instances the 'Ding' is seen as something no longer entirely earthbound, of being to some extent emancipated from the law of gravity. Both the 'Ding' likened to the meteor and the 'Kunst-Ding' of the letters claim for the work of art total autonomy, completeness in itself and an 'objectivity' which has strong overtones of transcendence.

The problem arises however, that this 'Ding' is to be made:

aus vielen Ungenaun und immer mir,
aus nichts als mir und dem, was ich nicht kenn,...

which contrasts rather oddly with 'allem Zufall fortgenommen, jeder Unklarheit entrückt' and 'ihre allseitige Loslösung vom Ungewissen'. An essential quality of the poem as 'Kunst-Ding' is that it should be 'ganz mit sich beschäftigt, teilnahmslos', in this sense 'objective' and not at the mercy of the same limiting and destroying forces as its human creator. It is not immediately visible how this transition from the situation of estrangement from 'das Irdische', of exclusion from 'das endgültig Daseiende' to the creation of a poem that is 'welthaft-irdisch wie ein Meteor' is to take place. There is awareness of this difficulty in Frau Hamburger's remarks on the poem,[3] but one may say more explicitly that there seems to be a necessary step omitted. We may see this step as similar to the 'nouvelle opération' demanded by Angela da Foligno. For the poem is as much a prayer for a change to occur in the poet's self as it is for poetic fulfilment. And such fulfilment would surely presuppose both a unity within the self, a harmony of intellect and emotion, and a meaningful relation of the self to its environment. Hence the lines:

> aus nichts als mir und dem, was ich nicht kenn,
> das Ding zu machen,

are, in terms of the situation which the poem presents, asking the impossible. The fact that the poem does not achieve any resolution of the tension between the protest of the self against its situation and the ultimate goal of the creation of the 'Ding' is strikingly emphasised by the poem's syntactic incompleteness – the infinitive construction of the main clause is never resolved into a finite verb.

Such a conflict within the 'lyrisches Ich' is by no means rare in the *Gedichte an die Nacht* and it will be shown that the disunity within the self which such conflicts may produce is of central importance in understanding these poems.[4] Such disunity is closely bound up with the theme of 'Fremdheit', of the alienation of the self from the external world, and contributes in large measure to the difficulty of giving certain of these poems an interpretation which is not ambiguous. This indicates the direction which the subsequent interpretations will take and explains why one may hesitate to see in the poem *only* the desire to produce a certain kind of poetry, for such an interpretation tends to overlook the obstacles which stand between the self and the creation of the 'Ding', obstacles which may be found within the structure of the 'lyrisches Ich'.

These obstacles may be seen as the feeling of alienation from the surroundings and the apparent division of the self into an observing consciousness and an aspect denoted by the word 'mir', which suffers from the lack of any *emotional* communication with the surroundings. The essentially unresolved character of the first poem of the trilogy prevents us from taking this line of interpretation further and so we shall consider the second poem.

> Warum muß einer gehn und fremde Dinge
> so auf sich nehmen, wie vielleicht der Träger
> den fremdlings mehr und mehr gefüllten Marktkorb
> von Stand zu Stand hebt und beladen nachgeht
> und kann nicht sagen: Herr, wozu das Gastmahl? (SW II, 44)

With the change to the third person much of the tension of the first poem has been lost. But nevertheless the first section of this poem is an enquiry into the problem of estrangement, of the lack of a meaningful relation among the objects of experience. The 'Dinge' – here the word is not used in the sense of 'Kunst-Ding' – are experienced as alien, much in the way that the various objects in *Aus dieser Wolke...* were, but with the additional factor that their accumulation in the memory does not make them more meaningful. In these lines the note of protest is more subdued than in the first poem: because the objects of experience seem alien, because the act of perception seems only to emphasise the lack of integration of the self with its environment, this sensitivity to 'Dinge' seems almost, in terms of the simile, an imposition. There are also indications of such a disunity within the 'Ich' as we observed in the first poem. For him experiences seem to make up:

> den fremdlings mehr und mehr gefüllten Marktkorb

– in other words, once experienced they are still not the property of the 'Träger'. So that if there *is* to be a 'Gastmahl', if these experiences are to culminate finally in some meaningful pattern or event he still:

> kann nicht sagen: Herr, wozu das Gastmahl?

He is in some way excluded from it.

The second part of the poem takes up this question again but with the important difference that the comparison with the figure of the 'Träger' has been replaced by that with the figure of the shepherd. The terms of the comparison are by no means as unambiguously negative as in the first five lines:

> Warum muß einer dastehn wie ein Hirt,
> so ausgesetzt dem Übermaß von Einfluß,
> beteiligt so an diesem Raum voll Vorgang,
> daß er gelehnt an einem Baum der Landschaft
> sein Schicksal hätte ohne mehr zu handeln...

Here the emphasis is not so much on the alien nature of what is experienced as on the further implications of this total receptivity to impressions. It might seem that the state of being 'beteiligt so an diesem Raum voll Vorgang' would be a complete solution to the problem of estrangement, so one must try to determine what such a 'Beteiligung' means. Something very close to what Rilke is here describing appears in a fragment written also in Ronda:

> Ich Wissender: oh der ich eingeweiht
> in alles Handeln bin und mich nicht rühre,
> fortwährend tritt der Held aus meiner Türe,
> hinausentschlossen, wie mit mir entzweit. (SW II, 389)

What emerges from this fragment is the degree to which this state of being 'eingeweiht/ in alles Handeln' means a lack of any active participation. For this reason there is the apparent 'Entzweiung' with the hero, whose nature represents the exact opposite. Such a destiny as one might have as 'Wissender' would be quite passive and derived from external influences – 'und mich nicht rühre' – 'ohne mehr zu handeln'. Rilke is here offering a different possibility of experience from that contained in the first poem in the trilogy. However, in a letter to Lou Andreas-Salomé of 10 August 1903, this state of total and indiscriminate receptivity is presented in a very negative light:

> alles jagt durch mich durch, das Wichtige und das Nebensächlichste und es kann sich kein Kern bilden in mir, keine feste Stelle: ich bin nur der Schauplatz einer Reihe innerer Begegnungen, ein Durchgang und kein Haus![5]

and one may detect an echo of this in the lines:

> ...Ihm dringt was anderen
> gerne gehört unwirtlich wie Musik
> und blind ins Blut und wandelt sich vorüber.

In order to gain a clearer understanding of this apparently very ambiguous form of 'Beteiligung' we must consider the figure of the shepherd. He, too, is 'beteiligt so an diesem Raum voll Vorgang', but the 'einer' of the second poem and the 'Hirt' are not identical. As we see from the third poem of the trilogy, the shepherd is an ideal figure:

> ...Noch immer dürfte ein Gott
> heimlich in diese Gestalt und würde nicht minder.

He is characterised by his complete congruity and oneness with his environment:

> Abwechselnd weilt er und zieht, wie selber der Tag,
> und Schatten der Wolken
> durchgehn ihn, als dächte der Raum
> langsam Gedanken für ihn.

What differentiates him from the 'einer' of the second poem is that the latter's sensitivity is too open and lacks the shepherd's stable orientation to his 'Tagwerk', to what 'belongs' to him in the landscape. Whereas the 'einer':

> ...hat doch nicht im viel zu großen Blick
> die stille Milderung der Herde. Hat
> nichts als Welt, hat Welt in jedem Aufschaun,
> in jeder Neigung Welt. Ihm dringt was anderen
> gerne gehört unwirtlich wie Musik
> und blind ins Blut und wandelt sich vorüber.

'Was anderen gerne gehört' – those experiences which for others remain part of the 'Kern' whose absence in himself Rilke laments in the letter quoted – are for the 'einer' of the second poem quite transitory: 'und wandelt sich vorüber' – 'ein Durchgang und kein Haus'.

But when we come to the third section of the second poem, it does seem as though this same mode of experience is shown in yet another, this time more positive light:

> Da steht er nächtens auf und hat den Ruf
> des Vogels draußen schon in seinem Dasein
> und fühlt sich kühn, weil er die ganzen Sterne
> in sein Gesicht nimmt, schwer – o nicht wie einer,
> der der Geliebten diese Nacht bereitet
> und sie verwöhnt mit den gefühlten Himmeln.

These lines are difficult because Rilke is here writing, as it were, poetic shorthand. The motif of the bird-call, the relation of 'Gesicht' to 'Sterne' and the implied rivalry of 'Nacht' and 'Geliebte' are all themes which occur in greater elaboration in other parts of the work. The latter two, particularly, are prominent among those themes explored in the later *Gedichte an die Nacht*. Here, because they occur at the end of the poem in a rather laconic formulation, the terms of which are not further developed in the trilogy, any interpretation must be tentative. One parallel, however, which may throw some light on the meaning of these lines, is to be found in the prose-piece from the year 1913 entitled '*Erlebnis*':

> Er gedachte der Stunde in einem anderen südlichen Garten (Capri), da ein Vogelruf draußen und in seinem Innern übereinstimmend da war, indem er sich gewissermaßen an der Grenze des Körpers nicht brach, beides zu einem ununterbrochenem Raum zusammennahm, in welchem, geheimnisvoll geschützt, nur eine einzige Stelle reinsten tiefsten Bewußtseins blieb. Damals schloß er die Augen, um in einer so großmütigen Erfahrung durch den Kontur seines Leibes nicht beirrt zu sein, und es ging das Unendliche von allen Seiten so vertraulich in ihn über, daß er glauben durfte, das leichte Aufruhn der inzwischen eingetretenen Sterne in seiner Brust zu fühlen. (SW vi, 1040)

The precise meaning of the passage itself and the degree to which it can be called an 'Erlebnis' are themselves matters of dispute,[6] but, to put it in its simplest terms, Rilke is positing or describing here the experience of a complete homogeneity of inner and outer worlds. And one may well conclude that the lines:

Da steht er nächtens auf und hat den Ruf
des Vogels draußen schon in seinem Dasein,

are intended to have a similar meaning. We are then faced with
the problem of how, within the second part of the trilogy, the
estrangement of the self from its environment, present in the
first five lines, becomes the complete homogeneity suggested
by the bird-call motif. The threatening aspect of exposure to the
'Übermaß von Einfluß', which we have previously noted, is
certainly not present in the lines:

Und fühlt sich kühn weil er die ganzen Sterne
in sein Gesicht nimmt, schwer –

and yet this state is left strangely without further development.
Whether 'die Sterne/ in sein Gesicht (nehmen)' is the same or
nearly the same thing as:

daß er glauben durfte, das leichte Aufruhn der inzwischen eingetretenen Sterne
in seiner Brust zu fühlen...

we are not in a position to say from the poem. In view of the
literal differences: 'schwer' as opposed to 'das leichte Aufruhn',
'Gesicht' as opposed to 'Brust', the more active 'nehmen' as
opposed to the quite passive and hesitant 'glauben durfte...zu
fühlen', one should be very wary of equating them. The degree
to which a particular 'Nuancierung' of a situation can alter its
meaning entirely for Rilke has been very adequately shown by
Mason,[7] and must always be considered when dealing with such
poems as this one.

The theme of the 'Geliebte' and the night, of the conflict
which arises in the poet over his devotion to both, is one which
will be dealt with in a later chapter. Here the lines:

...oh nicht wie einer
der der Geliebten diese Nacht bereitet
und sie verwöhnt mir den gefühlten Himmeln.

are best understood in conjunction with the two poems: *Oh wie
haben wir mit welchem Wimmern...Hinweg die ich bat, endlich
mein Lächeln zu kosten...*[8] There, as here, love for the woman

23

is seen as a kind of betrayal of the poet's truest self. The 'Geliebte' usurps, as it were, those feelings, that attention which should be reserved for the encounter with the night, or, in the second case, with the angel. However, we are told, the 'einer' with whom the second poem begins, does not allow this to happen, is presumably faithful to the night. And this raises the possibility that the transition from the highly equivocal value of 'Beteiligung' in the second part of the poem to the much more positive indications of the lines we have just treated, hinges on the word 'nächtens' – that the sensitivity which in the daytime is not quite equal to the 'Übermaß von Einfluß', which for want of 'die stille Milderung der Herde' cannot be as much at one with the landscape as the shepherd, through some quality inherent in the night then comes into its own.

A number of the poems which we shall examine indeed do justify this interpretation. But what is most immediately interesting about the poem is the extraordinary concentration of the material and the way in which the themes modulate into one another without obvious transitions. The quite negative state: 'fremde Dinge auf sich nehmen' of the first five lines becomes 'beteiligt [sein] an diesem Raum voll Vorgang', apparently an opposite state but containing its own negatives in the form of a too great openness to impressions and the lack of any kind of mitigation of this. Then this in turn becomes something very similar to the 'Vogelruf' passage in *Erlebnis* and, indeed, to the concept of 'Weltinnenraum'.[9] Moreover one cannot say that these states exclude one another, for they all seem equally to be possibilities of the self, and such a theme as the extreme openness to impressions may appear both in its negative aspect of 'Fremdheit' and in its positive form as the 'Beteiligung' enjoyed by the shepherd. As in the first poem of the trilogy, the persona of the poem is anything but simple and the transitions from one mode of experience to another, which remain unexplained, suggest once more that the 'lyrisches Ich' has itself become problematical. The enigmatic but apparently very positive conclusion of the poem becomes also tinged with doubt and ambiguity if we read it together with the original ending which Rilke subsequently rejected:

Ihm geht das nah, was nirgend sich bezieht:
als müßte einer der Gestirne Richtung
wie Liebe nehmen und des Sturmes Andrang
wie ein Gefühl nach seinem dumpfen Herzen.
Dies meint uns nicht, doch dieser steht im Weg. (SW II, 390)

These lines strongly suggest that there may be something illusory about the 'Beteiligung' with which the finished version of the poem ends, as if the figure in the poem were to experience things which are quite indifferent in themselves '*wie* Liebe', '*wie* ein Gefühl', whereas in fact 'dies meint uns nicht, doch dieser steht im Weg'. Of course, the poem must stand in the final form its author gave it, but here the adducing of a rejected continuation only serves to confirm what has been suggested: that the poem illuminates different aspects of the same problem, leaving both positive and negative answers open. That it is a poem written very much 'auf dem Wege', is evidenced by the fact that the parallels one may adduce for it reach back as far as 1903, and point forward to the poem *Es winkt zu Fühlung fast aus allen Dingen* of August–September 1914.

Whereas the first poem of the trilogy spoke from an immediate present, and the second in terms of a generality of experience, the third poem begins with a wish for the future:

Daß mir doch, wenn ich wieder der Städte Gedräng
und verwickelten Lärmknäul und die
Wirrsal des Fahrzeugs um mich habe, einzeln,
daß mir doch über das dichte Getrieb
Himmel erinnerte und der erdige Bergrand,
den von drüben heimwärts die Herde betrat...

The motifs of night and stars are not carried over from the second part of the trilogy. What does provide a continuity between the two poems is the figure of the shepherd, which comes to dominate the third poem. But before the shepherd is re-introduced, the poet projects forward to a time when he will again be living in the city, a time which, from the nouns used to denote it: 'Gedräng', 'Lärmknäul', 'Wirrsal', 'Getrieb', has overtones of estrangement and disorientation. In this time he wishes to retain the memory of 'Himmel' and 'erdiger Bergrund' to set against what he has around him. It then emerges from the next lines that this memory is not to be a simple recollection, but rather a re-creation of the landscape, and in particular of the figure of the shepherd in the poet's mind:

> Steinig sei mir zu Mut
> und das Tagwerk des Hirten scheine mir möglich,
> wie er einhergeht und bräunt und mit messendem Steinwurf
> seine Herde besäumt, wo sie sich ausfranst.

The wish 'Steinig sei mir zu Mut' is still projected towards some future time, but the description of the shepherd is in the present, the tense which comes to dominate the poem's syntax much as the figure of the shepherd its content. The motif of the herd appeared in the second poem in terms of the 'stille Milderung' which the poet lacks. Here the shepherd's 'Tagwerk' is seen initially as keeping the herd together, 'mit messendem Steinwurf...besäumt', of preventing it from scattering – that is to say the work consists of limitation, a restriction, but these in a positive sense. At the same time, as we have oberved above, the shepherd is seen as an ideal figure possessed of a certain splendour:

> Langsamen Schrittes, nicht leicht, nachdenklichen Körpers,
> aber im Stehn ist er herrlich. Noch immer dürfte ein Gott
> heimlich in diese Gestalt und würde nicht minder.
> Abwechselnd weilt er und zieht, wie selber der Tag,
> und Schatten der Wolken
> durchgehn ihn, als dächte der Raum
> langsam Gedanken für ihn.

In two senses the shepherd is a mediate figure. He is at once entirely congruous with the landscape, having through his 'Tagwerk' a stable orientation to the environment, and at the same time a complete openness to less earthbound forces: 'noch immer dürfte ein Gott...', 'als dächte der Raum...', so that he is 'beteiligt' both in the material world and in the realm of the more abstract cosmic forces, a meeting-point, as it were, of the two. The second sense in which he is a mediating figure is in his personal meaning for the poet:

> Sei er wer immer für euch. Wie das wehende Nachtlicht
> in den Mantel der Lampe stell ich mich innen in ihn.

The poet, by identifying in his mind with the figure of the shepherd attains the security which has been absent in the rest of the poem. The lack of orientation, the uncertainty and fluctuation of the various states of consciousness and feeling which we have observed, is here crystallised into the image 'wie das wehende Nachtlicht'. It is also significant that what begins as a wish for the future actually becomes fulfilled in the present, within the poem. Thus the trilogy is brought to a definite and positive conclusion:

> Ein Schein wird ruhig. Der Tod
> fände sich reiner zurecht.

Through the mediation of the figure of the shepherd the uncertainty and alienation have become transformed into a new sureness in existence, a confidence in the face of death.[10]

The discussion of the three poems has raised certain questions, which we shall attempt to answer as far as is possible at this stage. Firstly: in what way are the three poems connected to form a trilogy? In the three poems the confrontation of the poet with the same landscape plays an important part. The landscape is that of Ronda where Rilke stayed in December of 1912 and January of 1913. This experience of landscape must be understood in connection with the other major experience of his stay in Spain, that of Toledo. A good deal has been written about this, so that one need here recapitulate only the most salient points.[11]

The initial experience of Toledo was overwhelmingly positive:

> Fürstin, Ihnen das erste Wort, sei es: Hoffnung, und wenn schon gleich wieder
> ein Wunsch mitsprechen darf: es möchte lange kein anderes mir klarwerden,
> damit ich mich in diesem hier arglos und unbegrenzt einrichten kann. (B.
> 1907–14, 246f.)

There is at once a feeling of complete security – 'dieses unbeschreiblich sichere Genommen- und Geführtsein' – of being in the presence of great forces, of being at the meeting point of immanence and transcendence:

wie sehr alles hier im Außerordentlichen vor sich geht, im Überlebensgroßen...
sie (die Stadt) sei in gleichem Maße für die Augen der Verstorbenen, der Leben-
den und der Engel da – ja hier ist ein Gegenstand, der allen den drei, so weit
verschiedenen Gesichtern zugänglich sein möchte... (B. 1907–14, 249)

And it is not surprising that this situation should offer immense possibilities for poetic statement:

Ich muß immer wieder an einen Propheten denken bei dieser Gegend, an einen,
der aufsteht vom Mahl, von der Gastlichkeit, vom Beisammensein, und über
den gleich, auf der Schwelle des Hauses noch, das Prophezeien kommt, die
immense Sehung rücksichtsloser Gesichte...

Clearly there is here a reference to the major poetic task on which Rilke was engaged at the time, the Elegies. The hope of which he speaks to the Fürstin is partly that he himself may receive the 'Diktat', that prophecy may come upon him and bring about completion of the great work. However, this does not occur. For reasons which Rilke says were partly physical, and which in any case need not concern us in examining his poetry, the encounter with Toledo ends in failure,[12] and the letters from Ronda relate experiences which correspond very strongly to parts of the *Die spanische Trilogie*:

aber mir stürzt die Welt jeden Augenblick völlig ein, innen im Blut; und steht
dann draußen eine ganz fremde herum, so ist's eine Fremdheit über die Maßen.
(B. 1907–14, 255)

nun ist's, als wäre mein Herz um Meilen hinausgerückt, ich sehe viele Dinge,
die aufbrechen und die Richtung nehmen darauf zu –, aber ich erfahre nicht,
daß sie ankommen. (B. 1907–14, 258)

So that it is against a background of extremes of hope and despair, of 'Beteiligtsein' and alienation, of a reaching out to encounter transcendence and the lack of any meaningful orientation in the purely immanent world that *Die spanische Trilogie* is written. The focal point of the three poems is, as we have said, the land-scape of Ronda. The first poem raises the problem of 'Fremd-heit' at its most acute, the more so since it is in constant counter-point to a vision of a poetic fulfilment in which this alienation has no place. In the poem itself this dichotomy remains unhealed. The second poem then explores the dangers and the possibilities of a complete receptivity to impressions coming from outside, again in relation to the landscape, and introduces the figure of the shepherd. In the third poem there is firstly the hope that this experience of the landscape will provide some meaningful inner point of orientation in the future, and secondly, when the poet takes refuge as it were in the figure of the shepherd a point of rest is reached. This raises a further question: to what extent are all the problems raised in the trilogy answered in its conclusion? The endings of the first and second poems by no means entirely resolve the situations which they have presented. At the end of the third poem it is made clear enough that the poet *is* not the shepherd, but is able rather to identify with him as an ideal figure in which his own dichotomies do not exist. The words 'Sei er wer immer für euch' at the beginning of the lines where the identification takes place indicates that Rilke does not claim for what follows the same general validity as he later claims in the Elegies for the various solutions offered there. And in fact, as we shall see in examining the later *Gedichte an die Nacht*, the problems raised in *Die spanische Trilogie* are still very much problems. For one thing, the mediation between self and world which the figure of the shepherd here provides, will not always be possible.

Ulrich Fülleborn, in speaking of Rilke's intentions in writing the *Gedichte an die Nacht*, makes an observation which it would be well to discuss in connection with *Die spanische Trilogie*:

In den Nachtgedichten von 1913 und 1914 geht es Rilke um einen mythischen Zyklus, wobei das gestalterische Ziel unzertrennbar verknüpft ist mit dem Willen, unmittelbare religiöse Erschütterung in der Begegnung mit den numinosen Mächten des Kosmos nach dem Vorbild Hölderlins zu erfahren.[13]

Rilke in his initial encounter with Toledo had indeed hoped for some such encounter with numinous forces as is here suggested, and certainly in some of the *Gedichte an die Nacht* the night is sometimes spoken of as having numinous attributes, but this description does not sufficiently take into account the problems of purely immanent existence which have been seen to play a large part in the *Die spanische Trilogie*. This may, to some extent, be explained by Fülleborn's assumption that Rilke is writing directly 'nach dem Vorbilde Hölderlins'. This contradicts Rilke's own view of his relation to Hölderlin as expressed in the poem *An Hölderlin* written in August 1914. Of Hölderlin's poetry he says:

> Dir, du Herrlicher, war, dir war, du Beschwörer, ein ganzes
> Leben das dringende Bild, wenn du es aussprachst (SW II, 93f.)

whereas of the situation from which he is writing:

> ...aus den erfüllten
> Bildern stürzt der Geist zu plötzlich zu füllenden; Seeen
> sind erst im Ewigen. Hier ist Fallen
> das Tüchtigste...

The important phrase here is 'ein ganzes Leben', a unified vision and experience of life which Rilke sees as the basis of Hölderlin's poetry. Later in the poem he says:

> Keiner gab sie erhabener hin, gab sie ans Ganze
> heiler zurück, unbedürftiger...

But for his own situation this wholeness of vision is not a starting point, a basis of poetic expression, but rather an infinitely distant goal: 'Seeen/sind erst im Ewigen'.[14]

So that the poetry which is written from a situation of which Rilke says: 'Hier ist Fallen/das Tüchtigste', must needs be very different from that of Hölderlin. As evidence of the fact that this difference is not merely perceived after the event, that is: after he had failed to make the *Gedichte an die Nacht* 'mythical' poetry in a Hölderlinic sense, we may adduce a letter written from Toledo before the composition of the first *Gedichte an die Nacht*:

Was Sie...meine 'Welt' nennen, das reicht vorderhand nicht hin, jemanden zu nähren und zu erhalten, gerade dagegen muß man Gleichgewicht aufnehmen, um im ganzen zu sein. Mag sein, daß aus den Fragmenten, die man nach und nach vor sich bringt, einmal, im Uberblick, ein Welthaftes wird zu gewahren sein, – aber das hat noch gute Wege bis dahin, ich bin gerade jetzt mehr als je im Einseitigen...(B. 1907–14, 253f.)

This places a different emphasis on the composition of the

Gedichte an die Nacht from that which Fülleborn gives, and, indeed, one which is confirmed by our analysis of *Die spanische Trilogie.*

It has been said above that in the first poem of the trilogy there is not any way suggested in which the transition from the alienation of the self from its environment to the creation of the 'Ding' may come about except by some 'nouvelle opération', by some radical change within the self. This is another way of saying that, by virtue of its disunity and alienation, the self does not have the standpoint from which 'mythische Dichtung' in the Hölderlinic sense is an immediate possibility.[15] So it is that in *Die spanische Trilogie* there is no immediate encounter between the 'Ich' and numinous forces, and no 'unmittelbares Betroffensein' in Fülleborn's sense. That such a 'Betroffensein' is ardently desired goes without saying, but in these poems the problems within the 'lyrisches Ich' itself stand very much in the foreground, and I would venture to suggest that this is very much the case in others of the *Gedichte an die Nacht.* So that the poems, rather than setting out duplicate the achievement of Hölderlin without the necessary basis for doing so, are instead a series of attempts on Rilke's part to attain some standpoint, some unity within himself from which 'ein Welthaftes wird zu gewahren sein', that is to say: from which he as 'ein ganzes Selbst', will be able to reflect in his poetry 'ein ganzes Leben'.

There remains the question: what may we say of the function of the night in *Die spanische Trilogie?* It is difficult here, as in a number of the other poems, to assign it a clear symbolic or connotative value. At the beginning of the first poem it appears purely as an empiric phenomenon, something present 'für eine Zeit', neither threatening nor benevolent. Later in the first poem we have the formulation: 'das große dunkle Nichtmehrsein der Welt', which could be interpreted as denoting some kind of awesome presence. But as the poet contents himself with noting only the response of the herd to it, and does not appear to encounter it directly himself, it cannot be interpreted further at this point. Then in the second poem the word 'nächtens' seems to denote the time of a state of harmony of the inner and outer worlds, but again this is left as an indication, and not developed further. What we may note here is the exploratory nature of Rilke's approach to the night in these poems. In the following chapters we shall be encountering the night in many other guises and manifestations.

2. THE ENCOUNTER WITH
THE NIGHT

This chapter continues the interpretation of the poems begun with *Die spanische Trilogie*. Here and in the two chapters which follow the poems will be treated under broad thematic groupings. Another possibility would have been to take them in the order in which they appear in the 'Schreibbuch' presented to Rudolf Kassner.[1] Against this speaks the fact that too little is known of Rilke's intentions in preparing the *Gedichte an die Nacht* as a collection. The order in which they appear in the book presented to Kassner shows certain divergences from the strict chronological order in which they were composed, but Professor Ernst Zinn holds the view that it would be dangerous to draw conclusions from this as there is no way of telling what Rilke may have had in mind when copying the poems out in 1916.[2] All that one may be certain of is that Rilke felt that the twenty-two poems belonged together and took the trouble of preparing a version of them for a friend whom he held in very high regard. Because of the absence of any clear thematic progression in the poems, they cannot really be read as a cycle and instead one has the task of showing the thematic field of the poems.

Critics have already drawn attention to the apparent inconsistency of these poems. This is not just a matter of one poem failing to begin where another leaves off but is also evidenced by the often bewildering transformations of the chief figures and symbols. The night and the angel, the stars and the 'Geliebte' tend to change their meanings and their relation to the self from poem to poem in a way which often seems quite capricious. It can also happen that what the night appears to represent in one poem is taken over by the angel in another and for this and other delinquencies Rilke has been taken severely to task.[3] Inevitably such questions arise as whether Rilke's angels are real angels, whether they are objective or subjective or both, and this has led to a lot of polemical writing both for and against Rilke. Such issues usually depend on the critic's personal attitude to Rilke, on whether he wants to find in Rilke's work a valid answer to certain religious or philosophical questions, or whether he wishes to attribute to it the splendid isolation of 'absolute Dichtung'. It is also the case that Rilke, perhaps more than any other German writer, tends to bring out some of the irrational presuppositions of 'Literaturwissenschaft', particularly where they are implicitly normative or prescriptive. So the battle rages around works like subjective and objective, 'verbindlich' and 'unverbindlich', 'transzendent' and 'welt-immanent', genuine and spurious, usually without the emotional assumptions of the combatants being admitted as such. Such controversies are signs of a very genuine problem facing Rilke-criticism. It is on the one hand very tempting to try and get at the existential basis of Rilke's poetry, especially as it is so elusive. But attempts to do this often lead to condemnations of the man Rilke which appear strange alongside the intense fascination which his poetry obviously has for the critics concerned. The alternative to this seems to be to take no external point of view whatsoever, but rather to paraphrase and re-paraphrase Rilke's work entirely in its own terms. The great disadvantage of this method is that it is mainly directed towards showing harmony and consistency in Rilke's poetic thought. Furthermore, the attitude here towards the most controversial Rilkean concepts tends to be reverent and uncritical. But Rilke's poetic thought is basically not harmonious and consistent, and one does the work a disservice to gloss over all the inconvenient contradictions and thus make it appear much more harmonious and complete than it is.

In the controversies of Rilke-criticism, Hans Egon Holthusen has always steered a moderate course between these two extremes and he says of the problem of what is real and what is fictitious in Rilke's work:

Der Dichter ist als solcher einer existentiellen Infrageziehung nur schwer zugänglich, denn die Wahrscheinlichkeit seiner Errungenschaften gibt ihm die gleiche Sicherheit, als andere aus dem überzeugendem Besitz der Wahrheit empfangen.[4]

34

My own view is that the question as to the experience of Rilke's poetry needs to be asked, but that it is certainly the most difficult question even to begin to answer. The categories which one may derive from Dilthey's view of 'Erlebnislyrik', from Freudian psychology or from various brands of fashionable philosophy do not seem to have been altogether equal to the task, and I would venture to doubt whether criticism has adequate categories at its disposal yet. A phenomenology of the 'lyrisches Ich' since Rimbaud has yet to be written and until such time as it is, one has to resort to more or less makeshift devices. The method employed here will be to refrain as far as possible from condemning this poem as 'subjektiv-unverbindlich' or praising that as the record of an 'Urerlebnis', but to nevertheless keep the problem of the experience of Rilke's poetry alive by drawing attention to the ways it is treated in Rilke-criticism and by showing the obstacles in the poetry which stand in the way of a plain answer to it. In attempting to show the whole thematic field of the *Gedichte an die Nacht*, the following discussion will often dwell as much on inconsistencies as on consonances. The reasons for this will become apparent in the second part of the book in the chapters devoted to the origins of the ambivalence of 'Nacht' and to the conflicts within the human situation of the poems.

> So angestrengt wider die starke Nacht
> werfen sie ihre Stimmen ins Gelächter,
> das schlecht verbrennt. O aufgelehnte Welt
> voll Weigerung. Und atmet doch den Raum,
> in dem die Sterne gehen. Siehe, dies
> bedürfte nicht und könnte, der Entfernung
> fremd hingegeben, in dem Übermaß
> von Fernen sich ergehen, fort von uns.
> Und nun geruhts und reicht uns ans Gesicht
> wie der Geliebten Aufblick; schlägt sich auf
> uns gegenüber und zerstreut vielleicht
> an uns sein Dasein. Und wir sinds nicht wert.
> Vielleicht entziehts den Engeln etwas Kraft,
> daß nach uns her der Sternenhimmel nachgiebt
> und uns hereinhängt ins getrübte Schicksal.
> Umsonst. Denn wer gewahrts? Und wo es einer

3-2

gewärtig wird: wer darf noch an den Nacht-Raum
die Stirne legen wie ans eigne Fenster?
Wer hat dies nicht verleugnet? Wer hat nicht
in dieses eingeborne Element
gefälschte, schlechte, nachgemachte Nächte
hereingeschleppt und sich daran begnügt?
Wir lassen Götter stehn um gohren Abfall,
denn Götter locken nicht. Sie haben Dasein
und nichts als Dasein, Überfluß von Dasein,
doch nicht Geruch, nicht Wink. Schön wie ein Schwan
auf seiner Ewigkeit grundlosen Fläche:
so zieht der Gott und taucht und schont sein Weiß.

Alles verführt. Der kleine Vogel selbst
tut Zwang an uns aus seinem reinen Laubwerk,
die Blume hat nicht Raum und drängt herüber;
was will der Wind nicht alles? Nur der Gott,
wie eine Säule, läßt vorbei, verteilend
hoch oben, wo er trägt, nach beiden Seiten
die leichte Wölbung seines Gleichmuts. (SW II, 52f.)

In this poem the night is much more in the foreground than in *Die spanische Trilogie*. In the first line it is presented not merely as a region in which events are observed or take place but as a force in itself: 'die starke Nacht'.

The opening lines indicate a group of people in company whose laughter is presented by the poet with overtones of ugliness and falsity:

> werfen sie ihre Stimmen ins Gelächter,
> das schlecht verbrennt.

but this is as specific as the situation becomes. Already in the next words the generalisation is complete:

> ...O aufgelehnte Welt
> voll Weigerung.

The word 'Welt', and particularly the adjective 'welthaft', often have in Rilke's writings the connotations of a complete and harmonious existence.[5] However, here it is clearly used to mean rather 'die gedeutete Welt' common to all human beings, with the possible exception of the poet himself, who perceives but does not take part in the 'Weigerung'. Their refusal is clearly

connected with their resistance to the night, a refusal to acknowledge it, to admit to a relationship which does or should exist:

> ...Und atmet doch den Raum,
> in dem die Sterne gehen.

In these lines the 'Raum' is seen as something of which humanity
essentially partakes. Whereas in other poems, such as *Die große
Nacht*, the accessibility of this region comes as a sudden discovery,
here it is assumed and furnishes the starting point for the poem.
In this way the rightness or wrongness of various human
attitudes towards it becomes a central issue. The next lines:

> ...Siehe, dies
> bedürfte nicht und könnte, der Entfernung
> fremd hingegeben, in dem Übermaß
> von Fernen sich ergehen, fort von uns.

– although their logic is hard to reconcile with the previous use
of 'atmen' – stress the degree to which the 'Nacht-Raum' has
become personified and is seen as an entity capable of volitional
action. They also emphasise indirectly that such alienation as
exists is to be blamed on the 'aufgelehnte Welt'. It is interesting
to note that although the 'Nacht-Raum' is personified as a
benevolent power, it is still presented as 'dies' and 'es':

> Und nun geruhts und reicht uns ans Gesicht
> wie der Geliebten Aufblick; schlägt sich auf
> uns gegenüber und zerstreut vielleicht
> an uns sein Dasein.

Here we may see traces of the conflict, which is virtually permanent in Rilke's thought at the time, as to whether the cosmic
forces which he invokes are to be seen anthropomorphically,
or as completely other and incommensurable. Both attitudes are
taken on different occasions, as we shall see when discussing the
figure of the angel. But even in this one poem the two possibilities
are very much in evidence. For if on the one hand the night is
seen as 'dieses eingeborne Element', the gods who later appear
in the poem are seen as indifferent, silent and unapproachable:
'Nichts ist so stumm wie eines Gottes Mund.' In this part of the

37

poem, however, Rilke is most anxious to stress the possibility of contact between 'es' and man, whereby the night is both the entity encountered and the region in which the contact takes place. This concept of the night as the meeting-place of immanence and transcendence is already fully formulated in the poem *Sterne hinter Oliven* written five years previously:

> ...Ich glaube
> die Erde ist nicht anders als die Nacht.
>
> Sieh, wie im selbstvergessenem Geäste
> das Nächste sich mit Namenlosem mischt;
> man zeigt uns dies; man hält uns nicht wie Gäste
> die man nur nimmt, erheitert und erfrischt. (SW II, 356)

And here, too, the same dualism is presented. Even though the earth may not be 'other than the night', the meeting is still between 'das Nächste', that which is most accessible to human feeling, and 'das Namenlose'. And yet this meeting is under the auspices of yet another anonymous power: '*man* zeigt uns dies'. In this earlier poem, however, the conflicts of the situation are by no means so acute as in *So angestrengt...*, and so the certitude of the above lines gives place in the later poem to a more cautious tone: 'und zerstreut *vielleicht* an uns sein Dasein'. For in the later poem the emphasis is much more on the failure of man to be equal to what the night has to offer:

> ...Und wir sinds nicht wert.

The distinction which exists earlier in the poem between the poet and the 'aufgelehnte Welt' has disappeared, and humanity, the poet included, appear henceforth as 'wir'. With this the initial reproach against the 'Weigerung' has gained something more. For it is no longer simply a question of refusing to acknowledge a relationship which exists, but also of the difference in value between man's actual existence and his possible existence. However, the next lines, again with the caution of a conjecture, re-emphasise the possibility of some interaction between the immanent and transcendent spheres taking place:

> Vielleicht entziehts den Engeln etwas Kraft,
> daß nach uns her der Sternenhimmel nachgiebt
> und uns hereinhängt ins getrübte Schicksal.

This is the first and only mention of angels in the poem. Here they appear almost as a cipher for everything which humanity is not. They are used to suggest the possibility of a non-human, transcendent existence, but more importantly, to stress the role of the night as a possible mediator between the two spheres, much as in *Sterne hinter Oliven* 'das Nächste' mingled with 'das Namenlose'. But this possibility is not taken further at this point, for immediately follow the restrictions:

> Umsonst. Denn wer gewahrts? Und wo es einer
> gewärtig wird: wer darf noch an den Nacht-Raum
> die Stirne lehnen wie ans eigene Fenster?

Here the reproach against the wilful blindness towards the night is once more mixed with the theme of the discrepancy between the two spheres. This latter theme forms one of Rilke's characteristic thought patterns at this time – indeed, the poem *Der du mich mit diesem überhöhtest*...[6] is about little else – and plays an important part in determining the structure of the Elegies. The opening sections of the first two Elegies are both directed towards fixing a seemingly impassable gulf between man and the angels, thus throwing the inadequacy of the human condition into stark relief and providing a tension which the rest of the Elegies must seek to resolve. By resolving this tension, in terms of the poems, Rilke succeeds in imbuing aspects of human existence with something of the same intensity originally posited as characterising the existence of the angels. But in *So angestrengt*... Rilke is not yet concerned with resolving the tension, but rather with exploiting the dissonance to its utmost:

> Wer hat dies nicht verleugnet? Wer hat nicht
> in dieses eingeborne Element
> gefälschte, schlechte, nachgemachte Nächte
> hereingeschleppt und sich daran begnügt?

Of most significance for the *Gedichte an die Nacht* in these lines is the concept of the night as 'dieses eingeborne Element'. Again and again in these poems Rilke struggles with the question of whether the transcendent powers to which he addresses himself are an intensification and extension of something already innate in man or whether they represent something quite other and inaccessible. The fact that this problem does not come near to being solved within the framework of the *Gedichte an die Nacht*, but that rather each apparently definite affirmation either way is tinged with conjecture and at best only provisional is, in part, the cause of what Fülleborn terms 'die Unverbindlichkeit'[7] of these poems. Here Rilke is at once eager to stress the close relationship between night and man, but with the purpose, it seems, of doubly emphasising man's shortcomings. To see how close Rilke may present this relationship as being, let us examine a fragment, originally conceived as part of the Elegies and written in the same month as *So angestrengt...*:

> Unwissend vor dem Himmel meines Lebens,
> anstaunend steh ich. O die großen Sterne.
> Aufgehendes und Niederstieg. Wie still.
> Als wär ich nicht. Nehm ich denn Teil? Entriet ich
> dem reinen Einfluß? Wechselt Flut und Ebbe
> in meinem Blut nach dieser Ordnung? Abtun
> will ich die Wünsche, jeden andern Anschluß,
> mein Herz gewöhnen an sein Fernstes. Besser
> es lebt im Schrecken seiner Sterne, als
> zum Schein beschützt, von einer Näh beschwichtigt. (SW II, 53)

Here what is implicit in the concept 'dieses eingeborne Element' is taken a stage further. At one extreme one could interpret 'Himmel meines Lebens' purely as a metaphor for the greatest possibilities the poet sees awaiting him. Yet the distance he places between these heavens and his actual self at that moment, suggests again the siderial distances of the *Gedichte an die Nacht*: 'Wie still./Als wär ich nicht. Nehm ich denn Teil?'

One might almost say that what Rilke here gives with one hand, he takes with the other. For if in the first line he characterises the heavens as being those of his own life, which taken in isolation might be tantamount to reducing the 'Nacht-Raum' purely to a projection of the self, he at the same time qualifies this by bringing out his own ignorance and uncertainty in the face of what he is positing. Indeed, if the heavens are an extension of the self, it is still very dubious whether there is any more contact between the two than between the 'wir' and the 'Nacht-Raum' of *So angestrengt*...:

> Wechselt Flut und Ebbe
> in meinem Blut nach dieser Ordnung?

What is then achieved by positing the 'Himmel meines Lebens'? Firstly to stress the incompleteness of existence as it is experienced; secondly to postulate a direction in which thoughts and feelings must be turned if some meaningful completeness is to be attained. This function is close to that of the angel in the Elegies. As in the first section of *So angestrengt*... the situation is poised between an extreme negative on the one hand and on the other an 'unsägliche Hoffnung'.[8] So it is clear that the problem is not merely whether the transcendent point of reference is to be understood as on the one hand a 'Hypostase innerer Seelenkräfte',[9] or one of the 'numinose Mächte des Kosmos'[10] on the other, but to see rather what states of the self Rilke is positing and exploring.

This is not to say that one must resort to an 'existentielle Reduktion'[11] in the sense of O. F. Bollnow, which rests on the assumption that the metaphysical element in Rilke is not to be taken entirely seriously, 'hat nicht den gleichen Grad an Verbindlichkeit wie die Deutung des menschlichen Daseins selbst'.[12] For firstly, as Fülleborn points out, how is one to determine what is and what is not 'die Deutung des menschlichen Daseins selbst'?[13] It may, indeed, be the case that what Rilke in his early prose-work *Worpswede* says of the actual landscape may be equally true of the imaginary landscape of his later works:

Immer aber kommt es auf dieses Verhältnis an, nicht zuletzt in der Dichtung, die gerade dann am meisten von der Seele zu sagen weiß, wenn sie die Landschaft gibt, und die verzweifeln müßte, das Tiefste von ihr zu sagen, stünde der Mensch in jenem uferlosen und leeren Raume, in welchen ihn Goya gerne versetzt hat. (SW v, 16)

In this sense the transcendental points of reference which Rilke takes, may well be as revelatory of the human condition as any others. Secondly, Bollnow justifies his existential reduction as the only possible way: 'Rilke wirklich verbindlich ernst zu nehmen.' But has this anything to do with the study of poetry? If one is to require of poetry that it be 'verbindlich' in any sense, this surely implies an ulterior purpose to which one then wishes to put it, else one would be content with the 'Wahrscheinlichkeit' of which Holthusen speaks. In my view the poetry cannot be made responsible for the degree to which it, taken as a whole, suits or does not suit such purposes, conveys what to one writer may appear genuine 'Grunderfahrungen des Herzens'[14] or to another pure speculation.

To return to the lines under consideration, even if the meaning of 'Himmel' is in part that of a projection of the self, it is still a sufficiently far and daring projection to produce 'Schrecken' and 'Staunen' in the situation from which it is projected:

> mein Herz gewöhnen an sein Fernstes. Besser
> es lebt im Schrecken seiner Sterne, als
> zum Schein beschützt, von einer Näh beschwichtigt.

To interpret here 'sein Fernstes' as a cipher for Rilke's own poetic fulfilment is indeed tempting, especially in terms of the rejection of 'das Menschliche' implicit in the last line. However, one must consider that the 'Himmel meines Lebens', unlike the 'Ding' of *Die spanische Trilogie* which is envisaged as something yet to be created, is seen from the beginning of the fragment as something already existing in its entirety, something of which the poet can ask: 'Nehm ich denn Teil?' and the task which he sees before him is: 'mein Herz gewöhnen', which would be a quite uncharacteristic attitude for Rilke to have towards his future writings. Instead, one might suggest that, as in the later poem *An Hölderlin*, the problem of 'ein ganzes Leben' in the sense in which it is meant there is very much in the foreground. The 'Himmel meines Lebens' may be the vision of just such a completeness as Rilke saw in Hölderlin's poetry. The 'Schrecken' and 'Staunen' then serve to bring out the incompleteness of the present, the distance between the actual and the potential.

Moreover, from the limited situation of the present, the nature of 'sein Fernstes' must remain a matter of conjecture. It may be that what is ultimately to complete 'ein ganzes Leben' is the integration with some external transcendent power, or it may be the realisation of certain powers already latent in the self. Whichever it is, the fulfilment symbolised by the 'Sternenhimmel' is still too far removed from the given situation for one to exclude either possibility. Hence if one were to perform an 'existentielle Reduktion' in Bollnow's sense, that is: not take both possibilities equally seriously, then one robs the purely immanent situation of precisely that uncertainty which makes it most interesting. For there is no reason why we should be more eager to apply a final 'either/or' to these situations than Rilke himself was; the dilemma itself, with all its succession of hope, despair, speculations and provisional solutions, is the subject matter of these poems.

The example of this fragment has served to illustrate some of the complexity inherent in the concept of the night as 'dieses eingeborne Element'. The fragment also sheds some light on the 'gefälschte, schlechte, nachgemachte Nächte' of the poem *So angestrengt...* Here Rilke speaks of a perversion or distortion of the experience of the night, of which all are apparently guilty. This is in part the refusal of humanity to admit of the night as something which concerns them, which offers them a higher form of existence. But we may also detect in the lines the theme of the love-experience as something standing between the self and a meaningful encounter with the night. The last lines of the fragment certainly contain this theme:

> ...Besser
> es lebt im Schrecken seiner Sterne, als
> zum Schein beschützt, von einer Näh beschwichtigt.

and make more explicit the false contentment indicated in *So angestrengt...*:

> hereingeschleppt und sich daran begnügt

which again recalls the lines from the second poem of the *Die spanische Trilogie*:

> ...o nicht wie einer,
> der der Geliebten diese Nacht bereitet
> und sie verwöhnt mit den gefühlten Himmeln.

The theme of the 'Geliebte' and the night is one which, because of its complexity, will be treated at length at a later stage. Let it suffice to say for the present that the most extreme expression of the usurping of the place of night by the 'Geliebte' is to be found in the poem *Die Geschwister I*.[15]

In his treatment of the concluding sections of the poem Wodtke says of the transition from the theme of the night to that of the gods:

> Merkwürdigerweise führt er diesen an die Engel verknüpften Gedanken nicht weiter, sondern mißt plötzlich das Versagen des Menschen an den Göttern, deren gleichmütiges Dasein freilich in allem dem Wesen seiner Engel entspricht.[16]

It is true that there is a considerable similarity between the gods here and the angels elsewhere in the poems. However, the immediate question raised by this transition is whether there is a corresponding change in the human attitudes and situations which Rilke has been presenting in the poem. Indeed, the first lines of this section echo the previous condemnation of humanity's wilful blindness towards the night:

> Wir lassen Götter stehen um gohren Abfall,
> denn Götter locken nicht. Sie haben Dasein
> und nichts als Dasein...

but in the next lines the tone of reproach is not sustained. Instead Rilke develops the theme of the uncommunicativeness and otherness of the gods:

> ...Überfluß von Dasein,
> doch nicht Geruch, nicht Wink. Nichts ist so stumm
> wie eines Gottes Mund. Schön wie ein Schwan
> auf seiner Ewigkeit grundlosen Fläche:
> so zieht der Gott und taucht und schont sein Weiß.

The element of the gods is clearly no longer 'dieses eingeborne Element' of the previous section. One may well ask why the gods, rather than the angels which they so much resemble, are named at this point. A possible explanation is that Rilke may here have felt the need to establish a 'Fernstes', a furthest transcendent point of reference, a mode of existence which is still quite inaccessible to humanity. For in the earlier part of the poem the night is 'dieses eingeborne Element', and in this context Rilke has gone so far as to venture the conjecture:

> Vielleicht entziehts den Engeln etwas Kraft,
> daß nach uns her der Sternenhimmel nachgiebt...

which seems to place the sphere of the angels not altogether out of reach. The gods, however, with their complete indifference and silence, are one remove further off. We may, therefore, see the introduction of the gods here as adding a furthest limit to the definition of the region in which the meeting of immanence and transcendence may take place. The poem represents this region as follows: at one extreme there is the world of those who categorically refuse to acknowledge the possibility of this meeting, then there is the night, at once humanity's native element and the sphere of the angels – the place of the possible encounter – and finally, as the other extreme, the existence of the gods with whom no possible contact is envisaged.

In this poem then the positing of the transcendent entities is far from being an 'unverbindliche Zutat'.[17] For it is precisely by these entities that the position of man is defined, and the problems and conflicts which here form the human situation would hardly be meaningful without these entities as points of reference. It is surely significant that, after the introduction of the gods and the theme of their self-sufficiency and inaccessibility, the condemnatory tone of the earlier lines vanishes and the 'wir' are now seen rather as victims than as criminals:

> Alles verführt. Der kleine Vogel selbst
> tut Zwang an uns aus seinem reinen Laubwerk,
> die Blume hat nicht Raum und drängt herüber;
> was will der Wind nicht alles?

It is as if the evocation of the gods forces a re-appraisal of the inadequacies of human existence. These lines could be read as offering some extenuation of the blame for humanity's failure to respond to the night. For in these lines, which recall the second poem of *Die spanische Trilogie*, Rilke touches upon those aspects of experience which, being for him inseparable from an extreme sensitivity to the world of objects, endanger the unity of the self and work against any feeling of identity. If the individual is at the mercy of these forces and influences, then this failure to grasp whatever possibilities of higher existence the night may offer need not be seen solely in terms of a wilful refusal, but may be explained to some extent by his confusion and disorientation in the world of immediate experience. Such a situation is familiar to us both from Rilke's letters and his work. The letter to Lou Andreas-Salomé quoted above, where Rilke laments his inordinate sensitivity to impressions: 'alles jagt durch mich durch... und es kann sich kein Kern bilden in mir, keine feste Stelle', announces a theme which is further elaborated in *Malte Laurids Brigge*, and which recurs in a number of fragments written in the years which follow. We shall briefly examine two of them. The first is dated April 1910:

> Dasein, Beschränkung, was sein und was nicht?
> Was heute sein, was morgen und was nie?
> Nacht ist, die Brunnen gehen, bist du sie?
> Und Sterne stehn, die großen Sterne und
> du hast nicht Kraft vor ihrem Hintergrund
> dich auszuhalten.... (SW II, 375)

The syntax of the first lines indicates that the distinction between the self and the other is far from clear, or constant, and results in confusion as to where the boundaries between the self and the inanimate world lie:

> Nacht ist, die Brunnen gehen, bist du sie?

The 'Beschränkung', which is seen here as a necessary condition of existence, may be understood in the sense of a limitation of the sensitivity, in particular of the capacity for emotional identification with objects in the external world. Such identification is a constant quality of Rilke's poetic experience. In the poem *Fortschritt* from *Das Buch der Bilder* Rilke celebrates it as an aspect of his own poetic development:

> Mit meinen Sinnen, wie mit Vögeln, reiche
> ich in die windigen Himmel aus der Eiche,
> und in den abgebrochenen Tag der Teiche
> sinkt, wie auf Fischen stehend, mein Gefühl. (SW 1, 402)

Here, the power of empathy appears as something entirely productive and desirable, as does the closely related experience:

> ...O, der ich wachsen will,
> ich seh hinaus und *in* mir wächst der Baum.

of the poem *Es winkt zu Fühlung fast aus allen Dingen*. However, Rilke does not always represent this capacity for identification in such positive terms. It has for him other aspects in which it appears as dangerous to the individual's existence, as for example a state in which there is 'keine feste Stelle' in the self, in which existence is felt to be confused and insubstantial. In the fragment we are examining, the dilemma 'was sein und was nicht?' leads directly into one of the main themes of the *Gedichte an die Nacht*:

> Und Sterne stehn, die großen Sterne und
> du hast nicht Kraft vor ihrem Hintergrund
> dich auszuhalten...

Here the impermanence and mutability of the individual is measured against the opposite qualities of the stars, resulting in much the same feeling of weakness and inadequacy as is expressed in the opening lines of the fragment *Unwissend vor dem Himmel meines Lebens*. A connection with the concluding lines of *So angestrengt wider die starke Nacht* may be seen in the fact that the inability to carry out the necessary 'Beschränkung' of one's existence is, if looked at from the other direction, very close to the situation of being helpless to resist the 'Zwang', the distracting and disorienting force of impressions coming from the outside world:

> Alles verführt. Der kleine Vogel selbst
> tut Zwang an uns aus seinem reinen Laubwerk,
> die Blume hat nicht Raum und drängt herüber...

Moreover, in both instances human existence is compared to or confronted with being of another kind – in the poem: 'Götter', in the fragment 'die großen Sterne' – and found wanting. However the comparison with the gods does not give rise to the same bitter condemnations as mark the earlier part of *So angestrengt . . .*, and the words of the fragment 'und hast nicht Kraft' express sorrow rather than self-condemnation. We may use this to explain the change in attitude which occurs in *So angestrengt . . .* after the transition from 'Nacht-Raum' to 'Götter'.

Rilke began the poem by condemning humanity, and by implication himself, for not realising the possibilities offered by the night; the 'Nacht-Raum' is seen as something benevolent and accessible ('und atmet doch den Raum,/in dem die Sterne gehen'). As the poem continues, the tone of reproach is sustained, but the accessibility of the 'Nacht-Raum' becomes more equivocal ('. . . wer darf noch an den Nacht-Raum/die Stirne lehnen wie ans eigne Fenster?'). The transcendent point of reference then changes to the gods, who are quite indifferent and inaccessible, and at the same time humanity is shown, no longer as being in a state of revolt, but rather as being distracted from its true direction by the very nature of its experience of the immediate world ('Alles verführt . . .') and there is a corresponding change of tone from one of denunciation to one almost of lament. Some light has been shed on these transitions by connecting the last section of the poem with the theme of too great openness to outside impressions – the negative converse of 'Weltinnenraum' – which we encountered in the second part of *Die spanische Trilogie* and which may be observed in many variations throughout Rilke's writings. In *So angestrengt . . .* this theme is not elaborated, the poem concludes by reaffirming the distance and self-sufficiency of the gods, and so none of the possibilities of lament are given expression. However, in another fragment from autumn of the same year: *O Herz, vom Leben langsam abgeschnürt . . .*, which is written in a tone of complete despair, this theme appears in perhaps its most violent and extreme formulation in Rilke's work:

Bist versucht
von allen Munden, die an Sinnen saugen,
hineingetaucht in alle Augen,
bist, wie Geruch, von Hunden angespürt...

O Mutter Qual in deinen dichten Stoffen
wo sankest du, Abtragende, zusamm,
an welcher Gramwand...
                      Laß den Mantel offen.
Ich bin zu groß. Dir werd ich wieder Kind,
ich bin zu sichtbar unter diesen Dingen,
Geliebte können mich nicht unterbringen,
die Sonne glänzt mit mir, mich bauscht der Wind.   (SW II, 399)

This is an extreme instance of what appears in the final section of *So angestrengt wider die starke Nacht* in much more enigmatic and restrained terms. This fragment is also interesting in that it has side by side two major themes of *Die spanische Trilogie*: that of the alienation of the individual from life around him:

O Herz, vom Leben langsam abgeschnürt,
wo du es anrührst, schließt sich eine Türe;
...So aufgedeckt wie ein einziges Haus
inmitten Sümpfen, wie der alte Pfahl
an dem verfeindet sich die Wege trennen,
den alle einmal, zweimal, noch ein Mal
anstarren so als müßten sie ihn kennen:
Du Aufgezeigter, wo ist eine Qual
die dich verbärge...

and that of being exposed and helpless in the face of natural forces. Only the latter theme is evident in *So angestrengt wider die starke Nacht*, but the two are closely related, represent equally threatened and negative states of existence and appear with differing nuances and intensities. They may be temporarily resolved, as in the third poem of *Die spanische Trilogie*, one of them may be introduced and not further developed, as in the final section of *So angestrengt wider die starke Nacht*, or they may, as in this fragment, combine in such a desolate vision of life that the poet sees no refuge but in suffering itself: 'O Mutter Qual...'. For in suffering may be found a last proof of existence, if proof can be found nowhere else. And both these states, the one where the individual feels quite cut off from the world around him, the other where he feels too diffused and distracted by the objects of experience to be able to make anything meaningful of them, contribute to the 'Ichverlust', the estrangement from oneself and from the world about one which forms the central experience of *Die Aufzeichnungen des Malte Laurids Brigge* and which, as this fragment so clearly shows, is liable to recur in the period of the *Gedichte an die Nacht*.[18]

The poem *So angestrengt*... is more directly concerned with the possibility of an encounter with 'die starke Nacht' than with the above considerations. Yet from the predominantly pessimistic tone of the poem, and from the connections established between the last section and other variations of the same theme, it seems that the relation of the poet to the night is only one aspect of a complex of problems which includes those raised but not finally solved in *Die spanische Trilogie*. The poem also presented the night in two aspects: firstly, as a force to be encountered and secondly, as an element or medium ('dieses eingeborne Element') which is not inaccessible to humanity. The dual nature of the night is the central theme of the next poem to be examined.

'GEDANKEN DER NACHT' (SW II, 67)

In this poem, written in December 1913, the opening shows no trace of the despair or estrangement present in the poems we have so far examined:

> Gedanken der Nacht, aus geahnter Erfahrung gehoben,
> die schon das fragende Kind mit Schweigen durchdrang,
> langsam denk ich euch auf –, und oben, oben
> nimmt euch der starke Beweis sanft in Empfang.

Here the connection between the individual and the night is established. The 'Gedanken der Nacht' are seen as originating in the poet, and as having been latent in him from childhood. They are directed upwards and in some way received, approved by 'der starke Beweis'. The expression 'aus geahnter Erfahrung' offers some difficulty. The experience, which is presumably that of a meaningful encounter with the night, has existed up till now only as an intimation which now becomes actuality. This implies that the encounter with the night was something predestined and that there was in the child some presentiment that it would take place. Because it is unknowable for what it is until it *has* taken place, the result of the child's asking what this presentiment might mean could only be silence:

> die schon das fragende Kind mit Schweigen durchdrang,

Now, however, this becomes explicit as thoughts of the night, which are offered, perhaps speculatively, and confirmed by whatever entity is up there waiting for them. What is remarkable about this stanza is that the inner and outer worlds are represented as one uninterrupted and homogeneous space. The thoughts originate within, are associated with memories from childhood. Then the verb 'aufdenken' has both a literal meaning – in the sense of conjuring up the thoughts – and a metaphorical meaning: actually ascending into the night to be received by 'der starke Beweis', which is again an abstraction, but which here is made to seem as tangible as the thoughts themselves have become. Such a merging of the inner world into the outer recalls the passage from *Erlebnis* which we referred to in dealing with Part II of *Die spanische Trilogie*:

> ...da ein Vogelruf draußen und in seinem Innern übereinstimmend da war, indem er sich gewissermaßen an der Grenze des Körpers nicht brach, beides zu einem ununterbrochenen Raum zusammennahm, in welchem, geheimnisvoll geschützt, nur eine einzige Stelle reinsten, tiefsten Bewußtseins blieb...

In this passage the unification is brought about by something coming from outside ('ein Vogelruf draußen'), while in the poem a similar effect is achieved by having the thoughts – with no mention of a transition from inner to outer world – take on an almost tangible reality as they rise towards the heavens.

But this unity and wholeness is not only to be seen in spatial terms. For the 'Gedanken der Nacht' have always been present in the poet as a potential experience which would some day take place, and so the confirmation which they now receive unites the present moment of fulfilment to all those presentiments which extend back into childhood. Malte, who feels as estranged from his past as he does from the world about him, says:

Hätte man doch wenigstens seine Erinnerungen. Aber wer hat die? Wäre die Kindheit da, sie ist wie vergraben.   (SW VI, 721)

and the theme of the lack of continuity of the self in time also occurs in a fragmentary poem of early 1913:

> Wir wissen nicht, was wir verbringen: siehe,
> Benanntes ist vorbei und jedes Sein
> erfindet sich im letzten Augenblick
> und will nichts hören... (SW II, 391)

But in the poem *Gedanken der Nacht...* exactly the opposite is the case. Just as there is no estrangement of the self from the outside world, so here the encounter with the night confirms the continuity of the self in time, unites the present experience with those of childhood by resolving the apparent paradox of 'geahnte Erfahrung'. Whereas in other poems the fact that the heavens are seen as eternal and unchanging seems to intensify the poet's awareness of the transience of his own life, here it produces no such reaction. Instead the 'Beweis' of this poem would seem to answer already the questions which appear in a poem written over ten years later:

> Gestirne der Nacht, die ich erwachter gewahre,
> überspannen sie nur das heutige, meine Gesicht,
> oder zugleich das ganze Gesicht meiner Jahre,
> diese Brücken, die ruhen auf Pfeilern von Licht?   (SW II, 177)

In the later poem, too, the poet is eager that his experience of the night should provide proof of the unity and meaningfulness of all his past experience ('das ganze Gesicht meiner Jahre'). But whereas the later poem remains questioning and speculative:

> Wer will dort wandeln? Für wen bin ich Abgrund und Bachbett,
> daß er mich so im weitesten Kreis übergeht –,
> mich überspringt und nimmt wie den Läufer im Schachbrett
> und auf seinem Siege besteht?

the poem we are discussing continues on a note of strong affirmation:

Daß ihr *seid* ist bejaht; daß hier, im gedrängten Behälter,
Nacht zu den Nächten hinzu sich heimlich erzeugt.
Plötzlich: mit welchem Gefühl, steht die unendliche, älter,
über die Schwester *in* mir, die ich berge, gebeugt.

The italicisation of *seid* emphasises that these thoughts do not
merely exist in the poet's mind, but have been confirmed and
proven by some higher power. The verb *sein* when written in
italics generally denotes in Rilke's work some higher and more
valid plane of being on which the problem of transience has been
overcome.[19] Here the poet seems to have attained this in that
'Nacht', which is something eternal, is constantly being created
within him:

...daß hier, im gedrängten Behälter,
Nacht zu den Nächten hinzu sich heimlich erzeugt...

and in the last two lines of the poem this takes the form of a
personal encounter with the night.

What appeared in *So angestrengt*... as a possibility which was
not, or could not be realised, is here presented as fulfilment. From
this poem the sense in which the night might be 'dieses eingeborne Element' becomes clear. For 'Nacht' is indeed seen as
something innate in man: something which is present in the
beginning and which accumulates in the course of time, producing
the thoughts which finally bring about the encounter with 'die
unendliche, älter'. This encounter means the giving of security
and protection: the poet speaks of the night within him as 'die
Schwester *in* mir, die ich berge', and we may understand 'gebeugt'
as a similar protective gesture on the part of the elder, greater
power towards whom the 'Gedanken der Nacht' were directed.
Again, in the conclusion of the poem, the lack of any division
between inner and outer worlds is stressed. The night stands
stooped over its 'sister', in the poet, denoting not only a reciprocity of feeling between man and some cosmic power, but also
a fusing of inner and outer reality into one. The infinite night
and the poet's consciousness share the same space. It is interesting
to note that whereas the initial approach to the night was by way
of thought, the meeting explicitly culminates in feeling: 'Plötz-

lich, mit welchem Gefühl'. This may be seen as another of the reconciliations which the poem effects. For in it present and past, inner and outer reality, 'Ich' and 'Nacht' and finally thought and feeling all partake of the same wholeness and reciprocity. One may well ask what has become of all the problematical and negative aspects of the situation which *So angestrengt wider die starke Nacht* portrays, and by asking this one is brought to one of the central difficulties of interpreting the *Gedichte an die Nacht*.

Neither the experience of this poem, nor the closely related one at the conclusion of *Die große Nacht* provide Rilke with a permanent standpoint from which he can see man's existence as justified and the problems of the human situation as solved by the 'starker Beweis' or the 'auf weite Ernste verteiltes/ Lächeln' of the night. Fülleborn is right in denying on these grounds that the *Gedichte an die Nacht* form a true cycle. But admitting that this paradox exists, that poems which have every appearance of being 'verbindlich' are in fact not so, that an apparent mystic union does not serve to place the relation of self and world in Rilke's poetry on a new basis of religious confidence, does not mean that one must also concur with Fülleborn's strictures against Rilke. It seems more important to inquire with as much detachment as possible into the nature of this paradox, rather than rush to judgment on a writer whose complexity and nearness to us in time makes such evaluation very difficult. For without enquiring whether the man Rilke did or did not have such and such an experience of the night – which is surely idle – we may still ask to what extent are the problems of existence as Rilke has posed them in *Die spanische Trilogie* and *So angestrengt* susceptible of being solved by the poetic representation of such an experience as we find in *Gedanken der Nacht*. Certainly a number of things which appear as negatives in these other poems appear in *Gedanken der Nacht* as positives.

But this is not to say that these themes need not recur again in just as negative a form. There is in fact more to solving these problems than simply presenting their opposites as actual experiences, and this is borne out by the fact that the *Gedichte an die Nacht* do not form a complete mythical cycle. For within the whole thematic field of the poems, such statements as the conclusion of *Gedanken der Nacht* have a similar function to the description of the gods at the end of *So angestrengt*. There they represent a complete and fulfilled mode of being and, though humanity can apparently have no part of this, the introduction of the gods into the poem significantly alters the perspective of the human situation. The appearance of the gods expands and modifies the field of the poem, obliging the reader to re-assess what has been understood from the preceding lines. In the same way, the fulfilment of *Gedanken der Nacht* illuminates another segment of the thematic field of the whole collection and provides a thematic counterpoint to other poems which speak only of suffering and privation. It obliges us to enquire *why* such apparent solutions are only aspects of a crisis and do not mean its overcoming.

But to proceed for the moment with the thematic analysis, the poem *Gedanken der Nacht* demonstrates further the range of meanings which the word 'Nacht' may contain. As in the first part of *Die spanische Trilogie*, the night is present as an external phenomenon. However, these thoughts have something of the quality of the gradual coming to awareness of the 'höheres Ich' of which Novalis speaks in *Heinrich von Ofterdingen* and in a number of fragments. In Novalis' sense, they are an *a priori* phenomenon: something latent in the individual as a presentiment of his higher self and of his original and future existence. At the appropriate time they become explicit and are then recognised as having been always there *in posse*, so that in this poem the night is perceived and experienced as 'dieses eingeborne Element'. Then there is the question of 'der starke Beweis'. It is not stated who grants or performs this proof – it may be the night itself, or it may be some still higher, anonymous power, reminiscent of *Sterne hinter Oliven*.[20] We should not neglect this possibility, for it is sometimes the case that the night is not the ultimate reality, but rather an instrument or mask for something or someone beyond it:

Der du mich mit diesen überhöhtest:
Nächten – ist es nicht, als ob du mir,
Unbegrenzter, mehr Gefühl gebötest,
als ich fühlend fasse? (SW ii, 68)

However, the poem does not permit any final conclusion on this point. The 'proof' can indeed be seen as something abstract and intellectual, and so would correspond to the fact that the initial approach to the night is by way of thought. But it is typical of Rilke's tendency to endow abstractions with an almost tangible reality, that the 'Beweis' comes to have a power of its own.

In the second stanza of the poem, the idea of the night as an innate element of the self is extended to the statement that it is something being continually created within the poet, though the word 'heimlich' suggests that this process is something he is not always conscious of. This is what the poet sees as 'die Schwester in mir' – something which is both part of himself and of the same nature and substance as 'die unendliche', so that the night in this poem is at once 'das Nächste' and 'das Namenlose', the unification of immanence and transcendence. Furthermore, the night and the poet's consciousness together form a single region or medium in which the encounter takes place.

It is clear from this that the night cannot be seen entirely as one of the 'numinose Mächte des Kosmos', but that the single word may have a wide range of meanings, extending from the partly known region of the poet's self towards those regions which for Rilke ultimately remain unknown.[21] The problem of what is meant to be transcendent, in the sense of the completely other, and what is not, is thus complicated by the difficulty of knowing what aspects of the total possible meaning of night Rilke is presenting on each separate occasion. Wodtke has rightly drawn attention to the fluidity and ambivalence of such symbols as this one in Rilke's poetry, and concludes that such transcendence 'entsteht von Fall zu Fall im existentiellen Augenblick'. However, the fact that these symbols cannot be assigned one definite meaning need not prevent us from exploring as many possible meanings as are contained in the *Gedichte an die Nacht*, from establishing connections from poem to poem where they are evident and from noting such inconsistencies as may arise. Moreover, this variability is not so much a question of the poet seeing differently in each 'existentieller Augenblick', but rather of Rilke's continually expanding and modifying the field of reference of these poems by presenting certain central problems and situations in a wide variety of forms. We can know very little of what experiences contributed directly or indirectly to the composition of these poems. The excellent analyses by which Fülleborn attempts to effect the 'Rückgang auf das Ausgedrückte' nevertheless show precisely what is questionable in this procedure by passing all too rapidly into somewhat polemical evaluation – '...so erhellt daraus, in welchem Maße der Mensch bei einem solchen "Erlebnis" leer ausgeht'[22] – or by dismissing as 'uneigentlich' the complexity of the surface of the poem. The analysis of *Gedanken der Nacht* has very clearly raised the problem and indicated some of the obstacles which stand in the way of a simple solution. However, one cannot attempt to solve it until one has seen what other forms it takes in others of the *Gedichte an die Nacht*.

'DIE GROSSE NACHT' (SW II, 74)

Oft anstaunt ich dich, stand an gestern begonnenem Fenster,
stand und staunte dich an. Noch war mir die neue
Stadt wie verwehrt, und die unüberredete Landschaft
finsterte hin, als wäre ich nicht... (SW II, 74)

In the first lines the striking use of 'anstaunen' as an inseparable verb has been rightly explained by Fülleborn as giving the poem an immediate and forceful beginning.[23] The word 'oft' presents grave difficulties of interpretation; it refers back in time, but how far back? It refers initially to the verb 'anstaunen', but does it also extend to the rest of the poem as well?[24] Now it is by no means clear that the word 'oft' is meant to refer to the whole poem. The situation which Rilke recounts in great particularity need extend no further back in time than the yesterday of his arrival in the strange city and need embrace only what has taken place since the arrival. There is no suggestion in such statements as:

> ...Und dann weinte ein Kind. Ich wußte die Mütter
> rings in den Häusern, was sie vermögen –
>
> ...Dann schlug eine Stunde –
> aber ich zählte zu spät, sie fiel mir vorüber.

that Rilke is describing a series of similar occasions, or, indeed, that this occasion is meant to be representative of many. The word 'oft' certainly refers to 'anstaunen', and this astonishment may well be seen as occurring on occasions before the actual time of which the poem speaks but 'anstaunen' alone does not imply the rest of the experience. One might paraphrase the beginning of the poem as follows: the poet has often felt astonishment and incomprehension in the face of 'die große Nacht' – indeed, this astonishment in the form of '*an*–staunen' has something conscious and directed about it – and at the window at which he yesterday 'began', that is: which became from the time of his arrival in the new city the place from which he directed his thoughts and feelings towards the outside world, this act of 'anstaunen' is repeated.

The poet is aware of the greatness and splendour of the night but it is just as inaccessible to his feelings and understanding as is the city and the landscape around it:

> ...Noch war mir die neue
> Stadt wie verwehrt, und die unüberredete Landschaft
> finsterte hin, als wäre ich nicht...

Thus 'anstaunen' does not imply that the union with the night will necessarily follow. Rilke in fact uses it elsewhere in a context where such a union emphatically does not take place, in the fragment already quoted above:

> Unwissend vor dem Himmel meines Lebens,
> anstaunend steh ich. O die großen Sterne.
> Aufgehendes und Niederstieg. Wie still.
> Als wär ich nicht. Nehm ich denn Teil? Entriet ich
> dem reinen Einfluß? (SW II, 53)

Here again doubt and incomprehension are inextricably bound up with the feelings of wonder, and the occurrence of the words 'als wär ich nicht' in both cases suggests that in the act of 'anstaunen' there may be initially a feeling of exclusion from any close participation with its object. This is something which Rilke may well have often felt towards the night, without the situation resulting in any union with it. In the case of *Die große Nacht* this is the starting-point, and the poem goes on to record one instance where this incomprehension gave way to understanding, and where a contact with the night did take place.

There is a close thematic similarity between this poem and the first poem of *Die spanische Trilogie*. There is the same feeling of alienation from the surroundings and the same desire to overcome this:

> ...Nicht gaben die nächsten
> Dinge sich Müh, mir verständlich zu sein. An der Laterne
> drängte die Gasse herauf: ich sah, daß sie fremd war.
> Drüben – ein Zimmer, mitfühlbar, geklärt in der Lampe –
> schon nahm ich Teil; sie empfandens, schlossen die Läden.

The word 'fremd' indicates that once more the poem is directed towards the finding of some kind of 'Beteiligung'. Whereas in the *Die spanische Trilogie* this was seen in terms of the 'Ding' yet to be made, here the poet reaches out much more directly towards something which is 'mitfühlbar' and is much more explicitly rejected. Again the poem takes up the theme of 'wissen von' and 'nicht kennen':

> Stand. Und dann weinte ein Kind. Ich wußte die Mütter
> rings in den Häusern, was sie vermögen – und wußte
> alles Weinens zugleich die untröstlichen Gründe.
> Oder es sang eine Stimme und reichte ein Stück weit
> aus der Erwartung heraus, oder es hustete unten
> voller Vorwurf ein Alter, als ob sein Körper im Recht sei
> wider die mildere Welt.

In these lines the poet's attention is directed away from the night and towards 'die nächsten Dinge' and the other people whom he knows to be in the houses about him. It is interesting that these recall the old men and children of the first poem of *Die spanische Trilogie*:

> ...aus den Schlafenden,
> den fremden alten Männern im Hospiz,
> die wichtig in den Betten husten, aus
> schlaftrunknen Kindern an so fremder Brust...

Here there is a recapitulation of one of the central themes of the *Gedichte an die Nacht*: the isolation of the self in a world that seems closed to it. The poet is unable to fasten on to any object or person or event in the world around him:

> ...Dann schlug eine Stunde –
> aber ich zählte zu spät, sie fiel mir vorüber.

Then follows the image of the children playing with a ball:

> Wie ein Knabe, ein fremder, wenn man endlich ihn zuläßt,
> doch den Ball nicht fängt und keines der Spiele
> kann, die die andern so leicht an einander betreiben,
> dasteht und wegschaut – wohin – ?

This has been interpreted by Bollnow as follows:

Das Verhältnis des Menschen zur Nacht wird mit der Lage des Kinds verglichen, das von den Kameraden zum Ballspiel aufgefordert wird und doch nicht mitspielen kann... Die Nacht, oder um die Symbolik aufzulösen: das Unheimliche wird hier personifiziert und vom Menschen angeredet...[25]

But the image of the ball-game is not one of the poet's relation to the night, but rather to what the poem has been speaking of for the last fifteen lines: the immediate surroundings, from which he feels excluded like a child shut out by the others from the game: 'sie empfandens, schlossen die Läden' – a game to which he cannot synchronise his own thoughts or movements: 'aber ich zählte zu spät, sie fiel mir vorüber'. So these lines are a summation of the theme of 'Fremdheit', of the lack of any contact with 'die nächsten Dinge'. Nor is the night a symbol for 'das Unheimliche'. After the initial 'anstaunen' directed towards the night, the poet turns to his immediate environment and such 'Unheimlichkeit' as there is arises from his own feeling of exclusion from it. The actual turning of the poem comes not at the beginning of the image of the game, but at the end:

dasteht und wegschaut – wohin – ? stand ich und plötzlich
daß *du* umgehst mit mir, spielest, begriff ich, erwachsene
Nacht und staunte dich an.

Just as a child, who has tried to join in the game going on around
him and failed to do so through not knowing it or being too
clumsy, may give up, lose interest and look *elsewhere* for something to do, so the poet accepts that his immediate surroundings
remain closed to him, and turns his attention away from them:
'wegschaut, – wohin – ?' In doing so he realises ('begriff ich')
that he has been seeking 'Beteiligung' in the wrong direction,
that in fact it was there all the time but in the quarter where he
least expected it: not in the 'children's game' of his immediate
surroundings but with the 'erwachsene Nacht' which up till
now had perhaps seemed more distant and less accessible still.
This is not as Bollnow says:

Wie das Kind den Ball, so soll der Mensch das Gefühl der Unheimlichkeit *fangen*
und weiterwerfen, also in einer bestimmten Weise darauf reagieren.[26]

for the contact with the night does not come about by anything
so active. The poem defines the transition as looking away and
understanding. There is no mention of the ball-game being
resumed, or of feelings being thrown in any direction. After the
single act of *understanding* the poet's role becomes entirely
passive.[27] Again the word 'anstaunen' is used, but this time with
a different content: it is now the astonishment which results
from the realisation that the night does not share the indifference
of his surroundings, but rather that this 'adult' power has a
benevolent interest in him. We must distinguish, as we have
done with other poems, between night as merely an aspect of the
surroundings, and night as a supernatural entity. What manner
of game the night is playing the poem does not say, however,
the fact that the verbs 'umgehst' and 'spielest' are in the present
suggests that this is something which has been going on the
whole time and that the poet only now becomes aware of it.
This accords with the concept of the relation of man to night
present both in *So angestrengt* and *Gedanken der Nacht*. In the
former, the contact with the night is seen as a possibility which is

always open but rarely perceived, and in the latter the contact takes place as a result of the poet becoming aware of the night as something innate in him and formulating this in thoughts.

So we may conclude that the 'Umschlag' of the poem, from 'Fremdheit' to 'Beteiligung' comes about by a new and sudden understanding within the poet himself. However, the poem does not immediately go on to a triumphant conclusion. Instead there is a recapitulation of the theme of 'Fremdheit':

> ...Wo die Türme
> zürnten, wo abgewendeten Schicksals
> eine Stadt mich umstand und nicht zu erratende Berge
> wider mich lagen, und im genäherten Umkreis
> hungernde Fremdheit umzog das zufällige Flackern
> meine Gefühle –

Here the city and the landscape are not merely indifferent, but also menacing: 'wider mich lagen, hungernde Fremdheit'. Bollnow is right to ask:

Warum aber wird diese unheimliche Situation des Menschen zum zweiten Mal geschildert? Ist es nicht einfach eine Wiederholung?

but the answer he gives is hardly convincing.[28] What this repetition does is to stress the fact that the alienation of the self from its immediate environment has *not* been overcome, that it is co-existent with the new contact with the night. Bollnow, by interpreting 'die große Nacht' as a personification of 'Unheimlichkeit' rather than as its opposite, misses the difference between the benevolent entity whom Rilke addresses as 'erwachsene Nacht' and 'du Hohe' and the 'hungernde Fremdheit' of the poet's immediate environment. It is wrong to see the turning of the poem in a sudden resolution to look this 'Fremdheit' or 'Unheimlichkeit' in the face, for this is what the poet has been doing from the beginning in the detailed enumeration of the instances of his failure to make contact with the things and people around him. The turning comes when the poet gives up the attempt and looks away, becoming aware that the night has always been offering what he has vainly looked for in this 'Fremdheit'. The sense of the repetition is then that, although this alienation from his surroundings remains, he has found contact on a higher level: the two things exist in his consciousness at the same time. The self is not reconciled to its environment, any more than it is in the first poem of *Die spanische Trilogie*, but finds refuge in a power which stands outside and above the place where:

> ...im genäherten Umkreis
> hungernde Fremdheit umzog das zufällige Flackern
> meiner Gefühle –:

His feelings remain fortuitous in relation to the city and his immediate surroundings, it is only in the reciprocal feeling of the night that they acquire a direction and meaning:

> ...Dein Atem
> ging über mich; dein auf weite Ernste verteiltes
> Lächeln trat in mich ein.

To this extent Bollnow is right in terming what the poet achieves at the end of the poem a 'Halt im Unendlichen' – so it is, but one which leaves the problem of a 'Halt im Endlichen' still unsolved. This admittedly dualistic interpretation is in no way un-Rilkean, but is perhaps in need of some further justification.

The poem *Gedanken der Nacht* can be seen as a prefiguration of the conclusion of *Die große Nacht*. In the former poem the contact is instigated by the poet's directing his thoughts towards the night and having the rightness of this confirmed. He does not do so because of any stimulus from outside, but because he becomes aware of certain possibilities which have been always present in him, of a part of himself which is 'Nacht' and which calls forth a response in terms of feeling from the benevolent 'elder' entity – a striking parallel to the 'erwachsene Nacht' – which secures his existence. In the latter poem the poet's initial attitude to the night is that of 'anstaunen', which is apparently fruitless as he then turns to his surroundings, the description of which occupies the greater part of the poem. But when the unresponsiveness of these reaches a maximum in the image of the child who cannot join in the ball game, he turns away and in that moment, as it were, makes contact with the night in himself and hence *realises* the relation that exists between him and the power which before he could only regard with wonder and confusion. This gives a new quality to his astonishment, as he sees that while he was suffering in his lack of contact with immanent reality, he was 'known' all the time by some transcendent power. As in *Gedanken der Nacht* his coming to awareness of this enables the contact – 'Dein auf weite Ernste verteiltes/Lächeln trat in mich ein' – to take place. The 'astonishment' here is thus quite different from that at the beginning of the poem. So far the similarities between the two poems. However, the differences between them are equally interesting. For in *Gedanken der Nacht* there is no mention of anything but the poet and the night: the encounter takes place in no specific surroundings and there is no hint of any obstructing or negative element in the experience. However in *Die große Nacht* the theme of 'Fremdheit' is developed as fully as in *Die spanische Trilogie* and stands in clear opposition to that of the union with the night. To dismiss this as Fülleborn does: 'Alles bisherige war nur Kontrastfolie für das "plötzlich" eintretende Geschehen...' is to distort the meaning of the poem.[29] Precisely the recapitulation of the 'Fremdheit'-theme *after* the contact with the night has been established shows that it is not simply a foil, but that the two states must be seen as existing together. The continued 'Fremdheit' does not prevent the union with the night from taking place, but neither does the latter make, in the words of *Die spanische Trilogie*:

aus mir und alledem ein einzig Ding.

This interpretation explains to some extent why poems such as *Gedanken der Nacht* and *Die große Nacht*, for all that they may present experiences of union, are in a sense inconclusive, do not effect a fundamental change in Rilke's poetry by giving it a new and unshakable basis from which to develop. For just as the union with the night is only one of the themes developed in the *Gedichte an die Nacht*, so it may also be seen to secure only *part* of the poet's existence as he represents it in his poems. It does not in itself produce 'ein ganzes Leben', because it is essentially something apart from the problems which the self faces in the world of objects and other people. There is in the turning to the night an implicit turning away from these problems, a leaping over them, as it were, which leaves them unsolved and likely to re-assert themselves when the 'Lächeln' of the night is no longer present. In a letter written shortly after his return from Spain Rilke says:

...denn da ich mich, von Dingen und Tieren gründlich herkommend, danach sehnte, im Menschlichen ausgebildet zu sein, da wurde mir, siehe, das Übernächste, das Engelische beigebracht, und darum habe ich die Leute übersprungen und schau zu ihnen zurück mit Herzlichkeit. (B. 1907–14, 275)

The poetry Rilke writes in the next two years shows this to be *partly* true. For in the *Gedichte an die Nacht* there are clear signs of an attempt to substitute a relation with a higher power for any fulfilment in the human sphere.

Furthermore, several poems of the collection are concerned with encountering 'das Übernächste', sometimes in the form of the night, sometimes in the form of the angel. Yet what the letter presents as a *fait accompli*: 'darum habe ich die Leute übersprungen', does not always appear as such in the poetry. There it remains a problem which, in the poems to Benvenuta of February 1914, seems to be resolved by the poet's finding a new basis for his existence precisely 'im Menschlichen'. It was wholly premature for Rilke to see the problems of existence in the world as having been successfully avoided by his turning to 'das Übernächste', and the benevolent detachment from these problems which his letter claims – 'und schau zu ihnen zurück mit Herzlichkeit' – is rarely borne out by the poetry of the period. In fragments and rejected poems written over the period of the *Gedichte an die Nacht* one finds such statements as:

Ach die Pein der Liebesmöglichkeiten
hab ich Tag und Nächte hingespürt:
zu einander flüchten, sich entgleiten,
keines hat zur Freudigkeit geführt. (SW II, 400)

which shows that the problem of the relation of the self to 'das Nächste' can still give rise to bitterness and despair. This is not to say that poems representing an apparent solution in terms of 'das Übernächste' – such as *Gedanken der Nacht* and *Die große Nacht* – have to be rejected as spurious, but that such 'solutions' as they offer can only be partial because they involve a turning away from the problems of the self in the immediate world. So it is that the recapitulation of the theme of 'Fremdheit' at the end of *Die große Nacht* is not a mere rhetorical device, but rather shows that 'Fremdheit' in the sphere of 'das Nächste' and 'Beteiligung' in that of 'das Übernächste' are the negative and positive halves of the same experience. This dualism is in itself a problem which must be overcome before 'ein ganzes Leben' can be realised, as the Fourth Elegy, written in 1915, clearly states:

> Uns aber, wo wir Eines meinen, ganz,
> ist schon des andern Aufwand fühlbar. (SW 1, 697)

The contact with 'die große Nacht' which takes place at the end of the poem, and which gives it an undeniably positive conclusion can indeed be seen in terms of 'Eines meinen, ganz': it is presented with complete certainty as an experience of union with the night. However, at the same time 'des andern Aufwand', the theme of alienation, is still perceptible, indeed is deliberately re-stated after the union with the night has begun. Hence the ending of the poem is both conclusive and inconclusive at the same time. This is a contradiction in terms of ordinary logic, however, Rilke was from the beginning aware of the fact that the logic of his poetry did not present things always in terms of a simple 'A or not-A',[30] and saw no reason why apparently contradictory opposites should not coexist as aspects of the same situation without one cancelling the other out. Such contradictions do not necessarily impair the aesthetic unity of a poem, although they do complicate the task of rational analysis.

The above quotation from the letter of March 15th, 1913, expresses an intention on Rilke's part to direct his poetry towards 'das Engelische' at the expense of 'das Menschliche'. This he does in *Die große Nacht*, but in such a way that he remains aware of 'des andern Aufwand', of those questions he had raised in the period of *Malte Laurids Brigge* and which still lacked final answers. In *Gedanken der Nacht* these questions do not intrude, but the poem is the lesser for it. *Die große Nacht* is deservedly one of the best known of the *Gedichte an die Nacht*, for, by showing both the positive and the negative of a single situation, the poem presents a far greater thematic range and tension. It is partly because this tension is not entirely resolved in the concluding lines of the poem, that it remains 'unverbindlich'. But need poetry be 'verbindlich'?

'HINHALTEN WILL ICH MICH'

This poem, written close upon *Die große Nacht*,[31] is remarkable in that it does not take the concluding lines of the latter poem as its starting point, but rather presents, in counterpoint to the essentially passive rôle of the poet there, a new theme, which has been characterised as a 'maßlos ungeduldige, leidenschaftlich-subjektive Willensanspannung'.[32] However that be, we shall first examine the poem in detail before discussing its relation to the themes of *Die große Nacht*:

> Hinhalten will ich mich. Wirke. Geh über
> so weit du vermöchtest. (SW 11, 75)

The beginning of the poem certainly bespeaks a new confidence in the poet's approach to the night. The direct imperatives suggest that some kind of contact with the night is already there for there is none of the waiting for the 'Beweis' of '*Gedanken der Nacht*'. The situation seems to represent a successful overcoming of what the poet laments in the fragment of 1910:

> Und Sterne stehn, die großen Sterne und
> du hast nicht Kraft vor ihrem Hintergrund
> dich auszuhalten...

for now he feels able to be exposed to the night, welcomes whatever effect the night may have on him. The imperative 'Geh über' may be understood in the sense of a crossing of the barrier between two kinds of being: from the transcendent to the

immanent, whereby the latter hopes to be changed. Then follow
two examples of the form this change is to take:

> ...Hast du nicht Hirten das Antlitz
> größer geordnet, als selbst in der Fürstinnen Schoß
> unaufhörlicher Könige Herkunft und künftige Kühnheit
> formten den krönlichen Ausdruck?

The comparison between the shepherds and the royal embryos
points clearly in the direction of the letter quoted in connection
with *Die große Nacht*. The shepherds, being each one solitary,
but in constant communion with 'das Übernachste', with the
being of the night, have their faces 'größer geordnet' than even
those of future kings, who here represent a higher form of purely
human existence. Because in the case of the shepherds there has
been some 'Übergang' from the transcendent to the immanent,
their faces partake in some way of the eternal order. In Rilke's
poetry the night and stars have the quality of being removed
from time, as a fragment from autumn 1913 attests:

> Der Himmel singt in seiner Sicherheit,
> hoch über Zeit die reichen Sterne singen,
> wir treiben mit den abgehärmten Dingen
> zweischweigende Geselligkeit.   (SW II, 398)

Again in the late poem quoted above, the 'Gestirne der Nacht'
were seen as encompassing 'das ganze Gesicht meiner Jahre',
of providing a guarantee of the unity of the self in time. So it is
here that the 'order' of the shepherds' faces is seen as surpassing
even the 'unaufhörlicher Könige Herkunft und künftige Kühn-
heit' of a royal line. This suggests that the comparison with the
shepherds goes even farther than 'das ganze Gesicht meiner
Jahre' and that their faces, through constantly being directed
towards 'die große Nacht' or 'die reichen Sterne', are expressive
of that 'erfüllte Zeit'[33] which comes close to being timelessness.
It is, therefore, an escape from transience, one of the negatives
of the human condition, that the poet hopes for in his turning to
'das Übernächste, das Engelische', and which the effect of the
night on him is to bring about.

The second example introduces the image of ships' figure-heads:

Wenn die Galionen
in dem staunenden Holz des stillhaltenden Schnitzwerks
Züge empfangen des Meerraums, in den sie stumm drängend hinausstehn.

This image needs to be very carefully considered, as it touches on an important aspect of Rilke's concept of poetry. The figure-heads on the ship are rigid and motionless, suggesting a complete and exclusive directedness towards the 'Meerraum, in den sie stumm drängend hinausstehn'. Moreover, they project beyond the ship in the same way that the poet here wishes to project outside the sphere of immanent existence into that of the night. The effect, which he hopes for from the night, is in terms of the image of the figureheads 'Züge empfangen des Meerraums', that is: have his existence partake of the other, of the night, while at the same time remaining part of the ship. The ship may be thus equated with ordinary human existence. But, whereas the complete outwards-directedness of the figureheads is involuntary – they are made of wood – the poet's directedness towards the night is seen as an effort of will:

o, wie sollte ein Fühlender nicht, der *will*, der sich aufreißt,
unnachgiebige Nacht, endlich dir ähnlicher sein.

Such a goal must indeed involve an effort of the will, as it entails a turning away from the world of people and objects, in which the poet must continue to exist, and a solitary concentration on what lies beyond it, very much a 'Grenzsituation'. A similar, though not identical situation is presented in the prose piece *Über den Dichter*, written in Duino in 1912. Rilke there uses the account of a journey by boat to illustrate 'das Verhältnis des Dichters im Bestehenden'. The boat is propelled by rowers, whom Rilke describes at length. Then he breaks off his description and says of the man who represents the poet:

Da kann ich ihn nun länger nicht verschweigen, den Mann, der gegen den rechten Rand zu vorne auf unserer Barke saß...Ich weiß nicht, wie weit sich ihm die Verfassung unserer Mannschaft mitteilte, das alles war hinter ihm, er sah selten zurück und ohne ihn bestimmenden Eindruck. (SW VI, 1034)

The position of the man at the front of the boat, seldom looking back, is not unlike that of the 'Galionen' in the poem. He is not as completely directed towards the 'Meerraum' as a figurehead of wood, nevertheless he seems quite unconcerned with the ship and those in it: 'das alles war hinter ihm', whereas:

Was auf ihn Einfluß zu haben schien, war die reine Bewegung, die in seinem Gefühl mit der offenen Ferne zusammentraf, an die er, halb entschlossen, halb melancholisch, hingegeben war.

So that he is seen as the meeting place of something pertaining to the ship – not by any means 'die Verfassung der Mannschaft' but rather the less human and more abstract 'reine Bewegung' – and something which is beyond it: 'die offene Ferne'. This description, which is clearly to be reckoned among Rilke's self-interpretations, anticipates the image of the figureheads in the poem. Yet one must not be too ready to equate the two instances, for there are very marked differences between the two analogies. Whereas the figureheads are 'stumm drängend', the man in the boat sings, sings sporadically and without having regard for what the crew are doing, but in a way which nevertheless is meaningful to them:

In ihm kam der Antrieb unseres Fahrzeugs und die Gewalt dessen, was uns entgegenging, fortwährend zum Ausgleich – von Zeit zu Zeit sammelte sich ein Überschuß: dann sang er. Das Schiff bewältigte den Widerstand; er aber, der Zauberer, verwandelte Das, was nicht zu bewältigen war, in eine Folge, langer schwebender Töne, die weder hierhin noch dorthin gehörten, und die jeder für sich in Anspruch nahm.

In the poem we are dealing with, the situation has a quite different emphasis. In the image of the figureheads there is no question of an active transformation of 'was uns entgegenging' into something which exists between the allegorical spheres of 'Ferne' and 'Barke' ('die weder hierhin noch dorthin gehörten'). Rather, the aim is to become more like the 'Meerraum' and less like the ship:

unnachgiebige Nacht, endlich dir ähnlicher sein.

Furthermore, the poet-figure in the bark is seen as a point of 'Ausgleich', i.e. as not necessarily being changed by his 'Bezie-

hung zum Weitesten', for each time a certain intensity of experience of the other is reached, he expresses it in his singing. In the
poem, the poet wishes for a lasting change in his existence to
result from the effect of the night, a change which would leave
him permanently projecting 'outside' the ship, with no mention
of re-establishing the balance between immanent and transcendent being. The prose piece is clearly much more ambitious and
comprehensive in its claims than the poem we are treating. By
the use of the image of the 'Galionen', which are rigid and silent,
the situation of the poem is much more restricted than in the
earlier essay. There, for all the singer seems little concerned with
the 'Mannschaft', his 'Beziehung zum Weitesten' is seen as
actually pulling the boat along:

Während seine Umgebung sich immer wieder mit dem greifbaren Nächsten
einließ und es überwand, unterhielt seine Stimme die Beziehung zum Weitesten,
knüpfte uns daran an, bis es uns zog.

This shows the way in which the situation of the poem is not
resolved, as the rôle of the poet in the prose-piece is, and that the
image of the 'Galionen' implies much more strongly than the
figure of the man in the boat a 'Beziehung zum Weitesten' which
excludes any conscious 'Beziehung zum Nächsten'. In this way
the gesture: 'Hinhalten will ich mich', which has as its goal:
'Züge empfangen des Meerraums' may be likened to the 'wegschauen' (='vom greifbaren Nächsten wegschauen') of the poem
Die große Nacht. The two gestures are similar, however, only
in what they exclude; there is all the world of difference between
the act of 'sich aufreißen' in the later poem and that of 'begreifen'
in the earlier one.

This raises the question of the relation of *Hinhalten will ich...*
to the other poems we have dealt with. It is indeed confusing
that the benevolent 'elder sister' of *Gedanken der Nacht* should
have become without visible reason the 'unnachgiebige Nacht'
of the later poem. There is no suggestion at the beginning of
Hinhalten will ich... that contact with the night has been lost
altogether, that the night has become alien – rather the night is
addressed with a confidence and directness which is absent from

the openings of the other poems. One could resolve the difficulty by a simple appeal to the dualism of Rilke's poetic thought, which is especially evident where supernatural beings are concerned, and which in *Das Stunden-Buch* produces such extremely opposed positions within the same work as:

> Du bist so groß, daß ich schon nicht mehr bin,
> wenn ich mich nur in deine Nähe stelle. (SW 1, 269)

and

> Bin dein Gewand und dein Gewerbe,
> mit mir verlierst du deinen Sinn. (SW 1, 275)

but this would not go very far towards elucidating the thematic complexity of the *Gedichte an die Nacht*. Let us rather take the three poems: *Gedanken der Nacht, Die große Nacht* and *Hinhalten will ich mich*... and briefly examine their similarities and differences.

Gedanken der Nacht and *Hinhalten will ich mich*... both present situations in which there are only the poet and the night present. All interaction is between the poet and 'das Übernächste'; his immediate surroundings are not mentioned. But whereas in the former poem night is seen as something already existing in the poet and the contact with the night is complete, in the latter this is seen as a distant goal: 'endlich dir ähnlicher sein'. Further, the union in the former poem comes about without any effort or hindrance, as a result of a change in the consciousness of the poet himself: his beginning to think the 'Gedanken der Nacht'. In the latter poem everything is seen in terms of will and conscious effort: the poet must hold himself outside his immanent existence with total concentration, just as the figurehead always projects beyond the ship. Then chronologically between these two poems comes *Die große Nacht*, which differs from both of them in that the field of reference is much wider, encompassing also the poet's inability to come to terms 'mit dem greifbaren Nächsten'. However, the interpretation of *Die große Nacht* showed that although the union with the night takes place, the tension between this union on the one hand and the relation of the self to 'die nächsten Dinge' on the other is left unresolved.

The fact is, however, that a final solution to *all* the problems of existence raised in the *Gedichte an die Nacht* could only be in terms of an integration of the self *both* with 'das Nächste' and 'das Übernächste' and that for this reason the conclusion of *Die große Nacht* has the same character of a station on the way towards the goal of 'ein ganzes Leben' as the identification with the figure of the shepherd at the end of *Die spanische Trilogie*. As the poems demonstrate, this way cannot be seen as a linear progression. Successive poems may have quite different starting-points and proceed in quite different directions. In the poem *Hinhalten will ich mich*... the direction taken is clearly not towards 'das Nächste', but 'das Weiteste', with no suggestion in the imagery of any return to those things which remain unresolved. For this reason the poem has, in comparison with the essay *Über den Dichter* an incomplete and even fragmentary character, and in comparison with *Die große Nacht* an equally limited thematic range. It is quite possible that the poem *Hinhalten will ich mich*... expresses indirectly and in quite other terms something of the tension left unresolved by *Die große Nacht*.

It is also worth noting the correspondence between approach and response which occurs in the three poems under discussion. In *Gedanken der Nacht* we may observe two such correspondences: the initial approach to the night is by way of 'Gedanken' and the initial response is termed 'der starke Beweis'. Then, when the nature of the contact changes to one of feeling, the poet's feeling for 'die Schwester in mir, die ich berge' corresponds to the appearance of the night as the loving elder sister. In *Die große Nacht* the image of the poet as a child unable to join in the games of the others corresponds again to the manifestation of the night as a kindly adult. In the third poem the poet's exertion of will has the rigid directedness of a ship's figurehead and the night is correspondingly 'unnachgiebige Nacht'.

As critics have recognised, this poses a great obstacle to any satisfactory interpretation, whether the object of it be to discover a basis in experience for the poems or to establish the reality, if any, of the entities Rilke invokes. There is no simple way around this difficulty; however Käte Hamburger has suggested a fruitful way of approaching it. In speaking of the first two parts of *Das Stunden-Buch* she points to the problem of finding some kind of ordering principle in the 'hervorbrausende, chaotisch anmutende Fülle der Gebete, in deren Hin- und Herwogen keine klare Ordnung erkennbar zu sein scheint'.[34] She then shows that through these poems there exists a basic situation of 'Gegenüber', with the self of the poet on the one hand and whatever he chooses to denote as 'Gott' on the other:

> Es sind überall in den ersten beiden Büchern des *Stunden-Buchs* Bilder für die elementare Polarität von Ich und Sein (das Nicht-Ich) anzutreffen. Die Gebete wogen vom Seins- zum Ichpol hin und her, verlagern sich bald auf den ersteren, wo Gott als Name eingesetzt ist, und vor dem das Ich sich auszulöschen scheint, bald auf den letzteren, wo bereits die intentionale Polarität sich zur 'transzendentalen Subjektivität' zu vertiefen scheint...[35]

Let us for the moment consider the similarities and differences between the basic situation of *Das Stunden-Buch* and that of the poems we have been treating. In each case both the self and the object or entity towards which it is directed are liable to show drastic modifications of attitude or form from context to context. Moreover, it is as difficult to explain these changes in the *Gedichte an die Nacht* as it is to predict in what new guise 'Ich' or 'Gott' will appear in the earlier work. The situation of the self in the *Gedichte an die Nacht* likewise ranges from states where it seems barely to exist at all to extremes of arrogance. Finally, the *Stunden-Buch* is rich in such correspondences between self and 'intentionaler Gegenstand' as we have observed in the poems under discussion.

However, to take this comparison further is to see how much the 'Problematik der Intentionalität' has altered between 1900 and 1913. For in the *Stunden-Buch* the 'Ich-Gott' relationship is expressed throughout all its transformations with a fluency and confidence which contrasts strongly with the situation of most of the *Gedichte an die Nacht*. No single confrontation is held or developed long enough for the situation to become in any sense critical. When the persona of the monk says, for example:

> Du bist so groß, daß ich schon nicht mehr bin,
> wenn ich mich nur in deine Nähe stelle...

the reader registers this as one of any number of possible variations of the theme, and in no sense as a situation of despair from which a way out must be sought. The fact that 'Ich-Pol' and 'Seins-Pol' alike are so unrestricted in their metaphorical transformations expresses, somewhat paradoxically, a basic existential certainty. This gives the poems something of the character of a game which could be indefinitely prolonged. In the *Gedichte an die Nacht*, on the other hand, there is no such sweeping movement to bring about this kaleidoscopic interplay of opposites – rather each situation is taken for itself and worked out in its particular implications. More importantly, the relation between the self and the given intentional object has become problematical in two ways.

Firstly, there is a much greater circumspection in the use of divine attributes for objects in the empirical world, and a corresponding tendency to differentiate between what is 'transcendent' and what is not. Whereas in the *Stunden-Buch* the god is frequently represented in 'Bilder...gegenständlich-dinglicher Art, Sinnlichwahrnehmbares bezeichnend', which, as Käte Hamburger points out, may be seen to represent 'eine pantheistische Identität Gottes mit allem was ist',[36] the world of objects in such poems as the first part of *Die spanische Trilogie* and *Die große Nacht* has no such pantheistic implications. Instead, there is an increasing tendency for contact with transcendent entities to be sought outside what Rilke terms 'das greifbare Nächste'.[37] The spheres of immanence and transcendence no longer merge and overlap as easily and spontaneously as in the *Gebete* and the question is rather whether they can meet at all. Hence such questions arise as: can the gods at the conclusion of the poem *So angestrengt wider die starke Nacht*..., who are so removed from the sphere of human experience, be meaningfully considered as an 'intentionaler Gegenstand' in the sense of the

Studen-Buch? Secondly, the power of identification with the other – be it god, human or thing – which is constantly celebrated in the earlier work with such assurance – has itself become the object of an often anguished inquiry.

Poems such as *Die große Nacht* are concerned with reaching out towards the kind of 'Beteiligung' which appears in the *Stunden-Buch* as something given from the beginning. This raises an important aspect of the problem of intentionality which is not very much emphasised in Käte Hamburger's discussion. For in Rilke's poetry the problem of the 'Gegenüber' is never a purely intellectual one. The question of the nature and limitations of perception is always bound up with the problem of what *emotional* relationship exists between the self and what it perceives. The intense need for an emotional reciprocity between the self and the other is in fact the unifying theme of all the *Gedichte an die Nacht*, and hence to the more abstract problems of what is perceived? in what relation does it stand to the consciousness? – are added those of establishing an emotional rapport as well. In the *Stunden-Buch* there is scarcely any differentiation between thought and feeling as modes of intentionality, however, in the *Gedichte an die Nacht* an awareness or perception of something without the necessary emotional participation leads either directly to despair, or else to an attempt to establish some rapport. Not only, then, are the spheres of immanent and transcendent being likely to be divorced from each other conceptually, but emotional contact between either of them and the 'Ich' of the poems can also be extremely problematical:

> Da rauscht der Bach und dich, (der du ihn hörst)
> dich weiß er nicht. Und drängst du deine Klage
> den Lüften auf: er ringt durch reine Tage,
> die du nicht hast, die du nicht störst. (SW ii, 391)

> Was willst du fühlen? Ach, dein Fühlen reicht
> vom Weinenden zum Nicht-Mehr-Weinenden.
> Doch drüber sind, unfühlbar, Himmel leicht
> von zahllos Engeln. Dir unfühlbar. (SW ii, 97)

76

The development of the problem of intentionality between 1900 and 1913 could be seen as follows. Whereas in the *Stunden-Buch* the 'Gegenüber'-situation provided a basic structure for any of the various possibilities of opposition or identification among the three factors: 'Ich', 'Gott', 'Dingwelt', in the *Gedichte an die Nacht* this structure itself has become the focus of inquiry in a way which anticipates the theme of the eighth Elegy. It has done so largely as a result of the experiences presented in *Malte*, and, having become the object of scrutiny, it is shown to contain possibilities both of extreme privation and of fulfilment. The ease with which 'Ich' and 'Gott' are transposed into metaphors from the material world and thus related, as at the beginning of the *Stunden-Buch*, has quite disappeared, and instead the problem of whether the 'Gegenüber'-situation as such can be a meaningful relation becomes a central theme. For, as we have seen in the poems we have dealt with, if the immediate environment on the one hand is alien, and the gods or their equivalent are on the other hand 'unfühlbar' or inaccessible, then 'Gegenüber-sein' becomes for the self a state of isolation and despair. As Käte Hamburger rightly indicates, the poem *Es winkt zu Fühlung fast aus allen Dingen* presents 'Gegenüber-sein' as an ideal fulfilment where the objects which are felt are contained in the same 'Weltinnenraum' as the self, i.e. where all barriers are absent,[38] but in dealing with the *Gedichte an die Nacht* we are above all concerned with cases where this is not so. Rilke is rather exploring the possibilities of the 'Gegenüber'-situation in the hope of establishing an emotional participation which answers the needs of the self of the poems. That this attempt assumes the form of a crisis may be seen in two senses as the legacy of the breakdown of the *Stunden-Buch*-situation. Firstly, because the 'Gegenüber'-situation no longer implies an emotional relatedness of self and other, but presents the achieving of this relatedness as a major problem. Secondly, the drawing apart of the spheres of immanent and transcendent being creates a dilemma as to where this relatedness is to be sought: is participation to be found 'mit dem greifbaren Nächsten' or is the self to be directed towards 'das Übernächste, das Engelische'? This dilemma is clearly shown in the poems we have so far examined, perhaps best in *Die große Nacht*.

One thing which has been established is that 'Nacht' in these poems has a number of possible levels of meaning. It can simply be an aspect of the environment, it can represent a mode of human behaviour, or some aspect of the human psyche; as 'Nacht-Raum' it can be a region common to both man and the angels, and as 'die große Nacht' a cosmic power in its own right. This plurality of meanings makes it peculiarly appropriate to the crisis which we have outlined immediately above. For if it is true to say that 'Intentionalität' (in Käte Hamburger's sense) is the basic attitude in the *Gedichte an die Nacht* as it is in *Das Stunden-Buch*, it is equally true that while this attitude is given from the beginning, the identity of the object towards which the self is directed, is not an unambiguous datum, but is rather what Rilke is trying to *establish* throughout the poems. The form which this attempt takes is, however, conditioned by the second aspect of the crisis: the need for a meaningful relation *both* to the world of objects *and* to some transcendent power. One may see this as a need to achieve a meaningful synthesis of the immanent and transcendent spheres. Whether Rilke is ultimately successful in this or not, it is the imperative which determines the direction of his poetry at this time, and it is hence quite appropriate that this poetry should be written 'an die Nacht'.

For in the attempt to establish a meaningful 'Gegenüber' in the face of the 'Fremdheit' of the finite world and the indifference of the gods, the various levels of experience which the night offers provide a wide scale of possible objects. Furthermore, and perhaps more significantly, the night gives a possibility of mediation between the finite and the infinite. This possibility is present in Rilke's work well before the writing of the *Gedichte an die Nacht*, as we may see by recalling the lines from the poem *Sterne hinter Oliven* (1907 or 1908):

> Sieh, wie im selbstvergessenen Geäste
> das Nächste sich mit Namenlosem mischt;   (SW II, 356)

and it is taken up again and perhaps indeed over-exploited in the crisis of 1913. Above all it provides the possibility of a bridge between the world of phenomena of which it is part and that of the gods or angels, between the immediate and finite and the distant and infinite:

> Was könnte dein Lächeln mir was mir die Nacht nicht
> gäbe aufdrängen, die hier mit fast schüchternem Anfang an
>   meinem Gesicht
> beginnt und wo wo endet... (SW II, 392)

This desire to find a mediate object is also present in *Die spanische Trilogie* as a kind of prefiguration of the function of the night in the rest of the poems. The 'Ding' of the first poem is 'welthaft-irdisch' – it is 'irdisch' in that it is to be 'made' 'aus vielen Ungenaun und immer mir', which is to say out of 'das Nächste' in two senses, and at the same time the image of the meteor makes explicit that it is to be 'at home' in the 'Weltraum', is to transcend the gravity which binds the elements of which it is to be made. It is also through the mediation of the figure of the shepherd that the self of the trilogy is able to overcome the 'Fremdheit' of the landscape. However, the appropriateness of the 'Ding' to this rôle is questionable, and the figure of the shepherd is limited to the one particular situation. But night by its nature is not experienced as a single fixed state or object but rather as a mode of possible encounters. It is 'Richtung des Herzens'[39] and 'Gegenstand' at the same time.

3. THE NIGHT AND THE LOVERS

The theme of the 'Geliebte' in Rilke's poetry of this period can hardly be regarded as virgin soil. Indeed it has received a great amount of attention in Rilke-literature, the most significant contributions being Wodtke's treatment of the theme of 'die künftige Geliebte' and Fülleborn's analysis of the poem *Perlen entrollen*... [1]

A certain amount of confusion is evident in Rilke's attitudes towards the figure of the 'Geliebte' in the period from his visit to Spain to the end of the Benvenuta episode. On the one hand there is the letter to Karl von der Heydt of March 1913:

...denn da ich mich...danach sehnte, im Menschlichen ausgebildet zu sein, da wurde mir, siehe, das Übernächste, das Engelische beigebracht, und darum hab ich die Leute übersprungen und schau zu ihnen zurück mit Herzlichkeit. (B. 1907–14, 275)

which must be read more as a statement of intention than as an established fact. Nevertheless this attitude is amply documented in poems written in the following year. On the other hand there is the possibility raised in *Perlen entrollen*... and in the fragment *An die Erwartete* and taken up again so enthusiastically in the poems and letters to Magda von Hattinberg of a fulfilment precisely 'im Menschlichen'. The resultant conflict has been seen by both Fülleborn and Wodtke as being essentially that between art and life. Wodtke states:

Die Geliebte steht hier also der Begegnung mit dem Engel im Wege und wird mit unerhörter Schärfe fortgewiesen. Leben und Kunst stehen sich als unvereinbare Alternativen gegenüber; es ist immer die gleiche Entscheidung, die Rilke schließlich fällt; für seine Kunst opfert er auch die ihm entgegengebrachte Liebe. [2]

Here the conflict is presented as a simple either/or, whereas for Fülleborn the rivalry assumes a somewhat more complex form:

Die 'Geliebte' ist demnach Mittel zur Erreichung eines höheren Zwecks; von ihrem Erscheinen erhofft der Dichter dasselbe wie von der Epiphanie der

'Nacht' oder des 'Engels'. So werden 'Geliebte' und 'Weltraum' bzw. 'Engel' nahezu austauschbar als zwei Wege zum Gipfel des Spätwerks.[3]

For Fülleborn then the conflict between 'Nacht' and 'Geliebte' is not simply an allegory of that between art and life, but rather both are to be seen as pretexts, as 'gedichtete Erlebnisse' which:

jeweils genau in dem Maße uneigentlich wirken mußten, als sich in ihnen etwas vom Eigentlichen, eben der Künstlersehnsucht verbarg.[4]

Both critics are, therefore, in agreement that Rilke's own artistic fulfilment is the real subject matter of these poems, whether it be seen in the ascendency which the theme of the angel gains over the other themes, or whether it be seen as an 'Eigentliches', for which the other themes are merely disguises. In Wodtke's interpretation a decision for life and against art would still be possible, while in Fülleborn's, whichever way the conflict might be decided, the result is ultimately reducible to an expression of 'Künstlersehnsucht'. As these issues are obviously central to an understanding of the poems, it might be well to consider them here.

While it is beyond doubt that the problems of his own poetic art were a lasting preoccupation of Rilke's for the whole of his career, it has not been established that these problems must always be the 'real' theme of his poetry. Certainly, interpretations in this direction are possible and often valuable, but they have yet to be shown to exclude all others. As an example of this one might take Mason's interpretation of the angel of the fourth Elegy as a symbol for Rilke's own poetic inspiration,[5] which has taken its place among other possible interpretations but does not necessarily eclipse them. It is equally possible to regard the theme of Rilke's own poetic fulfilment as one element of a thematic complex, influencing and modifying but not necessarily dominating the other aspects. While it is not difficult to establish the presence of this theme at virtually any stage of the poet's development, it is questionable to insist on its primacy over all others. This is especially so when the theme is not explicit in the work itself but must be discovered by a process of reduction to lie somewhere behind the actual fabric of the poetry. Here, it is not the revealing of concealed themes as such which is dubious, but rather the further stage of assigning them a greater importance or reality than those themes which are already explicit. To make this standpoint somewhat clearer, let us return briefly to the first poem of *Die spanische Trilogie*.

There one may indeed follow the strong consensus of critical opinion and substitute 'das Gedicht zu machen' for 'das Ding zu machen' without seeing the poem as being exclusively about Rilke's own poetic fulfilment. For one thing, there is the paradoxical nature of the 'Ding' itself, and, for another, the fact that it is equally legitimate to see the theme of alienation in the poem as what is primary and real, and the 'Ding' as something produced in contrast to this as a distant and ideal resolution of a situation which admits of no immediate relief. One could indeed go further and discover 'behind' the 'Ding' as 'Kunst-Ding' an ideal of 'Beteiligung' disguised in the imagery as the creation of a particular kind of poem.

To assume the primacy of the theme of Rilke's own artistry even when this theme is not immediately visible in the poems under discussion, necessarily involves a process of reduction in order to arrive at what is genuine. This in turn implies that the surface of the poem must be to some extent discounted as 'das Uneigentliche' and the complexity of this surface simplified to what is basic. While this is one aspect of the abstraction from the work essential to all criticism, there is the obvious danger that distinctions present in the work are absent from the critical understanding of it. However, if one does not make this assumption, but rather sees Rilke's 'Künstlersehnsucht' as one theme among others, then such a reduction offers a distorted perspective. For as we have seen in the preceding chapter, there is no single constant meaning to be assigned to 'Nacht', rather it is characterised by a wide variation of possible meanings from context to context. As it seems that much of the thematic material of the *Gedichte an die Nacht* is connected with, though not necessarily *reducible to* the problem of Rilke's own artistry, there is every reason to question these simplifications, for the present discussion rests on the assumption that there is more to these poems than an indirect expression of the problems of writing the *Duineser Elegien*.

Wodtke's view that these poems present a genuine dilemma between 'Leben' and 'Kunst' which is always decided in favour of the latter, involves a less drastic abstraction from the work than Fülleborn's interpretation, but he nevertheless sees the choice as one between 'unvereinbare Alternativen'.[6] Firstly, can one when dealing with Rilke's poetry separate art and life into irreconcilable alternatives? Does this not overlook the fact that what Rilke says of the one is likely also to have relevance to the other and that the problems of both overlap in certain areas? That there is tension between them is certainly true and that Rilke attempts to resolve this tension in a variety of ways is evident from the poetry. But it is also the case that a fulfilment in terms of art need not exclude one in terms of life and vice versa – indeed, from *Die spanische Trilogie* one might conclude that they were interdependent.

Secondly, we find in the *Gedichte an die Nacht* repeated attempts at a reconciliation between 'das Nächste' and 'das Übernächste', between 'das Menschliche' and 'das Engelische', as well as a number of statements of their apparent incompatibility. So that while the conflict between 'Geliebte' and angel may be quite as Wodtke describes it, one may well question whether the 'Geliebte'-motif encompasses everything which one may understand by 'Leben' on the one hand and whether 'das Engelische' can be wholly equated to 'Kunst' on the other. In other words, the existence of the 'Leben-Kunst' conflict in the poems is readily admitted; the necessity for amalgamating all such polarities in the *Gedichte an die Nacht* into one irreconcilable conflict seems highly dubious. When dealing with Rilke's poetry, such simplifications are often more trouble than they are worth.

'DIE GESCHWISTER' I (SW II, 68)

This poem is remarkable among the *Gedichte an die Nacht*, firstly because it is a 'Rollengedicht' and secondly because it was written in two parts, only one of which was included in the collection presented to Kassner. Incest is, mercifully, not a major theme in these poems and it is obviously used here by way of hyperbole: to present the love situation as one of extremity. In the first stanza there are clear overtones of pain and guilt,

> O wie haben wir, mit welchem Wimmern,
> Augenlid und Schulter uns geherzt.
> Und die Nacht verkroch sich in den Zimmern
> wie ein wundes Tier, von uns durchschmerzt.   (SW II, 68)

yet a certain ambiguity surrounds their origin. I doubt that Rilke thought of incest as particularly sinful, yet it is the only apparent reason for the lovers' lack of enjoyment and for the unfortunate effect which their act has upon the night. In fact Rilke uses the opprobrium which incest connotes to express a condemnatory attitude towards the love-situation as such. Similar instances are not hard to find in which the terms of comparison are equally pejorative. To take two from poems which we have already treated:

> – o nicht wie einer
> der der Geliebten diese Nacht bereitet
> und sie verwöhnt mit den gefühlten Himmeln.   (SW II, 45)

> Wer hat nicht
> in dieses eingeborne Element
> gefälschte, schlechte, nachgemachte Nächte
> hereingeschleppt und sich daran begnügt?   (SW II, 52)

In these two instances the wrong committed is the failure to respond appropriately to 'die ganzen Sterne' and 'die starke Nacht' respectively: the energies which should be directed towards the encounter with the night are wasted instead on the 'Geliebte'. What remains puzzling in each case is the extremely negative emotion which colours the verse and which is reinforced in *Die Geschwister* by the use of the incest situation. Is this purely the violence of self-reproach or does it stem from some suffering inherent in the love situation? What is interesting about the first stanza of *Die Geschwister* is that this remains ambiguous. For the third and fourth lines of this stanza could be read either as postulating some *nefas*: that the night is in some way profaned by what the lovers are doing; or that the misery of the situation itself – 'mit welchem Wimmern' – has communicated itself to the night, establishing a correspondence of the kind which we observed in the preceding chapter. Or, to phrase this problem in another way, is the night a metaphor for some 'higher' aspect of the self which is denied or betrayed in the love situation or is it simply an image designed to illustrate the suffering? This ambiguity is both sustained and developed in the two stanzas which complete the poem:

> Wardst du mir aus allen auserlesen,
> war es an der Schwester nicht genug?
> Lieblich wie ein Tal war mir dein Wesen,
> und nun beugt es auch vom Himmelsbug
>
> sich in unerschöpflicher Erscheinung
> und bemächtigt sich. Wo soll ich hin?
> Ach mit der Gebärde der Beweinung
> neigst du dich zu mir, Untrösterin.

What is immediately interesting for our study of the night-motif, is the way in which the figure of the 'Geliebte' has become, as it were, the night. The figure of the sister corresponds almost exactly to the night in the concluding lines of the poem *Gedanken der Nacht*...:

> Plötzlich: mit welchem Gefühl, steht die unendliche, älter,
> über die Schwester in mir, die ich berge, gebeugt. (SW II, 67)

In a strange reversal of roles, the night has become a metaphor for the 'Geliebte'. The 'unerschöpfliche Erscheinung', which one might reasonably expect from other poems to characterise the night as a transcendent entity, here functions as a metaphor for the way in which the 'Ich' of the poem feels entirely dominated by the sister. This metaphor is a further extension of what we saw in the poem *Gedanken der Nacht*. There the night was

used to denote an aspect of the self – 'die Schwester in mir' –
and here the 'Nacht'-motif has become so much more fluid as
to be used as an image of a human situation; a situation which,
strangely, is elsewhere given as the very antithesis of the encounter with the night.

Clearly, the sister has usurped the place of the night in the
lover's experience. This gives rise to the same tone of reproach
as in the fragment:

> Was könnte dein Lächeln mir was mir die Nacht nicht
> gäbe aufdrängen...   (SW ii, 392)

where it is a question of the comparative *value* of the two modes
of experience. The relation to the 'Geliebte' is rejected in favour
of an approach to 'das Übernächste': the human sphere cannot
offer experience of the same order as the night. But in the poem
we are examining, it does. The 'Geliebte', by usurping the place
of the night, has assumed its attributes. And yet the experience is
still entirely negative.

This problem is closely related to the ambiguity in the first
stanza and bears on a basic contradiction of attitudes towards
the 'Geliebte'. On the one hand there is the discrepancy of
value between the finite and the infinite, between human and
angelic experience which is continually emphasised in these
poems, for example:

> Siehe, Engel fühlen durch den Raum
> ihre unaufhörlichen Gefühle.
> Unsre Weißglut wäre ihre Kühle.
> Siehe, Engel glühen durch den Raum.   (SW ii, 69)

This produces the intention to seek fulfilment outside the human
sphere which Rilke announces in the letter to Karl von der
Heydt and which is the substance of the ending of the poem
Hinhalten will ich mich... The night which is present within the
poet corresponds to this intention, and the rivalry between night
and 'Geliebte' is clearly that between 'higher' and 'lower'
modes of experience.

On the other hand, this apparently simple choice of direction is complicated by the fact that the love-relationship is an inescapable datum in these poems and that it continually intrudes upon the attempt to go beyond the limitations of finite experience. This intrusion generally takes the form of suffering in the love-relationship itself and cannot always be ignored in the invocation of the night or the angel. This is because Rilke is never able to give up completely the possibility of such a fulfilment and so it becomes a strong thematic undercurrent in the *Gedichte an die Nacht*, and an explicitly dominant theme once more in the Benvenuta episode.

Signs of this conflict may be found in the poem which we are examining. Rilke could, and does elsewhere express the rivalry between 'Nacht' and 'Geliebte' and the rejection of the latter without having recourse to so drastic a device as that of incest. Whereas in other contexts the negative connotations appear to arise from the *comparison* of the 'Geliebte' with some possibility of transcendent experience, the immediate and strong connotations of incest represent the love-relationship as *intrinsically* one of suffering. So that interwoven with the theme of the rivalry of 'Nacht' and 'Geliebte' we have that of the 'Pein der Liebesmöglichkeiten' which can also appear in this period as a theme in its own right:

> Ach die Pein der Liebesmöglichkeiten
> hab ich Tag und Nächte hingespürt:
> zu einander flüchten, sich entgleiten,
> keines hat zur Freudigkeit geführt. (SW II, 400)

Much of this interpretation is a result of considering the poem within the context of the *Gedichte an die Nacht*. Were it to be read solely in conjunction with its companion piece *Die Geschwister II*, which was not included in the collection, then the interpretation would receive a quite different emphasis. For in the second poem the incestuous love is resolved by an evocation of the Last Judgment:

> Wenn die Menge einst der Aufersteher
> uns entschwistert, und wir, irgend zwei,
> bei der jäh enttötenden Fanfare
> taumeln aus dem aufgestürzten Stein:
> o wie wird dann diese sonderbare
> Lust zu dir den Engeln schuldlos sein. (SW II, 69)

Clearly, if the two poems are read together, one is disposed to take the incest-theme more at face value and consider them as 'Rollengedichte' with a not necessarily serious admixture of eschatological speculation. However, it is quite possible to see why Rilke included the first in the *Gedichte an die Nacht* and excluded the second. While the imagery of the first poem is entirely based on the 'Nachtmetaphorik', this is quite absent from the second poem. Furthermore, the situation of the incestuous lovers in the first poem can be readily understood as an extreme representation of the general problem of love in the *Gedichte an die Nacht*, however its resolution in the second poem goes quite outside the thematic field of these poems. For in Rilke's depiction of the Last Judgment the human situation no longer exists as such. In this projected state the barriers between immanent and transcendent no longer exist and the problems of the individual identity have disappeared in an ideal anonymity. As Wodtke points out:

Rilke sieht dagegen im Tode den Übergang in die Anonymität, für ihn ist mit dem höchsten Bereich des Geistes der Begriff der Namenlosigkeit eng verknüpft.[7]

From this we may attempt to clarify the ambivalence of night in the poem. Involvement in the love-situation does not merely render the night inaccessible to the self of the poem but the inherent suffering – 'mit welchem Wimmern' – is imparted to the night itself: 'von uns durchschmerzt'. Hence the night appears in a dual rôle: as a metaphor for the pain of the lovers and for that aspect of the self of the poem which desires fulfilment *beyond* the 'Geliebte'. Then in the following two stanzas the 'Geliebte' assumes the attributes which are 'rightfully' those of 'Nacht' thus presenting an unusual extreme of the rivalry with which we are familiar. At the same time the other metaphorical function of night is carried over into the lines:

> Ach mit der Gebärde der Beweinung
> neigst du dich zu mir, Untrösterin.

These lines express not only that the sister has usurped the place of the night but also that there is something intrinsically false in the love-relationship itself: the sister is really 'Untrösterin' – unable or unwilling to console, but offering false consolation 'mit der *Gebärde* der Beweinung'. As the two figures in the poem are not just any pair of lovers this 'wrongness' of the love-relationship is present in the poem from the very beginning; but since, as Wodtke sees, the incest is merely 'Symbol einer äußersten menschlichen Grenzsituation', it is the suffering implicit in the situation of lovers as such which leads Rilke to exploit the connotations of incest. It is the unresolved conflict between the need for fulfilment in love (which the 'Untrösterin' does not give) and the need for fulfilment beyond the human sphere (which the night *may* offer) which creates such a 'Grenzsituation'.

While Rilke is not altogether averse to positing ideal solutions to the problems of human existence which form the themes of these poems, the Last Judgment is clearly inappropriate for a number of reasons.[8] However, the first poem, which leaves the problem of love quite unresolved and establishes the conflict between 'Nacht' and 'Geliebte' leads directly into the main themes of the *Gedichte an die Nacht*.

'EINMAL NAHM ICH ZWISCHEN MEINE HÄNDE' (SW II, 72)
and
'ATMETE ICH NICHT AUS MITTERNÄCHTEN' (SW II, 70)

These poems will be discussed together because they show a certain similarity in their treatment of the love-theme. In the first of them the 'Geliebte' is present, but there is no question of fulfilment:

> Einmal nahm ich zwischen meine Hände
> dein Gesicht. Der Mond fiel darauf ein.
> Unbegreiflichster der Gegenstände
> unter überfließendem Gewein.
>
> Wie ein williges, das still besteht,
> beinah war es wie ein Ding zu halten.
> Und doch war kein Wesen in der kalten
> Nacht, das mir unendlicher entgeht.

These first two stanzas again present the theme of 'Fremdheit'. But whereas before the estrangement was from the world of objects it is here expressed as an absence of any personal communication. In spite of the presence of some strong emotion in the 'Geliebte' – 'unter überfließendem Gewein' – this is not communicated and remains quite inaccessible to the self of the poem, who sees her face virtually as an inanimate object: 'Unbegreiflichster der Gegenstände...beinah war es wie ein Ding zu halten.' The sense of the word 'doch' in the next line is somewhat puzzling as it seems to imply that experiencing a woman's face 'beinah...wie ein Ding' should make it more 'begreiflich' or facilitate emotional communication.[9] However, the intention of the lines is clear enough. The 'Wesen' of the woman's face (and hence the being of the woman herself) escapes the poet 'to a more absolute degree' than anything else in the night. This implies that the personal situation is one element of an all embracing 'Fremdheit' such as Rilke presents at the beginning of *Die große Nacht*. The night is cold, unresponsive, and in it everything eludes the self, the other person most of all. As in *Die große Nacht* the estrangement is in terms of both understanding and emotion. For not only is there no emotional transference between the lovers, but the phrase 'Unbegreiflichster der Gegenstände' recalls the lines:

> ...Nicht gaben die nächsten
> Dinge sich Müh, mir verständlich zu sein.

The theme of the 'Geliebte', then, has been subsumed into the greater one of the isolation of the self in a world experienced as alien. In this poem there is no such attempt as in *Die spanische Trilogie* to resolve this and the last two stanzas become lament:

> O da strömen wir zu diesen Stellen,
> drängen in die kleine Oberfläche
> alle Wellen unsres Herzens,
> Lust und Schwäche,
> und wem halten wir sie schließlich hin?

> Ach dem Fremden, der uns mißverstanden,
> ach dem andern, den wir niemals fanden,

> denen Knechten, die uns banden,
> Frühlingswinden, die damit entschwanden,
> und der Stille, der Verliererin.

In this poem there is no note of reproach, no suggestion that the 'Geliebte' is inadequate, on the contrary it is the *state* in which empathy is impossible and the other is inaccessible, which stands in the way of a fulfilled love. Hence, of the two aspects of the problem which were isolated in examining *Die Geschwister* only one may be said to be present here. Moreover, it appears without any overtones of guilt or falsity: the wrongness is to be found here rather in the structure of experience itself, in the alienation of the self from its environment. In this poem there is no turning to the night or the angel, but in the next poem we shall see the 'Liebesproblematik' developing in just such a direction.

> Atmete ich nicht aus Mitternächten,
> daß du kämest einst, um deinetwillen,
> solche Flutung?
> Weil ich hoffte, mit fast ungeschwächten
> Herrlichkeiten dein Gesicht zu stillen,
> wenn es in unendlicher Vermutung
> einmal gegen meinem über ruht.
> Lautlos wurde Raum in meinen Zügen;
> deinem großen Aufschaun zu genügen,
> spiegelte, vertiefte sich mein Blut.

From the beginning it is clear that this poem is directed to the 'künftige Geliebte' and that, in the first stanza at least, Rilke is endeavouring to integrate this theme with that of the encounter with the night. The eventual arrival of the 'Geliebte' is to provide the culmination of a number of experiences. This is very similar to the rôle of the 'im Voraus/verlorne Geliebte' of the later poem:

> ...Alle die großen
> Bilder in mir, im Fernen erfahrene Landschaft,
> Städte und Türme und Brücken und un-
> vermutete Wendung der Wege
> und das Gewaltige jener von Göttern
> einst durchwachsenen Länder:
> steigt zur Bedeutung in mir
> deiner, Entgehende, an.   (SW ii, 79)

But while in the later poem 'die großen Bilder' are drawn from the immediate, visual world, the poem we are examining uses abstractions which are both much less precise and at the same time have unlimited connotations: 'solche Flutung', 'Herrlichkeiten', 'Raum', 'unendlicher Vermutung'. This difference aside, the figure of the 'Geliebte' still gives a hypothetical unifying point for these experiences, some final meaning which is greater than whatever meaning the experiences have as an uncompleted series. This is not an uncommon idea in Rilke's verse at the time and provides, for example, the central theme of the second part of *Die spanische Trilogie*:

> Warum muß einer gehn und fremde Dinge
> so auf sich nehmen,...
>
> und kann nicht sagen: Herr, wozu das Gastmahl?

Here the feast stands for a longed-for and ideal relatedness of the 'fremde Dinge', a state in which these experiences are a unity and not just a meaningless collection of alien images in the memory, and in which, equally importantly, the 'Ich' is no longer the excluded servant but partakes of the feast. The poem we have before us has a quite different shading of the idea, but in the light of these parallels we may examine more closely the avowed intention of *Atmete ich nicht*...

The experiences enumerated in the first stanza are all supposedly 'um deinetwillen' – for the sake of the 'Geliebte' when and if she appears. So, it is implied, the 'Flutung' and 'Herrlichkeiten' are not experienced for their own sake but as means to an end: 'dein Gesicht zu stillen'...'deinem großen Aufschaun zu genügen'. But this process of preparation for the coming of the 'Geliebte' is at the same time one of change within the self:

> Lautlos wurde Raum in meinen Zügen;
> . . .
> spiegelte, vertiefte sich mein Blut.

The 'Ich' must be transformed, acquire 'Flutung', 'Herrlichkeiten', what you will, so as to be equal to the ideal beloved.

Hence the 'Geliebte' is both distant object and simultaneously a means to some kind of magnification of the self. Which of the two rôles is more important in Rilke's poetry of this period tends to be decided by the individual context. In *Perlen entrollen* it is her final appearance or non-appearance which receives all the emphasis:

> siehe, so wälz ich, wenn du nicht kommst, mich zu Ende. (SW II, 42f.)

If the 'Geliebte' does not come then the pearls can never be strung together: there can be no 'Gastmahl', no unity within the self. But in the later poem *Du im Voraus* – where the 'Geliebte' is already 'lost' before any encounter has taken place – she can, as a purely imaginary figure, provide a unifying point and hence an enhanced meaning for 'alle die großen Bilder'. This meaning is, as it were, independent of its eventual referent; not the woman herself but the function of her image in the poet is important. In the poem *Atmete ich nicht*... the situation is initially still strongly influenced by that of *Perlen entrollen*... – in the first stanza everything seems to depend upon the 'Geliebte' appearing – but in the latter part of the poem the emphasis shifts towards what we might call with Novalis a kind of *Selbsterhebung*:

> Wenn mich durch des Ölbaums blasse Trennung
> Nacht mit Sternen stärker überwog,
> stand ich aufwärts, stand und bog
> mich zurück und lernte die Erkennung,
> die ich später nie auf dich bezog.
>
> O was ward mir Ausdruck eingesät,
> daß ich, wenn dein Lächeln je gerät,
> Weltraum auf dich überschaue.
> Doch du kommst nicht, oder kommst zu spät.
> Stürzt euch, Engel, über dieses blaue
> Leinfeld. Engel, Engel, mäht.

The 'Geliebte' is given up for lost, but all the by-products of waiting for her, the great abstractions with all their weight of connotations remain: 'Erkennung...Ausdruck...Weltraum' and are 'objectified' into the image 'dieses blaue/Leinfeld' and offered to the angels. Reading the poem a second time, one might indeed see 'um meinetwillen' very strongly implied in the 'um deinetwillen' of the second line. Longing for the 'künftige Geliebte' is made in this poem into a means of drawing nearer to the angel, towards a self-realisation which is equally future, in effect what is expressed in the following lines:

> ...Wir ahnen kaum,
> wie wir uns nach unermessenem Rate
> um zur Orgel bauen, horchend, leis,
> für den Sturm der kommenden Kantate
> und den Engel, der sie plötzlich weiß. (SW II, 394)

Here, if one substitutes 'um deinetwillen' for 'nach unermeßnem Rate' and the image of 'Leinfeld' for that of 'Orgel' the meaning is approximately the same. Being the organ for a celestial cantata or having one's face mown by angels are equally unfortunate and strained metaphors for the integration of the self in some sort of transcendent order, that is: the imbuing of human existence with the emotional intensity represented by the angel.

Let us try and see from the structure of the poem how this is brought about. In the beginning the 'Flutung', the 'Herrlich-keiten' are derived from above – 'aus Mitternächten'. This, Rilke suggests, is because they are needed for the encounter with the 'Geliebte'. At the same time their acquisition cannot but have an effect on the self – 'Raum in meinen Zügen'. Once this 'Beziehung zum Weitesten'[10] has been established – 'und lernte die Erkennung' – it remains only for the beloved to appear and perform suitably – 'wenn dein Lächeln je gerät' – for everything which has been experienced for her sake to reach its culmination. But then Rilke interposes the bald and final statement:

> Doch du kommst nicht, oder kommst zu spät.

which entirely dismisses the 'Geliebte' from the poem. The self is then left, not in the desperate plight of *Perlen entrollen*, but rather still in possession of 'Weltraum' and lacking only a human object to which to transfer it. 'Weltraum', which carries all the accumulated emotional values of 'Mitternächten, Flutung, Herrlichkeiten, Raum, Nacht mit Sternen, die Erkennung,

Ausdruck', becomes virtually an attribute of the self. The appeal to the angels to come and harvest can be seen as a metaphor for the degree of 'transcendence' which the poem, by poetic sleight-of-hand, has attained.

The technique by which this is done is an elaboration of that already observed by Wodtke:[11] the treatment of emotionally charged abstractions as concrete objects or quantities. 'Erkennung', 'Ausdruck', etc., are not assigned to any specific objects or given any specific contents and in this way acquire a kind of independent existence within the poem. While what they denote remains quite vague, their 'transcendent' connotations are all the more active. This enables 'Weltraum' in the final stanza to become something almost tangible – 'Weltraum auf dich über-schaue' – and it is but a further step to reinforce this effect by a striking visual image: 'dieses blaue/Leinfeld'. So, by the time the angels are addressed, whatever is expressed on the poet's face has become, within the context of the poem, just as much a 'Seiendes'[12] as his physical being, the 'Geliebte', the night and indeed the angels themselves.

The discussion of the means by which Rilke prepares the invocation to the angels at the end of the poem, has led somewhat away from the 'Leibesproblematik'. Let us now return to it by considering the poem in relation to the one previously treated: *Einmal nahm ich zwischen meine Hände*. Both poems have in common a reaching out towards the figure of the 'Geliebte' and a failure to achieve any satisfactory result; however, the reasons for this failure are quite different in each case. Indeed, it is hard to see how they can be made consistent with each other, For in the poem we have just looked at, the turning to the angels ostensibly comes about because the 'Geliebte' does not appear:

> Doch du kommst nicht, oder kommst zu spät.

The angels are invoked, as it were, by default. In the other poem, the 'Geliebte' is present, yet she might as well be still absent for all the communication that is possible. One reason for trying to reconcile these apparent inconsistencies is the strikingly similar use which Rilke makes of the 'Gesicht'-motif in the two cases. Communication is supposed to occur 'von Gesicht zu Gesicht'[13] and does not – in the one instance because the 'Geliebte' is not there, in the other because it seems to be impossible anyway. Moreover, the difficulty does not seem to lie in *what* is to be communicated – whether it be ordinary human feeling:

> alle Wellen unsres Herzens,
> Lust und Schwäche...

or something more grandiose:

> das ich, wenn dein Lächeln je gerät,
> Weltraum auf dich überschaue.

– but in the act of communication itself.

There is little point in complicating the already tortuous logic of these poems by trying to explain away their differences; they exist and they reflect confusions and ambiguities in Rilke's poetic thought in this period which centre around the figure of the 'Geliebte'. For the 'Geliebte' has an entirely different function in both poems. In *Atmete ich nicht* she is essentially an idealised 'Richtung des Herzens'. She has not yet appeared, yet her face is conceived in more than earthly terms: 'in unendlicher Vermutung', 'deinem großen Aufschaun', at the very beginning of the poem. In order to encounter such an ideal figure adequately, the poet must have already established his 'Beziehung zum Weitesten' and the imagery of the poem does this abundantly. That it is this *direction* of the poet's feelings and not the 'Geliebte' herself which is important is shown by the brevity, verging on indifference, with which her failure to appear in the flesh is registered and accepted. The 'Geliebte' may come or not come as she pleases; her meaning, the emotional equivalent of her presence *within* the poet – is transformed by the imagery into 'ein Seiendes' and projected into the sphere of the angels.

In *Einmal nahm ich* she is much more 'Gegenstand' than 'Richtung des Herzens', but the *theme* of love can no more be taken for itself than in the other poem. For here the failure of the lovers to communicate 'von Gesicht zu Gesicht' is an aspect of the failure of the self to find any kind of emotional participation at all, as the lament of the last lines shows. So that the conflict which we saw in *Die Geschwister I* is further illustrated by the contrast between these two poems. There we saw the conflict as between the need to seek fulfilment in the human sphere and the compulsion to find it outside. One side of this conflict is stressed in each of these poems and the figure of the 'Geliebte' changes accordingly: where it is used to denote a directedness towards the splendours of transcendent being, there the figure is idealised and her human presence seems almost superfluous; when the failure of the love situation appears as an aspect of the larger theme of alienation, then she is present but seen almost as part of the inanimate world ('Ding', 'Gegenstand').

It would be but a further step to say that the 'Geliebte' in each instance is no more than a pretext, that the 'real' themes are on the one hand the attempt to go beyond human existence and on the other the isolation of the self within it. One might then go still further and nominate a single 'real' theme for which these are in turn pretexts. But there are good reasons for not doing this. For while the 'Geliebte' does not appear in our analysis as a wholly consistent and unified figure, there is a definite problem of human love attached to both the major themes of transcendence and isolation. That it is different in each case does not necessarily mean that it is spurious, rather that the conflicts within the poet are so far from resolution that it is impossible to synthesise a single, definite function for the 'Geliebte'. Nor, it seems, was Rilke able or willing to exclude the problem of human love when writing either of 'das Nächste' or 'das Übernächste'. So the inconsistencies remain. We may dismiss them or else examine them for indications of a unity still to be achieved.

> Hinweg, die ich bat,   endlich mein Lächeln zu kosten
> (ob es kein köstliches wäre),
> unaufhaltsam genaht   hinter den Sternen im Osten
> wartet der Engel, daß ich mich kläre.

Daß ihn kein Spähn, keine Spur   euer beschränke,
wenn er die Lichtung betritt;
sei ihm das Leid, das ich litt,   wilde Natur:
er traue der Tränke.

War ich euch grün oder süß,   laßt uns das alles vergessen,
sonst überholt uns die Scham.
Ob ich blüh oder büß,   wird er gelassen ermessen,
den ich nicht lockte, der kam...   (SW ɪɪ, 72)

In this poem we find every appearance of a completely satisfactory solution to the rivalry between angel and 'Geliebte'.
It could be read as beginning where either *Atmete ich nicht*...
or *Einmal nahm ich*... leaves off: 'Lächeln' here could easily
be substituted for 'dieses blaue Leinfeld', or, alternatively, the
turning to the angel might be seen as a positive answer to the
question: und wem halten wir sie schließlich hin?

The explicit rejection of the figure of the 'Geliebte' (singular or
plural)[14] is balanced by the assumption that the angel is both
able and willing to take over her rôle. Rilke endeavours to impart
an air of certainty to this assumption by the deliberately slow
movement of the verse and the formal and elevated tone of
address. Even so, there is a certain ambivalence about the angel's
presence. There is no doubt whatsoever about his interest in the
self of the poem, yet he is still 'hinter den Sternen im Osten'
and the actual encounter is still seen as something future. The
reason for the hesitation is apparently contained in the words
'daß ich mich kläre': the self of the poem must shed or discard
the impurities of finite experience, the limitations represented by
the 'Geliebte' herself or by the poet's experience of her or them.
The image here implies not only that the 'Geliebte' might in
some way limit the appearance of the angel by being present, but
also that the memory of love situations in the poet must be put
aside because of the limiting nature of the love-situation as such.[15]
This is the meaning of the rather difficult image in the second
stanza. The meeting with the angel is envisaged as taking place
in a clearing in a forest from which all trace of the 'Geliebte'
must be absent. Within this image the poet calls upon 'wilde

Natur' to be 'das Leid, das ich litt'. This means that his past suffering, in the form of 'wilde Natur', the forest surrounding the clearing, is to provide the context in which the angel drinks from the 'Tränke' which is a further metaphor for 'Lächeln'. But while the suffering must be present as a necessary contrast to the meeting with the angel, it too must be purified into 'wilde Natur', transformed into anonymity and so no longer recognisable as the 'Pein der Liebesmöglichkeiten', as the memory of specific love situations. This is the sense of the words 'laßt uns das alles vergessen' of the third stanza – the poet wishes to be freed from the specific details of his past experience and to acknowledge it only as a generalised 'Leid, das ich litt', as a negative contrast to the experience of the angel. The shame which this is meant to avert is already familiar from the poem *Die Geschwister I*. It is at once the impiety of having ignored the angel in favour of what is closer at hand and at the same time the shame attendant on the failure of the love-situation as such. Hence the intention is essentially to put all unsolved problems of finite existence, of which love is here representative, out of sight and mind until such time as the angel shall provide the final answer:

Ob ich blüh oder büß,   wird er gelassen ermessen...

There is a remarkable similarity between the intention in this poem and the interpretation given above to the poem *Hinhalten will ich mich*. 'Daß ich mich kläre' denotes a process of directing the self entirely towards the angel by excluding as far as possible the specific problems of the human situation. In the other poem the image of the figureheads implies a similar exclusive directedness outwards towards something greater than human:

unnachgiebige Nacht, endlich dir ähnlicher sein. (SW II, 75)

Both poems are concerned with establishing an absolute emotional direction from which all human confusion and indecision is absent. Moreover, the fulfilments towards which both poems look can be seen as complementary. The self which is wholly directed towards the angel, is a unified self, emerging trium-

99   7-2

phantly from the background of past sorrows and confusions which themselves are now unified into 'wilde Natur'. The self which has taken on 'Züge des Meerraums', which has become more like the 'unnachgiebige Nacht', is not only unified in this sense but has transcended the limitations of humanity. Such fulfilments are clearly ideal. The question, which Fülleborn has very properly raised, is why they do not work. In other words, why does not the ending of *Hinweg die ich bat*..., for example, establish the relation of self to angel once and for all and provide a single and definite answer to the problem of transcendence in Rilke's poetry in the period under discussion?

One answer which emerges from the study so far, and which can be placed beside the view that the poems are really only disguised expressions of 'Künstlersehnsucht', is that fulfilments of the kind in which the self of the poems appears directed exclusively towards some being or power outside the human sphere, must necessarily be only partial and provisional precisely because of what they exclude. In these cases the self appears to be unified, but this is so only because the problems of existence in the world have been ignored or excluded. Our analysis of other poems of the collection has shown the urgency and magnitude which these problems can assume. That they are absent in some poems and overwhelmingly present in others points to the basic disunity of experience from which the *Gedichte an die Nacht* are written. This disunity is itself part of the subject matter of the collection and, characteristically, appears sometimes in one form, sometimes in another. In such poems as *Hinweg die ich bat*... there is every appearance of unified experience and we are left to deduce the incomplete nature of it from other poems in the collection, and from the fact that the apparent finality of the ending is not consistent with the overall development of Rilke's poetry.

That the place of the self in finite existence and its relation to transcendent powers may sometimes seem in these poems to constitute two different sets of problems points to the disunity itself and allows us to conjecture what kind of ideal unity the poems may be striving towards. A precise understanding of this ideal can best be gained by a detailed examination of those factors which stand in the way of attaining it. In doing so we must be prepared for contradictions as it is the presence of these contradictions within the experience of the poems which lends force to the striving for a final unity. That they are sometimes explicit within the one poem and at other times only visible from a thematic comparison of a number of poems, adds to the difficulty of the undertaking and determines the form of the present analysis.

The theme of the 'Geliebte' provides an example of this difficulty. She is the object both of extreme longing and of complete rejection and there are widely differing formulations of the problem of love in different contexts. If an overall understanding of the function of the 'Geliebte' in these poems is still possible, then it is because the understanding itself is that of a contradiction. One may see this more clearly by considering the fragment *An die Erwartete*, written in Toledo in November 1912, and the poems to Benvenuta of February and March 1914.[16]

The beginning of this fragment, written shortly before the first of the *Gedichte an die Nacht*, presents an idea already familiar to us from the poems *Atmete ich nicht...* and *Du im Voraus...*:

> ...komm wann du sollst. Dies alles wird durch mich
> hindurchgegangen sein zu deinem Atem.
> Ich habs, um deinetwillen, namenlos
> lang angesehen mit dem Blick der Armut
> und so geliebt als tränkst du es schon ein.   (SW II, 388)

The appearance of the 'Geliebte' is to provide a meaningful culmination of the poet's experience up to that point. Like the 'Flutung' of the later poem, he has assimilated 'Dies alles' entirely for the sake of the future encounter – 'um deinetwillen'. The selflessness of this is stressed in the words 'mit dem Blick der Armut' – these experiences have not become 'Besitz' – nor have they been loved for their own sake, but only as a projection of the love he is later to feel: 'als tränkst du es schon ein'. Although the actual appearance of the 'Geliebte' is still necessary – the compromise of her being 'im Voraus/verloren' has not yet been thought of – we may nevertheless say in the words of the later poem that the longing for her gives 'Dies alles' some kind of unifying meaning – a meaning which can only become complete in the actual meeting of the lovers.

So far the fragment appears as a quite direct expression of the theme of 'die künftige Geliebte'[17] and the only obscurity is the precise nature of 'Dies alles'. The following lines, however, complicate the situation vastly by undertaking two things at once. For they cast doubt on the outcome of the eventual encounter and describe the form which it is to take by an extended explanation of 'Dies alles'. The tone of doubt, but not the reason for it, is introduced in the first words and the sense is left incomplete through several reprises, each of which adds more and more elements to the list of what is to be 'given' to the 'Geliebte':

> Und doch: bedenk ichs, daß ich dieses, mich,
> Gestirne, Blumen und den schönen Wurf
> der Vögel aus nachwinkendem Gesträuch,
> der Wolken Hochmut und was nachts der Wind
> mir antun konnte, mich aus einem Wesen
> hinüberwandelnd in ein nächstes – daß
> ich eines nach dem andern, denn ich bins,
> bin was der Tränke Rauschen mir im Ohr
> zurückließ, bin der Wohlgeschmack, den einst
> die schöne Frucht an meinen Lippen ausgab –
> daß ich dies alles, wenn du einmal da bist,
> bis rückwärts zu des Kindes niederm Anblick
> in Blumenkelche, da die Wiesen hochstehn,
> ja bis zu einem Lächeln meiner Mutter,
> das ich vielleicht gedrängt von deinem Dasein,
> annehme wie Entwendetes – daß ich
> dann unerschöpflich Tag und Nacht soviel
> entbehrend angeeignete Natur
> hingeben sollte – wissend nicht, ob das
> was in dir aufglüht Meines ist...

What the poet 'dann unerschöpflich Tag und Nacht... hingeben sollte' is expressed most succinctly in the first line by the word 'mich', but it is the way in which this is presented which deserves our interest. For the 'mich' is seen as a succession of sensory images reaching back in time to childhood and to be communicated to the 'Geliebte'. They are termed 'angeeignete Natur', which is a somewhat puzzling formulation. Presumably they have become part of the self – 'denn ich bins...' – as a result of being experienced, and yet the opening lines tell us that they have not been experienced for themselves, but rather 'um deinetwillen'. Hence they do not acquire their full meaning until they have been imparted to the 'Geliebte' and since they are, in effect, the poet's self, this self remains incomplete until she appears. This incompleteness is expressed in the word 'entbehrend' in the lines:

> ...daß ich
> dann unerschöpflich Tag und Nacht soviel
> entbehrend angeeignete Natur
> hingeben sollte –

If we take 'entbehrend' as modifying 'angeeignete', it is implied that these images or experiences were acquired while the self was suffering privation, felt the absence of what is to give them their final unity and meaning, namely the 'Geliebte'. Hence what is expected from the encounter is, in the words of *Perlen entrollen*, the 'starke Schließe, die sie verhielte, Geliebte'. In other words, the 'Geliebte' is to provide a proof or guarantee of the unity of the poet's existence, is to give a single and secure meaning to all these accumulated experiences. That this is so, is confirmed by the fact that when the tone of doubt which has permeated the whole enumeration becomes explicit, it is in these terms:

> ...wissend nicht, ob das
> was in dir aufglüht Meines ist:

The anxiety which undermines the longing for the 'künftige Geliebte' is that there may still be no visible unity in all these experiences and hence no proven unity of the self.

The resulting uncertainty proceeds in two directions. Firstly, the encounter with the 'Geliebte' was to guarantee the meaningful continuity of the self in time – 'bis rückwärts zu des Kindes niederm Anblick' – a continuity which may be made uncertain or precarious by the nature of experience itself:

> ...und was nachts der Wind
> mir antun konnte, mich aus einem Wesen
> hinüberwandelnd in ein nächstes...

Secondly, the encounter was to prove the relatedness of the self to the other, in that the 'Ich' would recognise 'Meines' in the 'Geliebte'. In the lines which conclude the fragment it is this fear of unrelatedness which predominates:

> ...vielleicht
> wirst du nur schöner, ganz aus eigner Schönheit
> vom Überfluß der Ruh in deinen Gliedern,
> vom Süßesten in deinem Blut, was weiß ich,
> weil du dich selbst in deiner Hand erkennst,
> weil dir das Haar an deinen Schultern schmeichelt,
> weil irgendetwas in der dunklen Luft
> sich dir verständigt, weil du mich vergißt,
> weil du nicht hinhörst, weil du eine Frau bist...

After a few more lines beginning with a renewed 'wenn ichs bedenke...' the fragment breaks off, as well it might – for the confident and hopeful tone of the opening lines has dissolved into complete uncertainty in the word 'Meines'.

This fragment has been interpreted instead of the finished poem *Perlen entrollen* not only because the latter poem has been given an excellent interpretation by Fülleborn, but also because the fragment, both in its description of the form the encounter is to take and in its statement of the doubts which surround it, is closer to the themes which we have examined in the *Gedichte an die Nacht*. The only disagreement with Fülleborn's interpretation is once more one of perspective. Of the 'Geliebte' in *Perlen entrollen* Fülleborn says:

Sie soll 'starke Schließe' sein: in verhaltender Kraft die Konzentration ermöglichen, aus der allein das Werk entstehen könnte...[18]

Again one can question the necessity of supplying the further stage, 'das Werk', and hence reducing the problems of existence in the poem to the single one of attaining the degree of concentration necessary for artistic production. The data in *Perlen entrollen* from which this point could be argued are somewhat meagre. But the fragment, in which the 'Geliebte' plays a very similar rôle, gives us the possibility of an interpretation in which the problems of existence as such need not be seen as secondary to those of artistic creation.

We saw that what was expected from the meeting with the 'Geliebte' was the establishment of a unity of the self by the poet's first giving himself and then recognising himself in the other person. This idea appears with a different emphasis in the epigraph to the poem *Mandelbäume in Blüte*:

Die Mandelbäume in Blüte: alles, was wir hier leisten können, ist, sich ohne Rest erkennen in der irdischen Erscheinung. (SW II, 43)

But the whole tone of doubt in the fragment we are examining stems from the fear that one might *not* recognise oneself in that aspect of 'der irdischen Erscheinung' on which one has placed most hope, namely the 'Geliebte'. For this 'sich ohne Rest erkennen' amounts to a proof of existence, and this proof must be sought in the other when it is not present as a spontaneous feeling in the self:

In trüben Spiegeln suchen wir Beweis
für unser Aufstehn, während unbewiesen
der Schlaf zurückbleibt. (SW II, 398)

It is the absence of such proof which makes past experiences appear as alien in the consciousness and which is expressed as a feeling of estrangement from the world in which one exists. Clearly it is this proof which the encounter with the 'Geliebte' is expected to provide. And it is the fear of a lack of reciprocity between self and other which comes out so strongly in the latter part of the fragment:

...was weiß ich,
weil du dich selbst in deiner Hand erkennst,
weil dir das Haar an deinen Schultern schmeichelt,
weil irgendetwas in der dunklen Luft
sich dir verständigt, weil du mich vergißt...

The fragment is ostensibly about the need for the self to attain some certainty as to the structure and value of its own existence and this need is expressed in terms which have no *prima facie* relation to the further problem of the creation of poetry. It may well be that Rilke did in fact desire this certainty as a basis for his poetry, but this is not the perspective which the poetry itself offers in the case of *An die Erwartete* and I do not see the need in this instance to go so far beyond what the fragment appears to be about.

An die Erwartete both offers the coming of the 'Geliebte' as the solution to certain problems and in the very same lines takes back this apparent solution by shrouding the whole future encounter in doubt – why? The answer would seem to be that love is subject to the very same ills which it is expected to cure, that instead of overcoming the alienation both within and around the self the meeting may only sustain and indeed intensify this feeling of alienation. This is the case in the poem *Einmal nahm ich*... and elsewhere and it seems to be part of the structure of experience itself, one of the determinants of 'Gegenüber-sein'. But if this feeling of 'Fremdheit' is given as one of the basic data of experience, so equally is the need to overcome it, to create or be granted some form of 'Beteiligung'. In the resulting conflict, which is not resolved within the framework of the *Gedichte an die Nacht*, Rilke again and again has recourse to the figure of the 'Geliebte' to illustrate the many possible forms which this conflict takes. Or, to put it in somewhat more human terms: despite the strong element of scepticism and disappointment which is always likely to colour his attitude towards the 'Geliebte' and despite such programmatic rejections as we find in the letter to Karl von der Heydt, Rilke is never able to renounce finally the possibility of a solution through love and the proof of this is in his compulsion to continue making poetry out of its difficulties and failures. The love situation often comes to represent the wider problem of the relation of self and world and, as it is the attempt to establish this relation as meaningful, in spite of the various negatives that are part of it, which provides the main themes of the *Gedichte an die Nacht*, so we find repeated expressions of the desire for love side by side with those of alienation and despair.

This would be complex enough in itself, but it is made more so by another factor which is strangely absent from the fragment *An die Erwartete*, but which is also a basic determinant of the general situation of the *Gedichte an die Nacht*. This is, broadly speaking, the need for transcendence. 'Hiersein' in the *Gedichte an die Nacht* is, on the whole, anything but 'herrlich'. The limitations of existence in the finite world and its inferiority to the existence of the angels is a frequent and emotionally weighted theme. So that when Rilke speaks of 'Beteiligung am endgültig Daseienden'[19] he means something more than an overcoming of the alienation between the self and the world of objects or the 'Geliebte'. He means in fact a form of human existence which also partakes of transcendence; he means being recognised by the angel or acknowledged by 'die große Nacht' as well. So it is that in these poems we find a reaching out both towards 'das Nächste' and 'das Übernächste', sometimes separately, sometimes together and with confusing results. The first poem of *Die spanische Trilogie*, for example, is primarily about the relation of the self to the immediate surroundings, yet at the end of it the need for transcendence takes over and we have the image of an object, or poem if necessary, which exists quite outside the limitations of finite reality. In this way the rivalry between 'Nacht' and 'Geliebte' arises and it persists because Rilke cannot ever really forgo the possibility of reaching a solution that either represents. Nor does he succeed in reconciling them.

This rivalry is anything but a static opposition. With the fluidity that is characteristic of the figures in these poems, 'Nacht' and 'Geliebte' are differently related from context to context and may even appear to exchange rôles. In the poem *Gedanken der Nacht* the proof with which the night responds, confirms the unity of the self in time, from childhood to the present – precisely what is hoped for from the 'Geliebte' in *An die Erwartete*. Conversely, in *Die Geschwister I* the sister assumes the 'unerschöpfliche Erscheinung' proper to the night. Again, in *Atmete ich nicht aus Mitternächten* it is for the sake of an idealised 'Geliebte' that the poet experiences the 'Flutung' of the night, whereas in other

attempt, as we have said, is not successful. As a proof of this, the rejection of the 'Geliebte' in favour of the angel which appears in such a poem as *Hinweg die ich bat*. . . is completely revoked by the poems addressed to Benvenuta of February and March 1914. In these poems there is, intermingled with the theme of the expected fulfilment in love, a strong note of renunciation. It is as if Rilke has given up the attempt at reconciliation and desires only fulfilment in the human sphere. In one of the poems he seems to review what he has attempted in the *Gedichte an die Nacht* and have second thoughts about it:

> Ach die Nacht verlangte nichts von mir.
> Doch wenn ich mich zu den Sternen kehrte,
> der Versehrte an das Unversehrte:
> Worauf stand ich? War ich hier? (SW II, 956)

One might read this as an admission that in the *Gedichte an die Nacht* too much was attempted, that the turning to the stars and the attempt to relate them to the self threatened the latter's existence in the immediate world. And in the second poem addressed to the newfound 'Geliebte' Rilke makes his renunciation quite plain:

> Schau ich aber leise auf, so heilt
> mir die Welt am milderen Gesichte –
> oh so war ja doch: daß ich verzichte,
> allen Engeln noch nicht mitgeteilt. (SW II, 957)

How the angels received the news must forever remain open to conjecture, but, more seriously, it is clear that this renunciation may be understood as meaning not only that Rilke no longer expects to encounter the angel, but, more importantly, the need to reconcile 'das Nächste' with 'das Übernächste' no longer creates the same acute tension as produced the bulk of the *Gedichte an die Nacht*. It is in a sense ironical that this renunciation was no more final or lasting than the Benvenuta episode itself and that most of the conflicts of the *Gedichte an die Nacht* were to reappear in various forms in the years which follow.

4. THE NIGHT AND THE ANGEL

In this chapter we are confronted with the vexed question of the nature of the angel, not only in these poems but ultimately in the *Duineser Elegien*. The difficulty of establishing what the angel is or is not, whether it is to be taken as an entity, a symbol or a quasi-allegorical figure, is amply shown by the many different interpretations offered in Rilke-criticism. Here it is not so much a question of fitting the angel into any particular theory of Rilke's work, but of establishing its function in particular contexts. There is a strong tendency in literature on Rilke to imply or assume an identity of the angel of the *Duineser Elegien* with that of the *Gedichte an die Nacht*. The preliminary investigation of the night-motif showed a diversity of possible meanings which it could assume according to context, and the analysis of the 'Geliebte' indicated that a single figure may be used to express conflicting directions within the overall thematic framework of these poems. It is thus open to question whether the figure of the angel has a simple and obvious unity, or whether one may not differentiate a variety of functions from context to context. As a first and necessarily somewhat crude justification for this approach, one may contrast the lines from the second Elegy, written in February 1912:

> Träte der Erzengel jetzt, der gefährliche, hinter den Sternen
> eines Schrittes nur nieder und herwärts: hochauf-
> schlagend erschlüg uns das eigene Herz.   (SW i, 689)

with those from one of the *Gedichte an die Nacht* written towards the end of 1913:

> So, nun wird es doch der Engel sein,
> der aus meinen Zügen langsam trinkt
> der Gesichte aufgeklärten Wein.
> Dürstender, wer hat dich hergewinkt?
>
> .   .   .
>
>   Daß
> *du* noch dürstest. Überlaß
> dich dem Durst. (Wie hast du mich gepackt.)   (SW ii, 71)

Clearly, if the angel in both cases is to be termed 'Gestalt der Transzendenz',[1] then what constitutes transcendence is in sore need of definition. Equally, if the angel is to be understood as a projection of the poet's subjectivity, then it remains to ask why this projection should have such a radically different appearance and function in the two contexts. With these questions in mind we shall proceed to examine the poem *An den Engel*, written in Ronda at the same time as *Die spanische Trilogie*: January 1913.

So as to give the problems which this poem presents as sharp a definition as possible, I shall take advantage of the perspective offered by two quite opposed interpretations, those of Wodtke and Buddeberg. The disagreement is most clear in the ways in which the ending of the poem is understood. For Wodtke the ending is unequivocally negative:

So bleibt die unüberbrückbare Ferne zwischen Mensch und Engel bestehen, auch wenn das Gedicht mit dem verzweifelten Wunsch schließt, der Engel möge ihn durch seinen Glanz so erhellen, daß er 'angeschauter bei den Sternen' werde...Aber diese Verwandlung vollzieht sich nicht, die Einheit mit allem Seienden stellt sich nicht her, und so bleibt ihm nichts als Verzweiflung.[2]

Buddeberg, on the other hand, sees it in equally positive terms:

Die negative Grenzerfahrung ist damit positiviert. Der Mensch erfährt von Jenseits der Grenze etwas, das ihm zuwächst: Erhellung...Grenze, zunächst Ausschließung, wird zur Brücke. Sie betretend, erfährt der Mensch nunmehr sein bisheriges Dahinschwinden in der Verwandlung zur Dauer. Er wird 'angeschauter bei den Sternen.' Seine Vergänglichkeit – der grundsätzlichen Möglichkeit nach wenigstens – ist geheilt.[3]

This difference hinges to a large extent on the way in which one understands the lines in the final stanza:

> Daß ich lärme, wird an dir nicht lauter,
> wenn du mich nicht fühltest, weil ich *bin*.

but underlying this there is a basic disagreement about the nature of the angel.

While for Buddeberg the angel is 'Gestalt der Transzendenz' in the fullest meaning of the word, Wodtke sees this 'Antithese von himmlischem und irdischem Sein' as 'in die Immanenz verlegt' and continues:

die im Engel zur mythischen Gestalt erhobene ideale Seinsweise der Vollkommenheit steht der ins Ungewisse, in den Irrtum geworfenen Existenz des Menschen schroff gegenüber. Der Standpunkt des Dichters aber ist auch bei ihm wie bei Klopstock identisch mit dem des Engels...⁴

There is the immediate distinction that if one accepts the angel as a genuinely transcendent entity, then whatever being it may have must lie beyond the limits of human experience, must represent a mode of being quite other than human existence. If we understand the figure of the angel as 'in die Immanenz verlegt', then the 'ideale Seinsweise der Vollkommenheit' may be seen as a kind of perfection which human existence may hope to realise in itself – or at least come closer to than it could to a mode of being which by definition transcends the immanent sphere. One's understanding of the poem therefore depends to a large extent on where one places the 'Grenze' between man and angel and how one evaluates the regions on either side of it. This is closely linked with the problem of the perspective of the poem. Wodtke seems to imply a certain dualism of perspective by implicitly contrasting the 'ins Ungewisse...geworfene Existenz des Menschen' with the standpoint of the poet which is 'identisch mit dem des Engels'. As the poem is entirely in the first person, there is the problem of which standpoint the 'Ich' of the poem represents. Again on the question of perspective, Buddeberg's interpretation calls for a re-understanding of the beginning of the poem in terms of its conclusion on the grounds that the poem exemplifies 'Verwandlung...innerhalb eines Gedichts',⁵ which is presumably meant to convey that the poem may be read differently by a change of perspective. It is with difficulties such as these that one must try to come to terms when interpreting the poem.

> Starker, stiller, an den Rand gestellter
> Leuchter: oben wird die Nacht genau.
> Wir ver-geben uns in unerhellter
> Zögerung an deinem Unterbau.

The opening stanza presents the first of a series of antitheses in which human existence is contrasted with that of the angel. The angel appears as a light in darkness and thereby distinguishes two kinds of darkness from each other. There is the darkness 'oben' which is made or seen to be 'genau' by the radiance proceeding from the angel and the darkness beneath, the 'unerhellter Zögerung' in which human existence expends itself. 'Genau' is not readily understandable as a visual image, unless it be taken to mean that the limits of the night become precisely defined, which is unlikely. Rather, it may be understood as a mode of being which is the antithesis of the confusion and uncertainty ascribed to humanity. This somewhat mannered distinction between darkness which is 'genau' and darkness which is 'unerhellt' does not make our understanding of the phrase 'an den Rand' any easier. In terms of the visual imagery the 'Rand' would seem to represent a horizon from which the angel illuminates the night above and does not illuminate mankind below, but there is also the possibility that 'Rand' is to be taken figuratively, so that one might see the angel as standing 'am Rande des Daseins', 'am Rande des Erfahrbaren'. If this is so and the 'Rand' represents the furthest limit of human perception and experience, then it is strange that the 'Genauigkeit' of the night above is known and perceived by those who live 'in unerhellter Zögerung'.

Though this may at first appear somewhat captious, it bears on the very real problem of establishing where the border lies between man and angel. Buddeberg's interpretation is anything but clear on this point. Beginning from: 'die Unüberbrückbarkeit des Abgrunds zwischen modernem Bewußtsein und Transzendenz' she initially places the angel in the beyond – 'denn er steht hier ganz jenseits der Grenze'. Later, however, and by no visible process, it is the angel 'der die Grenze besetzt hat', 'der auf der Grenze steht'.[6] Nor is the angel alone on the border drawn across the abyss, for: 'Sie betretend, erfährt der Mensch nunmehr sein bisheriges Dahinschwinden in der Verwandlung zur Dauer.'[7] Wodtke speaks much more consistently of an 'unüberbrückbare Ferne' between ideal and real existence and denies that any such *rapprochement* between man and angel as

Buddeberg envisages takes place. Remains the question: is there an abyss between man and angel or is the distance to be seen as a matter of degree? In other words, is the angel 'Transzendenz' in the sense of the completely other and unreachable, or else a more intense or pure form of 'Existenz'. From our analysis of the 'Nacht'-motif it is advisable to consider a third possibility: that the angel is sometimes one, sometimes the other in an attempt to establish a mediation. If we accept the third possibility then the problem of transcendence becomes in the first instance a problem of *definition*. We shall return to this after examining the rest of the poem.

The imagery of the first stanza, at any rate, does not permit us to reach any final conclusion. On the one hand the difference implied in the contrast of 'genau' and 'unerhellt' could represent 'das Absolute im Gegensatz zur Endlichkeit'.[8] On the other hand, the fact that 'wir' appear to be in contact with the angel's 'Unterbau' suggests a possible continuity between the two spheres. This possibility is reinforced by the next stanza:

> Unser ist: den Ausgang nicht zu wissen
> aus dem drinnen irrlichen Bezirk,
> du erscheinst auf unsern Hindernissen
> und beglühst sie wie ein Hochgebirg.

The first two lines may be read as an amplification of 'in unerhellter Zögerung'; the second two lines indeed stress the existence of impediments, painful or limiting aspects of human existence, but the fact that angelic radiance falls on them surely implies, as does the use of 'Unterbau' in the stanza before, that there is no *absolute* separation between human and angelic being. Buddeberg's interpretation is curious on this point. She begins by saying: 'Das Licht aber strahlt nur herauf und nicht herab.'[9] But then continues:

Die folgenden Verse rufen noch ausdrücklich den Eindruck herauf, als ob sein Licht keine Erleuchtung für uns, sondern nur die Bescheinung der Hindernisse bewirke...

Quite how the 'Bescheinung der Hindernisse' is achieved if the angel's light is directed exclusively upwards, is a very good question. This contradiction is in the interpretation rather than the poem itself. For if to live 'in unerhellter Zögerung' means that one's existence consists largely of obstacles, then any light falling on these will presumably (in terms of the imagery) throw them into sharp relief. If this light is a metaphor for a comparison of real with ideal or transcendent existence then the obstacles appear magnified by it – 'wie ein Hochgebirg'. Buddeberg's confusion lies in taking 'unerhellt' in a purely visual sense. Rather, human existence is 'unerhellt' because it is limited, transient and petty in comparison with that of the angel. This darkness, which is that of everything negative in the human condition, goes beyond the purely *visual* level of the imagery of the first stanzas and is in fact what is elaborated in the lament of the following stanzas:

> Deine Lust ist *über* unserm Reiche,
> und wir fassen kaum den Niederschlag;
> wie die reine Nacht der Frühlingsgleiche
> stehst du teilend zwischen Tag und Tag.

> Wer vermöchte je dir einzuflößen
> von der Mischung, die uns heimlich trübt?
> Du hast Herrlichkeit von allen Größen,
> und wir sind am Kleinlichsten geübt.

The inferiority and privation which are seen as part of the human situation make explicit what the 'unerhellt' implies. The force of the stanzas is once again to emphasise the distance between man and angel, the 'Herrlichkeit' of one and its absence in the other, yet Rilke refrains from making this distance an absolute one. The simile of 'die reine Nacht der Frühlingsgleiche' indeed brings the angel very close to human experience in one sense, while in another it emphasises the lack of any emotional reciprocity. The next stanza, although developing a further antithesis, treats human and angelic existence as essentially *comparable*:

> Wenn wir weinen, sind wir nichts als rührend,
> wenn wir anschaun sind wir höchstens wach;

Here the deprecatory tone of 'nichts als rührend' and 'höchstens wach' must imply: 'in comparison with the intensity of an angel's "Anschaun", ours can at best be described as just being awake.' So that the difference here seems to be entirely that of the intensity with which a certain action is performed by man or angel. In the next stanza the orderly progression of antitheses is interrupted and the lament becomes quite unrestrained:

> ...Engel, klag ich, klag ich?
> Doch wie wäre denn die Klage mein?
> Ach ich schreie, mit zwei Hölzern schlag ich
> und ich meine nicht, gehört zu sein.

Again, it is possible to interpret the angel's not hearing either as indifference to human suffering – in the sense of the equanimity of the gods in the poem *So angestrengt...* – or else as being indicative of an absolute difference between the two modes of being, such that no communication between them is possible. Buddeberg's contention:

> Man würde den Charakter dieser Wirklichkeit völlig verkennen, wenn man annähme, daß hiermit ein 'Antworten' des Engels im Sinne der Herstellung einer subjektiv-individuellen Bezogenheit eingeschlossen wäre.[10]

is certainly not supported by the tone of the poem at this point and if one looks at other of the *Gedichte an die Nacht*, such as the poem *Hinweg die ich bat...*, the urgent desire for a purely individual fulfilment is unmistakable. Rilke may indeed in the preceding stanzas adopt the more general 'wir'-form in delineating the negative aspects of human existence, but the tendency throughout the collection is to strive for 'Beteiligung' as an isolated individual.

The final stanza of the poem is that on which the overall interpretation hinges:

> Daß ich lärme, wird an dir nicht lauter,
> wenn du mich nicht fühltest, weil ich *bin*.
> Leuchte, leuchte! Mach mich angeschauter
> bei den Sternen. Denn ich schwinde hin.

Buddeberg sees the conditional clause: 'wenn du mich nicht fühltest' as implying a possible 'Seins-Verhältnis' between man and angel and continues:

Ist der Engel Gestalt der Transzendenz und die Bezogenheit des Menschen ein Seins-Verhältnis, so ist garnicht möglich, daß dieses Verhältnis in der Einseitigkeit einer nicht gehörten Klage sich erschöpfe. Engel und Mensch stehen zueinander als Seiende im fühlenden Bezug.[11]

It is possible to take the conditional clause in the sense in which Buddeberg does, that is: as implying a positive answer, but the possibility which this contains: that there is no absolute separation between angel and man, is already given from the beginning of the poem. It is present in phrases such as 'an deinem Unterbau', 'du erscheinst...und beglühst sie', and in the implication in stanza 5 that the difference between human and angelic being is one of degrees of intensity. It is not necessary to invoke 'Verwandlung' or to insist so heavily on one possible interpretation of one line in the last stanza to establish the possibility of communication between man and angel. The absence of this communication is constant throughout the poem and produces the lament; the ending of the poem, however, is left open. It is balanced between the despair on the one hand which is still present in the final words: 'Denn ich schwinde hin' and on the other the 'unsägliche Hoffnung' that awareness of and contact with the angel may produce some radical change within the self. In terms of the poem this change would mean that the angelic radiance, instead of serving only to illuminate the 'Hindernisse' would make the self 'angeschauter bei den Sternen'. But how does this relate to the problem of transcendence?

If we are to speak meaningfully of transcendence, then we should, strictly speaking, not use the word merely to denote a more intense form of human existence. Rather, it must denote otherness in the sense in which Jaspers defines it:

Transzendenz ist das Sein, das nicht Dasein und Bewußtsein und auch nicht Existenz ist, sondern alle transzendiert. Es ist das Absolute im Gegensatz zur Endlichkeit, Bezogenheit und Ungeschlossenheit von allem, was für Bewußtsein und im Bewußtsein ist. Dieser Begriff des Transzendenten meint nicht etwa, was über meine gegenwärtige Erfahrung hinausgeht, aber prinzipiell der Möglichkeit nach von mir erfahren werden könnte, sondern transzendent ist, was schlechthin nie Gegenstand werden kann wie Dasein, und nie als es selbst bewußtseinsgegenwärtig wird wie mögliche Existenz.[12]

In these terms, if the angel of the poem is to be seen wholly as 'Gestalt der Transzendenz' then the frontier between man and angel must be in principle uncrossable. The being of the angel must lie outside what 'der Möglichkeit nach von mir erfahren werden könnte'. Is this the case in the poem? Hardly, as from the very beginning of the poem the being of the angel is described and defined as something experienced in human terms. Certainly there is a complete lack of *emotional* reciprocity between man and angel, and certainly human existence is lamented as being far less splendid, but the imagery of the poem makes the postulation of an absolute 'Grenze' in *conceptual* terms highly questionable. Indeed, one may say that the angel is throughout the poem 'bewußtseinsgegenwärtig wie mögliche Existenz' – precisely as that possibility which the poet grasps at in the lines:

> ...Mach mich angeschauter
> bei den Sternen. Denn ich schwinde hin.

The obvious criticism of Buddeberg's interpretation is that she begins by postulating an unbridgeable 'Abgrund zwischen modernem Bewußtsein und Transzendenz' only to be able to cross it later:

> Das umfassende Seins-Verhältnis enthüllt sich erst in einer bejahenden Grenz-überwindung.[13]

But it is precisely the existence of such an absolute separation which the poem makes ambiguous, and this ambiguity is still present in the lines:

> Daß ich lärme, wird an dir nicht lauter,
> wenn du mich nicht fühltest, weil ich *bin.*

Either there is a 'Grenze', in which case no emotional communication is possible, or there is not, in which case the angel becomes accessible, is in Wodtke's terms 'in die Immanenz verlegt' as possible existence. But the real function of the poem is to preserve the tension between these alternatives by leaving both open. To conclude either: 'und so bleibt ihm nichts als Verzweiflung' or: 'Damit ist seine negative Grenzerfahrung verwandelt', is to overlook, from opposing points of view, the essentially unresolved character of the ending of the poem.

It is this lack of resolution which creates the problem of the perspective of the poem. It is because both possibilities are present that the self of the poem must in Wodtke's interpretation represent both the 'ins Ungewisse...geworfene Existenz des Menschen' and the 'Standpunkt des Dichters', and that Buddeberg calls for a second reading of the poem on the grounds of the supposed 'Grenzüberwindung' in the final stanza. What this means in effect is that the angel in the second reading is no longer the 'Gestalt der Transzendenz' in the sense in which her interpretation begins. If one recognises, however, that the figure of the angel is ambivalent from the beginning, then there is no 'Verwandlung', no 'Grenzüberwindung', but rather a *duality of perspective* which persists throughout the poem. This duality is very much a matter of nuances and is carried by the constantly changing and elusive metaphors in which man and angel are compared and by such semantic differences as that between 'beglüht werden' and 'unerhellt sein'.

Wodtke's and Buddeberg's interpretations have been compared because of the insight they afford into the problem of establishing the meaning of the angel with any certainty. The problem is aggravated when the definition of transcendence becomes as flexible as it does in Buddeberg's interpretation. If one begins by defining transcendence as that which lies on the other side of an unbridgeable abyss from human existence, well and good. Transcendent entities are then in Jaspers' terms 'was schlechthin nie Gegenstand werden kann wie Dasein'. However, if one then says: 'Engel und Mensch stehen zu einander als Seiende im fühlenden Bezug',[14] then the logical distinction between immanence and transcendence present in the previous definition no longer applies: the absolute 'Grenze' which the first definition posits no longer exists and hence the angel cannot be transcendent in the same sense. Admittedly, the ambiguity is present in the poem itself, and gives rise to Wodtke's quite opposite interpretation. But it is then the task of the critic to examine this ambiguity.

One may explain this further by comparing the figure of the angel in the first two *Duineser Elegien* with certain of the *Gedichte an die Nacht*. In the relevant sections of the first two Elegies two things are emphasised concerning the angels. Firstly, that they are terrible and secondly, that any attempt at contact on the part of man would be fatal, for:

> ...ich verginge von seinem/stärkeren Dasein. (SW 1, 685)
> ...hochauf-/schlagend erschlüg uns das eigene Herz. (SW 1, 689)

Here the complete otherness of the angel is clearly established, and the images which are used invoke a reality in which the laws which govern the sphere of human experience are reversed, for example:

> *Spiegel*: die die entströmte eigene Schönheit
> wiederschöpfen zurück in das eigene Antlitz. (SW 1, 689)

But in the poetry written in the years following there is a distinct tendency to make the angel a much more anthropomorphic figure and to represent him in terms of analogies with human experience. This is most obvious in the poem quoted in part above:

> So, nun wird es doch der Engel sein,
> der aus meinen Zügen langsam trinkt
> der Gesichte aufgeklärten Wein.
> Dürstender, wer hat dich hergewinkt?
>
> Daß du dürstest. Dem der Katarakt
> Gottes stürzt durch alle Adern. Daß
> *du* noch dürstest. Überlaß
> dich dem Durst. (Wie hast du mich gepackt.)
>
> Und ich fühle fließend, wie dein Schaun
> trocken war, und bin zu deinem Blute
> so geneigt, daß ich die Augenbraun
> dir, die reinen, völlig überflute. (SW 11, 71)

Here it is remarkable that not only does contact with the angel *not* result in the destruction of the self, but that the angel's indifference and self-sufficiency, by which he is virtually defined in the first two Elegies, have become the exact opposite. More importantly for our discussion, the angel can no longer be termed a 'Gestalt der Transzendenz' in the sense of the first two *Duineser*

Elegien but has become a mediate figure. Whereas before the angel as 'des Schrecklichen Anfang' represented the furthest limit of human perception, the imagery of this poem presents his being as the point where 'der Katarakt Gottes' may mingle with 'der Gesichte... Wein'. This possibility of mediation is essentially the same as that given by the figure of the shepherd in the third part of *Die spanische Trilogie* and in contexts such as these lines from *Sterne hinter Oliven*:

> Sieh, wie im selbstvergessenen Geäste,
> das Nächste sich mit Namenlosem mischt.[15]

This transition from an absolute to a mediate figure is, by the very nature of the *Gedichte an die Nacht*, not a clear and logical progression, nor is it an explicit theme in the poetry. We may gain some insight into it, however, by comparing the structures of the two poems *Siehe, Engel fühlen durch den Raum* and *Der du mich mit diesem überhöhtest*. (SW II, 68f.)

The first, which reads like an elaboration of the fifth stanza of *An den Engel*, has for its theme the comparison of human with angelic existence:

> Siehe, Engel fühlen durch den Raum
> ihre unaufhörlichen Gefühle.
> Unsre Weißglut wäre ihre Kühle.
> Siehe, Engel glühen durch den Raum.
>
> Während uns, die wirs nicht anders wissen,
> eins sich wehrt und eins umsonst geschieht,
> schreiten sie, von Zielen hingerissen,
> durch ihr ausgebildetes Gebiet.

From the point of view of humanity the comparison is overwhelmingly negative, as it is in *An den Engel*. Yet if one contrasts the representation of the angels here with such images from the second Elegy as:

> ... – Pollen der blühenden Gottheit,
> Gelenke des Lichtes, Gänge, Treppen, Throne...

the tendency to bring the angels closer to human terms is apparent. The angels have emotions which immeasurably surpass those of man, but the difference is given as one of intensity and not of essence.

Similarly the 'unerhellter Zögerung' in which humanity pursues its goals is contrasted with the complete certainty with which the angels pursue theirs, but at the same time the unqualified analogy with human behaviour is clearly a step towards a mediation. This becomes clearer in the structure of the second poem:

> Der du mich mit diesen überhöhtest:
> Nächten – ist es nicht als ob du mir,
> Unbegrenzter, mehr Gefühl gebötest,
> als ich fühlend fasse? Ach von hier
>
> sind die Himmel stark, wie voller Leuen,
> die wir unbegreiflich überstehn.
> Nein, du kennst sie nicht, weil sie sich scheuen
> und dir schüchterner entgegengehn.

At one extreme there is the 'Unbegrenzter', the unnamed god, whose power, expressed as 'Nächte', demands a response from the self which seems to exceed the human capacity for feeling. At the other extreme there is the human situation, from which perspective the heavens are 'stark wie voller Leuen'. But here the 'antinomische Metaphorik'[16] has the dual function of binding as well as separating. For though the heavens have quite different aspects when viewed from the human or from the divine perspective, they represent a medium between the two extreme limits. In other words, the heavens here serve to establish a continuity between the known and accessible and the unknown and inaccessible. We may take this structure as a paradigm of the change which occurs in the figure of the angel. In the period of the *Gedichte an die Nacht* the angel tends to lose its complete otherness and to be adapted in the search for a possible mediation.

The poem *An den Engel* is a stage in this process. The negative possibility derives from the opening situation of the first two *Duineser Elegien*, the positive points in the direction exemplified by the poem *So, nun wird es doch der Engel sein...* The two possibilities are balanced one against the other, as the transience of human existence is against a possible fulfilment 'bei den

Sternen'. It is because both remain open that the poem offers a dual perspective, making the figure of the angel so difficult to define.

In a prose fragment written in Ronda immediately after *An den Engel*, Rilke praises El Greco's manner of depicting angels in a way which sheds some light on the subsequent development of the figure in his verse. He says of El Greco's angel:

...nicht daß er fliegt ist ihm entscheidend, denn der Flug ist auf beiden Seiten begrenzt, ein Intervall des Aufruhens; er streckt sich sinnlich ins Übersinnliche, nur das Strecken ist unaufhörlich, parallel, hat seinen Anfang und entgeht in die Unendlichkeit.[17]

The words 'sinnlich ins Übersinnliche' contain the essence of the angel's function as a mediate figure. An entity which is perceptible to the senses, or which can be described in images from the world of sensory experience, and yet which at the same time 'entgeht in die Unendlichkeit', has the paradoxical quality of being at once immanent and transcendent. Because of the contradictions which this implies, it is virtually impossible to establish in the poems where what is 'sinnlich' ends and where 'das Übersinnliche' begins. And this merging of the two spheres is precisely what Rilke is trying to achieve in the period of the *Gedichte an die Nacht*. As a mediate figure the angel's function is virtually identical with that of 'Nacht' in the fragment:

Was könnte dein Lächeln mir was mir die Nacht nicht gäbe aufdrängen,
die hier mit fast schüchternem Anfang an meinem Gesicht beginnt
und wo wo endet... (SW ii, 392)

This could certainly not be said of the angel of the *Duineser Elegien* whose 'Schrecklichkeit' excludes any such proximity.

In the same prose piece, Rilke contrasts El Greco's angels with other representations of the supernatural which are 'nur... eine Übertreibung des Irdischen'. And this again raises the question of the nature of Rilke's angels themselves. For if they reach 'sinnlich ins Übersinnliche', if they mediate by virtue of their dual nature between 'das Nächste' and 'das Namenlose', the possibility is present that they may be also only 'eine Übertreibung des Irdischen'. Rilke at times comes close to suggesting this himself, as for example in one of the poems to Lou Albert-Lazard written in September 1914:

> Einzeln sind wir Engel nicht; zusammen
> bilden wir den Engel unsrer Liebe:
> ich den Gang, du seines Mundes Jugend. (SW II, 222)

where the angel is produced by the combined feeling of the two lovers – that is to say: represents a certain intensity of purely human emotion. One could object that the angel here has an obviously metaphorical function – very similar to that of the night in *Die Geschwister I* – and that the angel of other poems is an entity in its own right. But it is precisely that the angel may be seen here as a 'Metapher des Irdischen' and elsewhere as a 'Gestalt der Transzendenz' which reveals a scale of possible meanings for the figure analogous to that which we have observed in the case of 'Nacht'.

It is the fluidity of night and angel, manifested in their sometimes appearing to be no more than a metaphor for a particular state of human consciousness or emotion, while at other times representing something beyond the reach of human perception and feeling, which gives rise to so much of the controversy surrounding them. One direction in Rilke-criticism is eager to discredit them as 'Subjektiv-Unverbindliches',[18] another direction, less vocal recently, insists that they be taken as expressions of an often rather vaguely defined transcendence, and venerated accordingly. But one need espouse neither of these persuasions and thus refrain from the polemical statements to which the emotional attitudes implicit in both inevitably lead.

This is not compromise for its own sake, for it is clearly enjoined by the poems themselves. For the *Gedichte an die Nacht* should be taken not so much as records of experiences – be they real or figments of the poetic imagination – but rather of explorations of the problem of the relation of human consciousness and feeling to the empiric world and to what may transcend it. It is perhaps misleading to describe this as a single problem, for the poems present different aspects of it as if they were complete

THE NIGHT AND THE ANGEL

in themselves and as if a solution to one of them would have an all-embracing finality for the poet's existence. The perspective offered by Rilke's whole work shows this to be not so, but this does not condemn the poems aesthetically, nor does the often very dubious objectivity of figures such as 'Nacht' or 'Engel' prevent us from seeing the poems as a serious attempt to explore the problem of transcendence. This is done with apparent disregard for the rules of logical consistency and of the methodical progression which a philosophical treatment of the same theme would make necessary. The task of rational analysis is all the harder for it. Here I would agree with Mason that: 'Sein (Rilkes) Denken geht zuletzt gegen das Denken als solches...'[19] – if by 'Denken als solches' one may understand the formal obligations which discursive thought acknowledges and by which it is defined. But the antithesis is not complete. For the tradition of Rilke-criticism attests over and over again what Käte Hamburger has given its most recent formulation:

Die Unvergleichbarkeit seiner Lyrik mit jeder anderen beruht mit darauf, daß sie so beschaffen ist, um auf philosophische Fragestellungen antworten zu können...[20]

Rilke's thought indeed often shows a high degree of formal logic in its structure, and in places where this logic is not apparent it may be shown as implicit or else supplied by critical analysis without doing violence to the poetry. However, it is also the case, and the *Gedichte an die Nacht* give ample evidence of it, that logical consistency becomes elusive where critical reason most desires to find it. In general terms, this stems from a duality of attitudes, both of which are strongly evident in Rilke's poetic practice. The one is the affirmation of precision, which may also mean logical precision, expressed most clearly in the well-known sentence from *Malte Laurids Brigge*:

Er war ein Dichter und haßte das Ungefähre. (SW vi, 863)

and the other is that of fear or disdain of the limitations which adherence to the laws of formal logic may impose on the poetic consciousness:

Ich fürchte in mir nur diejenigen Widersprüche die Neigung haben zur Versöhnlichkeit. Das muß eine sehr schmale Stelle meines Lebens sein, wenn sie überhaupt daran denken dürfen, sich die Hände zu reichen, von Rand zu Rand. Meine Widersprüche sollen nur selten und in Gerüchten voneinander hören. (BT, 203)

It is interesting that these two quotations are characteristic of two different periods of Rilke's development, the latter of the *Stunden-Buch* and the former of the *Neue Gedichte* and *Malte*, for the legacy of both these periods is present in the thematic material of the *Gedichte an die Nacht*. The influence of the *Stunden-Buch* can be seen in the attempt to establish a transcendent entity as the other pole of an 'Ich-Du-Gegenüber', to recapture the 'Ich-Gott' polarity of the *Stunden-Buch*. The legacy of the *Malte* period is evident in the extremely problematical nature of the relation of the self to the world of objects. Within the *Gedichte an die Nacht* these influences can be seen to merge sometimes and sometimes to oppose each other, just as the poems permit in some respects an extreme precision of logical definition, while in others the analysis is confronted with all the difficulties arising from 'das Weltbild der Nuance'.

To accept this as an aspect of the poetry which in itself deserves neither praise nor blame, does not mean that one is indifferent to the grave problems of interpretation which it raises. For it is not sufficient to say that the angel is sometimes this and sometimes that and therefore neither purely a projection of the subjectivity nor a genuine numinous power. We must go further and inquire into the nature of the poetic experience which produces such a figure. This will be the prime concern in the second part of the book. It is now time to consider the theme of 'Strömung' in its relation to the night and the angel.

The first poem to be treated exists in two versions. The version in the collection presented to Kassner has three stanzas, however in 1919 Rilke submitted the first two stanzas for publication as a separate poem.[21] We shall look at the longer version:

> Ob ich damals war oder bin: du schreitest
> über mich hin, du unendliches Dunkel aus Licht.
> Und das Erhabene, das du im Raume bereitest,
> nehm ich, Unkenntlicher, an mein flüchtig Gesicht.

Nacht, o erführest du, wie ich dich schaue,
wie mein Wesen zurück im Anlauf weicht,
daß es sich dicht bis zu dir zu werfen getraue;
faß ich es denn, daß die zweimal genommene Braue
über solche Ströme von Aufblick reicht?

Sei es Natur. Sei es nur *eine*
einige kühne Natur: dieses Leben und drüben
jenes gestalte Gestirn, das ich unwissend anweine:
o so will ich mich üben, gefaßt wie die Steine
zu sein in der reinen Figur. (SW II, 66)

The content of the first stanza is already somewhat familiar
from the themes treated in the second chapter. The insignificance
of human existence is contrasted with the timeless splendour of
the night-sky. The second half of the stanza recalls both the
antithetical imagery of *An den Engel* and the possibility of communication offered in *Der du mich mit diesen überhöhtest*. For
there is firstly the 'Nuancierung' of the idea of darkness: the
night is 'du unendliches Dunkel aus Licht', which as well as
being a visual image suggests the clarity and precision of 'oben
wird die Nacht genau', while the self of this poem describes
himself as 'Unkenntlicher', implying a darkness in which he is
obscured, unrecognisable. This in turn comes close to the
meaning of 'unerhellt' in *An den Engel*. The parallel between the
two poems is strengthened by the phase 'mein flüchtig Gesicht'
which connects the 'Unkenntlichkeit' of human existence to
the awareness of its transience, just as in *An den Engel* the lament
of 'Unerhelltsein' crystallises at the end of the poem into the
words 'Denn ich schwinde hin'. Yet, despite the antithesis
between self and night there is nevertheless communication.
The self receives 'das Erhabene...an mein flüchtig Gesicht',
which may be seen as a way of overcoming 'Unkenntlichkeit'.
In much the same sense another poem turns toward the
angel:
Ach aus eines Engels Fühlung falle
Schein in dieses Meer auf einem Mond,
drin mein Herz, stillringende Koralle,
seine jüngsten Zweigungen bewohnt. (SW II, 77)

In this we may see again the tendency to bring night and angel
closer to human experience, while retaining all their emotional

values of intensity and splendour. The angel is no longer entirely terrible, the night is no longer entirely inaccessible. The comparability of human and angelic being which we observed in *An den Engel* has developed to the point where the self may participate in 'das Erhabene'. The further stage, that of seeing the night as essentially the same 'substance' as human feeling, is given in the opening stanza of one of the drafts for the *Gedichte an die Nacht*:

> Ist dort nicht Lächeln? Siehe, steht dort nicht
> in Feldern, die von Fülle übergingen,
> was wir zu einem kleinen Aufblühn bringen,
> wenn wirs bemühn in unser Angesicht? (SW II, 405)

It is on the assumption that the splendour of the night or the angel is only an intensification of human experience that the theme of 'Strömung' is based. For if sufficiently intense feeling is directed towards the night then human existence, or more specifically the 'Ich' from which these 'Ströme von Aufblick' proceed, becomes visible 'bei den Sternen'.

This is the possibility which the second stanza of the poem we are examining embraces. The human 'Wesen' is projected towards the stars and presumably thereby overcomes its 'Unkenntlichkeit'. But the third stanza does not sustain the theme of 'Strömung'. There is instead a very marked turning. The poet now invokes 'Natur', which does not mean animate or inanimate nature, but rather being as such:

> Sei es Natur. Sei es nur *eine*
> einige kühne Natur: dieses Leben und drüben
> jenes gestalte Gestirn, das ich unwissend anweine...

These lines contain the wish that what the second stanza has endeavoured to establish by an extreme exertion of will should rather be of its own accord, should not have to be produced by desperate exertion but should as 'Natur' be one of the basic determinants of human existence. This '*eine*/einige kühne Natur' is in fact the ideal unity of existence whose lack is felt so acutely throughout the *Gedichte an die Nacht* and which Rilke tries over and over again in the poems to establish.

So the third stanza provides a definite corrective of the second. For it is as if the whole possibility and probity of overcoming 'Unkenntlichkeit' by 'Strömung' is questioned. The line: 'jenes gestalte Gestirn, das ich unwissend anweine' places the 'Ströme von Aufblick' in a completely different perspective. It is as if the momentary intensity of feeling has spent itself, leaving the self worse off than before – or else, it may contain the same insight as the lines from *An den Engel*:

> Daß ich lärme, wird an dir nicht lauter,
> wenn du mich nicht fühltest, weil ich *bin*.

In other words, if man and angel or man and night are not united anyway as aspects of the same 'einige kühne Natur', then 'Lärmen' or 'Strömung' are equally futile measures of desperation. If, however, this unity *does* exist, then there is no need for any such deliberate intensifying of feeling so as to break out of the human sphere, but the self may exist 'gefaßt wie die Steine... in der reinen Figur'. The 'reine Figur' stands for the ideal unity of 'dieses Leben' and 'jenes gestalte Gestirn', a unity of immanent and transcendent being towards which the *Gedichte an die Nacht* continually reach out and sometimes capture as an image or imply as a future possibility, but, as the third stanza of this poem shows, never finally realise. The intrusion of 'das ich unwissend anweine' into the vision of the 'einige kühne Natur' is, like the words 'Denn ich schwinde hin' at the end of *An den Engel*, a sign that this unity is something longed for as an ideal possibility, not something firmly established.

In the light of this we may reconsider one aspect of the problem of interpreting these poems: that solutions in the form of 'komische Erlebnisse' are presented in a number of poems and yet remain without lasting effect, do not provide the longed-for unity of existence, do not make the self of the poems once and for all 'angeschauter bei den Sternen'. Comparing the two versions of this poem shows why this is the case. If the poem ends at the lines:

> faß ich es denn, daß die zweimal genommene Braue
> über solche Ströme von Aufblick reicht?

then it appears that the poet has succeeded in the 'Erwirkung eines "Daseins", das sich mit dem der Nacht vergleichen ließe'.[22] If one then reads the third stanza one sees the full precariousness of such a position, for it is at best an attempt to achieve by force the unity which, if it is to be at all, must be of itself. This is the same tension as is present in *An den Engel*. If the angel already feels man because human and angelic being are not irremediably other but are aspects of a unity, then there is no need for the lament – the state of 'Unerhelltsein' can be overcome. If on the other hand this unity does not exist *a priori*, then all efforts on the part of man to reach 'das Übernächste' are in vain and the situation is that of the lines from *Vor Weihnachten 1914*:

> ...Was willst du feiern, wenn
> die Festlichkeit der Engel dir entweicht?
> Was willst du fühlen? Ach, dein Fühlen reicht
> vom Weinenden zum Nicht-mehr-Weinenden.
> Doch drüben sind, unfühlbar, Himmel leicht
> von zahllos Engeln. Dir unfühlbar. Du
> kennst nur den Nicht-Schmerz. Die Sekunde Ruh
> zwischen zwei Schmerzen...   (SW II, 97)

In the period of the *Gedichte an die Nacht* this tension is not ultimately resolved. It often appears to be resolved in one form or another, but behind each apparent resolution there is implicitly 'des andern Aufwand fühlbar'. For this reason the poems do not form a finished cycle with one beginning where the other leaves off, because the essential ordering principle, the unity to be achieved, cannot be presented as a certainty. It can be glimpsed, as in the third stanza of *Ob ich damals war...*, but the situation of the 'lyrisches Ich' remains essentially that of the beginning of the poem *An Hölderlin*:

> ...aus den erfüllten
> Bildern stürzt der Geist zu plötzlich zu füllenden; Seeen
> sind erst im Ewigen...   (SW II, 93)

In this poem Rilke attributes to Hölderlin the unified vision of existence the absence of which he laments in his own poetry:

> Dir, du Herrlicher, war, dir war, du Beschwörer, ein ganzes
> Leben das dringende Bild, wenn du es aussprachst,
> die Zeile schloß sich wie Schicksal...

We may understand 'ein ganzes/Leben' as the '*eine*/einige kühne Natur' of the poem from the *Gedichte an die Nacht*. As this is for Rilke not 'das dringende Bild' as something given, but an elusive ideal of unity which is constantly counterbalanced by the despair of 'Fremdheit', the *Gedichte an die Nacht* are without the foundation in certainty which he attributes to Hölderlin's poetry and so in a sense never come to rest.

Hence Fülleborn is quite right to be suspicious of the numinous experiences which appear in the poems, because, as Rilke himself indicates the vision of 'ein ganzes Leben' in which the relation of human to divine being is an established certainty, is precisely that which it is hardest to attain. Each attempt to realise it occurs against a negative background of experience: 'Fremdheit', 'Unerhelltsein', transience, all of which speak for the other possibility: that the longed for 'Beteiligung am endgültig Daseienden'[23] may be only wishful thinking. Hence the ambiguity of the angel: for if this figure is 'nur...eine Übertreibung des Irdischen' or if it *is* 'Gestalt der Transzendenz', but nevertheless quite indifferent and inaccessible to man, then human existence means emptiness, isolation, and is, as it were, unproven:

> Der Himmel singt in seiner Sicherheit,
> hoch über Zeit die reichen Sterne singen,
> wir treiben mit den abgehärmten Dingen
> zweischweigende Geselligkeit.
>
> In trüben Spiegeln suchen wir Beweis
> für unser Aufstehn, während unbewiesen
> der Schlaf zurückbleibt. Vielleicht Schlaf von Riesen
> von unserm ganzen Blute heiß. (SW II, 398)

It is the constant presence of 'des andern Aufwand', which one may deduce from the *Gedichte an die Nacht* themselves and which is amply attested by the fragmentary poems of this period,[24] that makes the problem of transcendence in these poems such a vexed one. Nevertheless it seems possible to regard the *Gedichte an die Nacht* as an exploration of the problem of transcendence in terms of generalised human experience. It is a far from consistent and methodical exploration and it may at crucial moments present the reader with ambiguity where he most desires a single meaning, but this does not mean that it is not genuine. In other words, the poems may reveal possible structures of experience which are not exclusively determined by Rilke's desire to write a certain kind of verse and his frustration at not being able to do so.

To return to the theme of 'Strömung', there is an obvious affinity between it and the concept of 'intransitive Liebe' and that of prayer in the letter to Mimi Romanelli of 5 January 1910.

There Rilke says of prayer:

La prière est un rayonnement de notre être soudainement incendié, c'est une direction infinie et sans but, c'est un parallélisme brutal de nos aspirations qui traversent l'univers sans aboutir nulle part. (AB I, 277.)

and 'Strömung' similarly has the character of intense feeling projected from finite existence into infinity:

> ...In dir hörte ich auf,
> so aber streng ich mein Herz an, ströme, und immer
> hat der Raum nicht genug. (SW II, 392)

Further analogies may be drawn with certain aspects of the night and the angel. For it is night in the same fragment which:

> ...hier mit fast schüchternem Anfang an meinem Gesicht
> beginnt und wo wo endet...

and the angel of El Greco is seen as extending from the perceived world into regions beyond the senses. But one must be careful of taking these similarities too far. For in the way of any immediate identification of 'Strömung' with prayer or indeed night, there stands the problem of 'Gegenständlichkeit'. For the essence of 'prière' is that it quite transcends any object and is independent of any response. *What* it is directed towards is ultimately unimportant – it is the intensity of feeling attained in pursuing the emotional direction which constitutes its own value. In this sense prayer, as Rilke defines it in the letter, constitutes a form of escape from the situation of 'Gegenübersein', for if the 'rayonnement de notre être' continues to traverse the cosmos without ever impinging on anything, then the vexations of the subject-object relationship are avoided – the intensity of the subject is sufficient unto itself. In the *Gedichte an die Nacht*, however, Rilke is continually concerned with establishing an object and with eliciting from it some response. Night and angel do sometimes come close to being 'Richtung des Herzens' but equally important is their function as intentional objects.[25] Rilke may in 1910 show a sovereign disdain towards the 'god' he prays to:

S'il n'est plus ou pas encore: qu'importe. Ce sera ma prière qui le fera car elle est toute création telle qu'elle s'élance vers les cieux. Et si le Dieu qu'elle projette hors de soi ne persiste point: tant mieux: on le fera de nouveau, et il sera moins usé dans l'éternité. (AB I, 277)

but this attitude is not present in the period of the *Gedichte an die Nacht* and to interpret night and angel entirely in the sense of this quotation[26] is to ignore the problem of their 'Gegenständlichkeit'.

That 'Strömung' in the *Gedichte an die Nacht* still bears traces of this earlier concept of 'prière' is undeniable, however the importance of a possible response from the transcendent object is borne out by these lines from the poem *Überfließende Himmel verschwendeter Sterne*...:

...Hier, an dem weinenden schon,
an dem endenden Antlitz,
um sich greifend, beginnt der hinreißende Weltraum. Wer unterbricht,
wenn du dort hin drängst
die Strömung? Keiner. Es sei denn,
daß du plötzlich ringst mit der gewaltigen Richtung
jener Gestirne nach dir. . . . (SW II, 54)

Fülleborn concludes from the rhetorical question in these lines:

Die leidvolle Erfahrung, die sich hinter dem Weinen verschweigt: daß...
'einer die Strömung unterbricht' oder unterbrochen hat, muß somit einem
anderen Erlebniszusammenhang entstammen...Demnach muß angenommen
werden, daß das movens des Gedichts eine enttäuschende *negative Liebeserfahrung* ist.[27]

One could modify this conclusion so far as to say that the suffering from which 'Strömung' represents an escape may indeed be a 'negative Liebeserfahrung' but that the interpretation need not cease at this point. For as we have seen in the previous chapter,

133

the failure in love may in turn be representative of the overall alienation in which the self exists. 'Fremdheit' may appear as an absence of emotional communication between the self and its object, whether this be another person, a landscape or the immediate surroundings. For it is a negative possibility inherent in the subject-object relationship as such and in the *Gedichte an die Nacht* it may appear as a barrier which emotion cannot cross.

For Rilke this 'opacity' of objects to human consciousness or feeling is from the period of *Malte Laurids Brigge* an often repeated cause for lament and 'Strömung' presents one possibility of overcoming it. Other possibilities are contained in the concepts of 'Weltinnenraum' and 'das Offene':

Mit dem 'Offenen' ist also nicht Himmel, Luft und Raum gemeint, auch *die* sind, für den Betrachter und Beurteiler 'Gegenstand' und somit 'opaque' und zu. Das Tier, die Blume vermutlich, *ist* alles das, ohne sich Rechenschaft zu geben und hat so vor sich und über sich jene unbeschreiblich offene Freiheit, die vielleicht nur in den ersten Liebesaugenblicken, wo ein Mensch im anderen, im Geliebten, seine eigene Welt sieht, und in der Hingehobenheit zu Gott bei uns (höchst momentane) Äquivalente hat.[28]

In the period of the *Gedichte an die Nacht*, 'Himmel' and 'Raum' are not always included in the category of things which are 'opaque'. So we may see in the turning to 'der hinreißende Weltraum' an attempt to escape from the 'Gegenständlichkeit' of human experience, of which the failure in love may be part. Of course, if this 'Strömung' provokes a response from some transcendent object, such as 'die gewaltige Richtung jener Gestirne nach dir', then one might say that the self has only exchanged one form of 'Gegenständlichkeit' for another. This in turn leads into the question of the overall structure of the experience of the night and the angel in these poems and this will be treated in a later chapter.

PART II
DEVELOPMENTS AND
CONCLUSIONS

5. THE MEANING OF 'NACHT'

The analyses of individual poems have so far been directed towards elucidating the meaning of night in each particular context and with establishing similarities and differences from poem to poem. This has either been suggested by the text itself, in the case of obvious parallels, or else been made necessary when a precise meaning for lines or phrases does not emerge from their immediate surroundings. There has however been no satisfactory answer to the question of the overall meaning of 'Nacht', indeed this problem has, if anything, become more and more complex. This is largely the result of a conscious unwillingness to use Occam's razor after the manner of other writers on Rilke[1] or to attempt syntheses for the sake of critical neatness when a reading of the poems makes them very questionable. However, it is now time to draw some conclusions by showing the conditions which govern the various possible meanings of 'Nacht' and the relevance of these conditions to Rilke's poetry as a whole. One must begin by illustrating the principle of ambivalence which is inherent in Rilke's concept and use of 'Nacht'.

To state this principle simply: 'Nacht' may be used to transpose aspects of human consciousness into images of external reality and conversely to transpose external reality into images of human consciousness. There is nothing new or difficult about the principle as such – it is a commonplace of poetry that inner states should be expressed by an objective correlative and that aspects of the external world should be largely divested of their independent existence and become part of a purely inner landscape. The interest lies in the use to which this principle is put in Rilke's poetry. For to Rilke during most of his creative life the relation of inner and outer worlds presents itself not as something which he can assume with the sublime confidence of: 'Denn was innen, das ist außen',[2] but rather as a problem which he feels called upon to solve in his poetry:

> Komm her; wir wollen eine Weile still sein.
> Sieh diese Rose an auf meinem Schreibtisch;
> ist nicht das Licht um sie genau so zaghaft
> wie über dir: sie dürfte auch nicht hier sein.
> Im Garten draußen, unvermischt mit mir,
> hätte sie bleiben müssen oder hingehn –
> nun währt sie so: was ist ihr mein Bewußtsein? (SW I, 650)

So that while he continues to use images of external reality to represent thoughts or feelings purely as a poetic technique, the intellectual and emotional basis of this technique, that is, a relatedness of inner and outer worlds, has itself become what the poetry is trying to establish. The difficulties which this poses are reflected in the wealth of affirmation and denial – at either extreme 'Weltinnenraum' and 'Fremdheit' – and the many nuances of both which surround the question of this relatedness.

Furthermore, while making constant use of this principle in the cause of 'Bilder zu finden für meine Verwandlungen'[3] Rilke explores or posits states of consciousness which transcend the accepted limits of our direct experience of the external world. This means that his poetry at times attempts to express the act or content of transcendence in images taken from immanent reality. In this way the principle stated above may become a blade to cut in two directions. One may clarify this by an example of the metaphorical possibilities of 'Nacht'. Rilke may begin by establishing the night as the objective correlative of a certain state of consciousness which raises no claim to transcendence, in the sense of passing from the natural to the supernatural, and which may be readily communicated by an appeal to common experience, as in the opening lines of the *Titelblatt* of the series *Aus einer Sturmnacht* in *Das Buch der Bilder*:

> Die Nacht, vom wachsenden Sturme bewegt,
> wie wird sie auf einmal weit –
> als bliebe sie sonst zusammengelegt
> in die kleinlichen Falten der Zeit. (SW I, 460)

These lines scarcely pose any metaphysical problems at all – the night and storm correspond to a sudden feeling of expansion which calm nights do not evoke. Admittedly, the image of 'die kleinlichen Falten der Zeit' gives warning of the metaphysical speculation to come, but the point of departure of the poem is essentially within the region of familiar experience. However, the poem then develops the *idea* of the night as something infinite:

> Wo die Sterne ihr wehren, dort endet sie nicht
> und beginnt nicht mitten im Wald
> und nicht an meinem Angesicht
> und nicht mit deiner Gestalt.

which turns suddenly into the bold speculation:

> Die Lampen stammeln und wissen nicht:
> *lügen* wir Licht?

and by the final two lines the rather innocuous opening experience has become a problem in metaphysics:

> Ist die Nacht die einzige Wirklichkeit
> seit Jahrtausenden...

From these lines one might go on to conclude that what passes for reality is not reality but illusion and that the poet experiences in night that which transcends mere appearance. 'Nacht' appears at the beginning of the poem as a familiar phenomenon of external reality and at the end as (possibly!) an 'einzige Wirklichkeit' in contrast to which the rest of the world of phenomena may be mere illusion. Of course, this too may be seen as the objective correlative of a state of consciousness. Rilke may, in the footsteps of Novalis, be positing an inner world which is 'more real' than external reality and assigning to it the name 'Nacht'. This would accord with the first half of the principle of ambivalence.

It is the implementation of the second half, however, which makes the interpretation of 'Nacht' so difficult. For once 'Nacht' or 'Sternenhimmel' have been offered as *images* for a transcendent reality, they tend in Rilke's verse to lose the 'as if' quality of the image and to become to all intents and purposes the reality itself. This process occurs in the *Gedichte an die Nacht* and makes the problem of transcendence such a vexed one. For example, Rilke uses the spatial metaphor of the distance between himself and the constellations to differentiate between two modes of being: the finite and limited and often unhappy 'Hiersein' and the infinite and apparently quite other being of the angels. Were this to remain a metaphor for the otherness of what humanity cannot experience, then the interpretative problems would be relatively simple. But the fact that these images for otherness are at the same time experienced as phenomena complicates things no end. For the spatial metaphor, transposed *back* into conceptual terms makes this otherness quite relative: the consciousness perceives the 'Sternenhimmel', it responds to it emotionally, it may metaphorically project itself towards the stars in an endeavour to be acknowledged, in short, it may fix the 'Nachtraum' as an intentional object in much the same way as it may direct itself towards a thing, a work of art or another human being. In this way 'Nacht' or 'Sterne' may oscillate between representing 'Transzendenz' and 'mögliche Existenz'.[4] A failure to recognise this essential duality in the function of Rilkean metaphors is responsible for much of the controversy concerning the figure of the angel in this period.

But night above all lends itself to being used in this manner. For there is a strong tradition in which it represents certain stages of religious or mystical consciousness and with which Rilke must have been familiar. At the same time, as an aspect of the external world, it offers itself as an obvious theme to a poet seeking to establish a meaningful relationship between inner and outer reality. Furthermore, the manner in which it can be used both to denote the limits of human experience and to imply what may lie beyond corresponds to Rilke's constant attempts to penetrate 'die schwarzen Sektoren..., die das uns Unerfahrbare bezeichnen' of which he speaks in the prose piece *Ur-Geräusch*:

Stellt man sich das gesamte Erfahrungsbereich der Welt, auch seine uns übertreffenden Gebiete, in einem vollen Kreis dar, so wird es sofort augenscheinlich, um wieviel größer die schwarzen Sektoren sind, die das uns Unerfahrbare bezeichnen, gemessen an den ungleichen lichten Ausschnitten, die den Scheinwerfern der Sensualität entsprechen. (SW VI, 1091)

In the *Gedichte an die Nacht* the night has been seen to represent in a number of instances 'seine uns übertreffenden Gebiete' in the sense of 'das uns Unerfahrbare'. At the same time, however, the encounter with the night definitely takes place in one or more of the 'lichten Ausschnitte, die den Scheinwerfern der Sensualität entsprechen', as is particularly the case with the visual sense.

This is then the basic principle which determines the ambivalence of 'Nacht' in the poems which we have examined, but it remains to make this more understandable by showing something of the development of the theme of 'Nacht' in Rilke's poetry before his visit to Spain in late 1912.

In the first two parts of the *Stunden-Buch* night appears as a unifying point of 'Gott' and 'Ich':

> Doch wie ich auch mich in mich selber neige:
> *Mein* Gott ist dunkel und wie ein Gewebe
> von hundert Wurzeln, welche schweigsam trinken. (SW 1, 254)

> Du Dunkelheit, aus der ich stamme,
> ich liebe dich mehr als die Flamme,
> welche die Welt begrenzt... (SW 1, 258)

> Du bist der dunkle Unbewußte
> von Ewigkeit zu Ewigkeit... (SW 1, 276)

> Wie der Wächter in den Weingeländen
> seine Hütte hat und wacht,
> bin ich Hütte, Herr, in deinen Händen
> und bin Nacht, o Herr, von deiner Nacht. (SW 1, 293)

These quotations tend to emphasise the inwardness of 'Nacht' as that region or state of the poet's self where he is closest to his god, 'der dunkle Unbewußte'.[5] But just as this god continually assumes the forms of exterior reality as well, so 'Nacht' can appear as a phenomenon without forfeiting any of these connotations:

> Jemehr der Tag mit immer schwächern
> Gebärden sich nach Abend neigt,
> jemehr bist du, mein Gott. Es steigt
> dein Reich wie Rauch aus allen Dächern. (SW 1, 333)

And indeed in poems from *Das Buch der Bilder* written in 1900 'Nacht' is celebrated as the time and place of an ideal relatedness between the self and its surroundings:

Meine Stube und diese Weite,
wach über nachtendem Land, –
ist Eines. Ich bin eine Saite
über rauschende breite
Resonanzen gespannt... (SW 1, 400)

Nacht, stille Nacht, in die verwoben sind
ganz weiße Dinge, rote, bunte Dinge,
verstreute Farben, die erhoben sind
zu Einem Dunkel Einer Stille, – bringe
doch mich auch in Beziehung zu dem Vielen,
das du erwirbst und überredest... (SW 1, 401)

So that at this stage 'Nacht' is an aspect of the god, is likewise an aspect of the poet's consciousness, is a part of external reality and can symbolise an ideal relatedness of self and world. In this period, then, we have all the ingredients of the theme of night in the *Gedichte an die Nacht* but without any of the obstructions or tensions which characterise it in the later poems: there is no 'Fremdheit', no despair, no attempt by the self to establish contact by a desperate exertion of will. Rilke seems remarkably at ease with any contradictions which such an all-embracing concept of 'Nacht' might contain, while in the poems of 1912–14 the nature of what the poet experiences as night is approached as a problem to be solved. This is partly explained by the change in the 'Grundhaltung der Intentionalität' in the intervening period, but one may gain further insight into it by examining another poem from *Das Buch der Bilder* in which the seeds of future conflicts are contained:

ABEND

Der Abend wechselt langsam die Gewänder,
die ihm ein Rand von alten Bäumen hält;
du schaust: und von dir scheiden sich die Länder,
ein himmelfahrendes und eins, das fällt.

und lassen dich, zu keinem ganz gehörend,
nicht ganz so dunkel wie das Haus, das schweigt,
nicht ganz so sicher Ewiges beschwörend
wie das, was Stern wird jede Nacht und steigt –

und lassen dir (unsäglich zu entwirrn)
dein Leben bang und riesenhaft und reifend,
so daß es, bald begrenzt und bald begreifend,
abwechselnd Stein in dir wird und Gestirn.　(SW 1, 405)

It is as if one can see cracks appearing in the unity of 'Ich',
'Umwelt' and 'Gott' which is assumed so confidently in most
of the poems of this period. There is first of all the distinction
between two regions of darkness: 'ein himmelfahrendes' which
will later become the 'unendliches Dunkel aus Licht', the
'unnachgiebige Nacht' with which we are familiar, and 'eins,
das fällt' which prefigures the darkness of 'Unkenntlichkeit', of
the 'unerhellter Zögerung' of the human situation. Secondly,
there is implicit the idea of a reality which is no longer the
pantheistic nature of *Das Stunden-Buch* but instead a world of
objects which are alien, such as Rilke evokes at the beginning of
Die große Nacht. And thirdly, there is the conflict of direction
within the self – the need for identification with *both* 'das
Nächste' *and* 'das Weiteste'. This conflict is, within the poem,
still held in a kind of uneasy balance: 'dein Leben.../abwech-
selnd Stein in dir wird und Gestirn' but the words 'unsäglich
zu entwirrn' are indeed prophetic of the confusions which this
will cause in the period of *Gedichte an die Nacht*. For instead of
this alternation, which here suffices to keep the structure of the
experience together, one encounters contexts in which the 'Ich'
despairs of being able to identify either with the immediate
objects or the most distant ones. Characteristic of this earlier
period remains, however, the poet's vision of his own life as
'riesenhaft und reifend', so reminiscent of the poem *Fortschritt*.[6]
This vision of himself in effect prevents any of these latent
conflicts from becoming too explicit.

The poem which we have just considered has not been given
a definite date,[7] but its composition lies within the period 1902–
1906. The time between the completion of *Das Stunden-Buch*
in 1903 and the composition of the first of the *Gedichte an die
Nacht* in January 1913 sees radical changes in Rilke's attitude
towards the external world and towards his god. Whereas in the

Stunden-Buch, particularly the first two parts, the external world seems to be very much a function of the creative subjectivity:

> Meine Blicke sind reif, und wie eine Braut
> kommt jedem das Ding das er will... (SW I, 253)

there is an increasing tendency for the 'Dinge' to be no longer extensions of the self to be transferred at will, but rather for their independent and quite different reality to be acknowledged. Rilke himself was quite aware of this change and comments on it at some length in a letter to his wife of 13 October 1907:

> ...aber damals war mir die Natur noch ein allgemeiner Anlaß, eine Evokation, ein Instrument, in dessen Saiten sich meine Hände wiederfanden; ich saß noch nicht vor ihr; ich ließmich hinreißen von der Seele, welche von mir ausging; sie kam über mich mit ihrer Weite, mit ihrem großen übertriebenen Dasein, wie das Prophezeien über Saul kam; genau so. Ich schritt einher und sah, sah nicht die Natur, sondern die Gesichte, die sie mir eingab. (B. 1906–7, 377)

This situation of being 'vor der Natur' is evident in the success of many of the *Neue Gedichte*, but it has its negative effects also. For once the 'Dinge' are established as objects before which the consciousness stands, they are no longer extensions of the self in the sense of the *Stunden-Buch* and it is but a further step to the loss of that participation with the objective world which Rilke found so necessary. The final stage of this process is the alienation of the first poem of *Die spanische Trilogie* and the lament of the letter from Ronda of December 1912:

> ...und jetzt sitz ich da und schau und schau, bis mir die Augen wehtun, und zeig mirs und sag mirs vor, als sollt ichs auswendig lernen, und habs doch nicht und bin so recht einer, dems nicht gedeiht. (B. 1907–14, 265)

Clearly it is the negative aspect of Rilke's new attitude to the world of objects which is the origin of the problems of 'Gegenständlichkeit' which Rilke *appears* to solve in 1914 by the concept of 'Weltinnenraum' but which, nevertheless, provide the material for the eighth Elegy. Further insight into the development of this 'Gegenständlichkeit' and at the same time into changes in Rilke's experience of 'Gott' may be gained by considering parts of the *Improvisationen aus dem Capreser Winter* of December 1906.

The opening verses present a situation in which elements from the *Stunden-Buch* are mixed with the new theme of 'Gegenständlichkeit' producing a tone of rather confused desperation:

> Täglich stehst du mir steil vor dem Herzen,
> Gebirge, Gestein,
> Wildnis, Un-weg: Gott, in dem ich allein
> steige und falle und irre..., täglich in mein
> gestern Gegangenes wieder hinein
> kreisend...   (SW ii, 11f.)

That the god should be represented by 'Gebirge, Gestein' and that the poet should feel himself to be inside this is quite in accordance with the imagery of the *Stunden-Buch*: 'Du Wald, aus dem wir nie hinausgegangen...'[8] But at the same time this god does not merge into the poet's consciousness but stands 'mir steil vor dem Herzen', seems impenetrable, is 'Wildnis, Un-weg' and as such cannot be understood. God and the external world have become, as it were, equally unfathomable *objects* and the reaction of the self is to take refuge in the inner world in the hope of re-establishing some stability:

> Laß mich, laß mich, die Augen geschlossen,
> wie mit verschluckten Augen, laß
> mich, den Rücken an den Kolossen,
> warten an deinem Rande, daß
> dieser Schwindel, mit dem ich verrinne
> meine hingerissenen Sinne
> wieder an ihre Stelle legt.
> Regt sich denn Alles in mir? Ist kein Festes,
> das bestünde auf seines Gewichts
> Anrecht? Mein Bangstes und mein Bestes...
> Und der Wirbel nimmt es wie nichts
> mit in die Tiefen...   (SW ii, 11)

The realisation that the world of objects now stands 'steil vor dem Herzen', that instead of being able to identify with it in the sense of the poem *Fortschritt*:

> Mit meinen Sinnen, wie mit Vögeln, reiche
> ich in die windigen Himmel aus der Eiche
> und in den abgebrochenen Tag der Teiche
> sinkt, wie auf Fischen stehend, mein Gefühl. (SW i, 402)

the poet must confront it within the structure of ordinary human perception produces a lament on the theme of having a face. The evils of the subject-object relationship as Rilke understood them will be dealt with at length in the next chapter. For the sake of the present discussion, however, one may somewhat prematurely equate 'Gesicht haben' with 'Gegenüber-sein'. This negative aspect of 'Gesicht' has also been shown by August Stahl.[9]

> Hat der Wald ein Gesicht?
> Steht der Berge Basalt
> gesichtlos nicht da?
> Hebt sich das Meer
> nicht ohne Gesicht
> aus dem Meergrund her?
> Spiegelt sich nicht der Himmel drin
> ohne Stirn, ohne Mund, ohne Kinn? (SW II, 12)

Implicit in these lines is the concept of the purer existence of objects in their 'An-sich-Sein' and the idea that human perception in some way falsifies this reality.

Rilke's reaction to his confrontation with the problem of 'Gegenständlichkeit' in this poem is to appeal to the darkness of the *Stunden-Buch* as symbolising the emotional relatedness of 'Ich', 'Gott' and 'Dingwelt':

> ...Und wir?
> Tiere der Seele, verstört
> von allem in uns, noch nicht
> fertig zu nichts, wir weidenden
> Seelen,
> flehen wir zu dem Bescheidenden
> nächtens nicht um das Nicht-Gesicht,
> das zu unserem Dunkel gehört? (SW II, 12)

'Nicht-Gesicht' would represent a state in which one does not *perceive* things as objects but rather *feels* them as part of the darkness of the inner world, a state which Rilke celebrates in the *Stunden-Buch* but which he now cannot regain. For the darkness which was that of relatedness of the self to all things may now become that of the isolation of the individual:

> Mein Dunkel, mein Dunkel, da steh ich mit dir,
> und alles geht draußen vorbei;... (SW II, 13)

And the god of the *Stunden-Buch* is no longer present in this darkness, but very definitely outside:

> der immer wieder, sooft es tagt,
> aufsteigt: steilstes Gestein.
> Und türm ich mein Herz auf mein Hirn und mein
> Sehnen darauf und mein Einsamsein:
> wie bleibt das klein,
> weil *Er* es überragt.   (SW II, 13)

Perhaps the change in Rilke's attitude to the god of the *Stunden-Buch* and the corresponding state of the self is clearest in the third *Improvisation*:

> Und manchmal ist in einem alten Buche
> ein unbegreiflich Dunkles angestrichen.
> Da warst du einst. Wo bist du hin entwichen?   (SW II, 15)

One might well ask. It is striking to note that hand in hand with Rilke's recognising the world of objects as something independent of the creative individual, there develops the theme of despair at having lost contact with the god. This is first apparent in a poem written presumably in spring 1906:

> Ich brauche dich. Ich greife nach dem Horne
> das du mir einstens gabst damit ich bliese
> wenn ich in Not bin...
> Und nun versucht, zum ersten Mal vielleicht,
> mein Horn den hellen Hilferuf, den Schrei.
> Nun bet ich dich zum ersten Mal herbei,
> nun will ich dich, nun hungert mich nach dir,
> nun bin ich bange wie ein dürstend Tier
> und wie ein Sterbender ganz ohne Zeit
> voll Ungeduld und Leid und Einsamkeit.[10]

And three years later this cry for help is repeated, again without producing a response from the god who is now entirely a *deus absconditus*:

> Ach in der Kindheit, Gott: wie warst du leicht:
> du, den ich jetzt von nirgend widerbringe.
> Man lächelte nach seinem Lieblingsdinge;
> es rollte zu: da warst du schon erreicht.
> Und nun mein Herr, wo reis ich hin zu dir?
> Wo fahr ich ein? Auf was für Berge steig ich?
> Fragt einer dich: nach welcher Seite zeig ich,

Wo weht dein Hain? Wo geht dein Tier?
Wo ist das Wasser neu, daß ich mir wasche
Gesicht, Geschlecht: ich war noch niemals rein... (SW II, 367f.)

In fact there is no need to go as far back as childhood to find
the stage in which god was 'leicht', for one could substitute 'in
the period of the *Stunden-Buch*' for childhood without doing the
meaning of the lines any violence at all. Indeed, the first two parts
of the *Stunden-Buch* do represent, when viewed from the perspective of the *Gedichte an die Nacht*, a kind of poetic Eden in
which everything is potentially related to everything else in a
totality which is both human and divine and where all the later
problems of the subject-object relationship are still quite latent.
The distance and silence of god which Rilke laments in 1909
is echoed by the words: 'Der aber wollte noch nicht' at the end
of *Die Aufzeichnungen des Malte Laurids Brigge* and indeed
provides one of the aspects of the 'Ich-Verlust' against which
Malte struggles.[11] It would be extremely difficult to establish
the aetiology of the breakdown of the *Stunden-Buch* situation
without setting foot in the quicksand of psychological conjecture
by attempting to guess what thoughts or experiences Rilke did
not include in his letters or his poetry. It is enough to observe
that it took place and that its later manifestations are implicit
in a poem such as *Abend* and are clearly visible from the *Improvisationen aus dem Capreser Winter* onwards.

But what do the appearance of the theme of 'Gegenständlichkeit' and the loss of contact with the highly personal divinity
of the *Stunden-Buch* have to do with the development of the
theme of 'Nacht'? To answer this we must trace two distinct
threads from the *Stunden-Buch* to the *Gedichte an die Nacht*;
their separateness is, in fact, the result of the changes which we
have just delineated. The first proceeds from the aspect of night
as a state of consciousness, expressed most emphatically in the
Buch vom mönchischen Leben as: 'und bin Nacht, o Herr, von
deiner Nacht'. This reappears in the later collection in the idea
of night as 'dieses eingeborne Element' but even more explicitly
in the poem *Gedanken der Nacht*:

148

Daß ihr *seid*, ist bejaht; daß hier, im gedrängten Behälter,
Nacht, zu den Nächten hinzu, sich heimlich erzeugt.
Plötzlich: mit welchem Gefühl, steht die unendliche, älter,
über die Schwester *in* mir, die ich berge, gebeugt.   (SW II, 67f.)

Rilke does not often have recourse to this theme in the period
between the completion of the *Stunden-Buch* and 1913, for he
is much more intent on establishing the relation of the self to the
external world and to some transcendent power *outside* the self.
This provides the second theme which must be traced in some
detail.

With the loss of the *Stunden-Buch* situation there is a corresponding need to re-establish it, or at least come closer to the
god who is so distant and unknowable. In a fragment written at
the same time as the *Improvisationen* this takes the form of the
gesture of reaching out towards some means of expression which
may bring the self once more into the god's proximity:

Wie, wenn ich jetzt aus diesen Einsamkeiten
die Hände hübe, die sich mir entzwein;
wie, wenn ich sie ausstreckte in die Weiten:
ob sie nicht eine Harfe fänden: Saiten
um DIR in ihnen wieder nah zu sein?   (SW II, 330)

Compare this with the fragment written in September 1907 in
which the same gesture is repeated with the difference that the
god is no longer mentioned and the situation of the self has
become a lamentation: 'daß wir nicht sind'.

Immer noch und wie am ersten Tage
ist uns dies: daß wir nicht sind, zuviel,
und wir heben diese schwere Klage
immer wieder in das Saitenspiel
wenn die Liebesklagen, die wir hoben,
es nicht füllen. Ach sie waren leicht.
Aber diese schwere bleibt nicht oben:
kaum hat sie den Rand erreicht
fällt sie wieder... [12]

The 'schwere Klage' which will not remain aloft is a later and
much more despairing form of the attempt to find 'Saiten/um
DIR in ihnen wieder nah zu sein'. But the attempt to overcome
despair of 'non-existence' by unrestrained lament is fruitless,

just as in *Malte* pure, unrelieved 'Elend' is not sufficient to produce the 'Umschlag'.[13] What remains important, however, is the *gesture* of reaching upwards 'in die Weiten' outside the self, for this becomes in the later poems the pattern for the directedness towards the night. This is, in 1907, still a long way from realisation, but in poems written from this time onwards there is not only an increasing preoccupation with the night as part of the external world but also a tendency to establish aspects of the night in a kind of ascending scale of values, so that by the time the first *Gedichte an die Nacht* come to be written, the *Sternenhimmel* has acquired many of the attributes of the lost or distant god. We shall therefore look at a number of poems written during this period in which the tendency to regard the night as both *numen* and *phenomenon* may be seen developing.

The first poem was written on Capri in March 1907 and is entitled *Die Nacht der Frühlingswende*. In the first two stanzas Rilke is chiefly intent on evoking the visual and sensuous reality of the night:

> Ein Netz von raschen Schattenmaschen schleift
> über aus Mond gemachte Gartenwege,
> als ob Gefangenes sich drinnen rege,
> das ein Entfernter groß zusammengreift.
>
> Gefangener Duft, der widerstrebend bleibt.
> Doch plötzlich ists, als risse eine Welle
> das Netz entzwei an einer hellen Stelle,
> und alles fließt dahin und flieht und treibt...[14]

One might argue that the mention of 'ein Entfernter' invokes the distant god of the *Capreser Aufzeichnungen*, but it is important to recognise that this is contained within the framework of the 'als ob', that this reference is used as a means of making the visual reality more vivid and impressive. The image of the net containing 'Gefangenes' and then tearing to allow this to escape is essentially to convey the movement of moonlight and shadows as the wind moves throught the trees and bushes. That 'Gefangenes' becomes 'Gefangener Duft' serves mainly to add another sensory dimension to the visual reality. However, in the third stanza one may find the beginnings of that contrast which is invoked so often in the *Gedichte an die Nacht*:

> Noch einmal blättert, den wir lange kannten,
> der weite Nachtwind in den harten Bäumen;
> doch drüber stehen, stark und diamanten,
> in tiefen feierlichen Zwischenräumen,
> die großen Sterne einer Frühlingsnacht.

What is the sense of the opposition expressed by the 'doch'? It is firstly that between what is near and well known – 'den wir lange kannten,/der weite Nachtwind' – and 'die großen Sterne' which are distant and majestic. Secondly, there is the opposition between the area of immediate experience where everything is in motion and holds no firm contours: 'und alles fließt dahin und flieht und treibt...' and the clarity and fixity of the stars. The words 'Noch einmal blättert...in den harten Bäumen' may even suggest a certain triviality or meaninglessness about this movement,[15] whereas the stars are placed 'in tiefen feierlichen Zwischenräumen'. However, this opposition is in no sense an absolute one, for the immediate surroundings and 'die großen Sterne' are both aspects of the same experience, are elements of 'Die Nacht der Frühlingswende'.

In this poem, then, there are outlines of a structure of experience of external reality which provides a continuity from that which is near and well-known to that which is 'stark', 'groß', 'feierlich' and distant. In another poem, written in 1908 or 1909, a similar process takes place:

> STÄDTISCHE SOMMERNACHT
>
> Unten macht sich aller Abend grauer,
> und das ist schon Nacht, was da als lauer
> Lappen sich um die Laternen hängt.
> Aber höher, plötzlich ungenauer,
>
> wird die leere leichte Feuermauer
> eines Hinterhauses in die Schauer
> einer Nacht hinaufgedrängt,
> welche Vollmond hat und nichts als Mond.

Und dann gleitet oben eine Weite
weiter, welche heil ist und geschont,
und die Fenster an der ganzen Seite
werden weiß und unbewohnt.   (SW II, 35)

Once more in the depiction of a specific visual reality we may
see the poet of the *Neue Gedichte* standing 'vor der Natur' – the
self in no way intrudes. At the same time the poem shows the
same tendency as *Die Nacht der Frühlingswende*, for it establishes
aspects of 'Nacht' in an ascending order of intensity. The darkness which is gathering in the streets is 'schon Nacht' but in no
way splendid or intimidating. Then, as the gaze travels upwards
the night acquires a distinct awesomeness and splendour. In the
third stanza this movement goes even further and the night
becomes correspondingly more distant and abstract: 'Und dann
gleitet oben eine Weite/weiter...' In the contrast between the
'lauer Lappen' of the first stanza and this 'Weite...welche
heil ist und geschont' the antithesis of *Die Nacht der Frühlingswende* is repeated and a similar structure of experience is established. The last two lines are somewhat obscure, but the word
'unbewohnt' suggests that under the influence of this 'Weite'
and the light of the full moon the houses lose their quality of
human habitations and partake of the otherness of the distant
night sky. What is clear is the way in which the spatial terms of
external reality are employed to suggest transitions between
intensities of experience. 'Nähe' and 'Weite' are not simply
spatial concepts but are used to imply a contrast between the
commonplace 'Nacht' of the immediate environment in the
first stanza and the connotations of awe and solemnity which it
acquires in the rest of the poem.

In the *Gedichte an die Nacht* night is often a mediator between
the known and the unknown, ultimately between immanent and
transcendent being. It is obvious that the structure of these
poems lends itself ideally to such a mediation for it presents what
is close and what is most distant – with all that this implies – as
complementary poles of a single experience of the external world.
So it is that in a poem of 1911 we find the *rapprochement* of

'Nähe' and 'Ferne' anticipated, which is striven for in so many of the *Gedichte an die Nacht*:

MONDNACHT

Weg in den Garten, tief wie ein langes Getränke,
leise im weichen Gezweig ein entgehender Schwung.
Oh und der Mond, der Mond, fast blühen die Bänke
von seiner zögernden Näherung.
Stille, wie drängt sie. Bist du jetzt oben erwacht?
Sternig und fühlend steht dir das Fenster entgegen.
Hände der Winde verlegen
an dein nahes Gesicht die entlegenste Nacht. (SW ii, 38)

From this it could be said that in the theme of night as he develops it between 1906 and 1912 Rilke has found what he longs for in the *Capreser Aufzeichnungen*, namely:

wie, wenn ich sie ausstreckte in die Weiten:
ob sie nicht eine Harfe fänden: Saiten
um DIR in ihnen wieder nah zu sein?

for there is a definite tendency for 'Nacht' and 'Sterne' to take on the attributes of a transcendent reality. But this does not mean that the situation of the *Stunden-Buch* can be re-established. For there is an essential ambivalence in 'Nacht' which derives from the problem of 'Gegenständlichkeit', that is to say: from the situation of being 'vor der Natur', and no longer in the 'Dunkel' of the *Stunden-Buch*.

This can be seen by comparing the poem *Sterne hinter Oliven* (Capri or Paris, 1907–8), which has been often used as an example in previous chapters, with the poem *Nächtlicher Gang* written approximately at the same time. *Sterne hinter Oliven* presents night as an experience of unity which is somewhat unexpected in the poetry of this period:

Geliebter, den so vieles irre macht,
neig dich zurück bis du im lautern Laube
die Stellen siehst, die Sterne sind. Ich glaube
die Erde ist nicht anders als die Nacht.

Sieh, wie im selbstvergessenen Geäste
das Nächste sich mit Namenlosem mischt;
man zeigt uns dies; man hält uns nicht wie Gäste
die man nur nimmt, erheitert und erfrischt.

Wie sehr wir auch auf diesen Wegen litten,
wir haben nicht den Garten abgenützt,
und Stunden, größere als wir erbitten,
tasten nach uns und gehn auf uns gestützt.   (SW ii, 356)

The line 'die Erde ist nicht anders als die Nacht' implies: 'das Nächste ist nicht anders als das Namenlose' and further, that the human consciousness is the unifying medium between the world of objects and 'das Namenlose'. There is no barrier of alienation between the self and the surroundings and the initial confusion is outweighed by the affirmations of the rest of the poem. Moreover, and most significantly, 'das Namenlose' no longer stands 'steil vor dem Herzen' as does the god of the *Improvisationen aus dem Capreser Winter*, but mingles with 'das Nächste' – nothing interposes between them. It is in effect the unity of inner and outer worlds observed in the poem *Gedanken der Nacht* and similar to that of the prose piece *Erlebnis*. In this unity any 'Gegenständlichkeit' which night may possess has been absorbed into the overall *feeling* of relatedness, much as in the *Stunden-Buch* the basic attitude of intentionality is oblivious of any emotional separation between subject and object, at least as far as the first two sections are concerned.[16] But this is only one aspect of 'Nacht'.

For in the new attitude which Rilke takes to external reality in the period of the *Neue Gedichte*, there is implicit the danger of the loss of all empathy with what is perceived, of a complete alienation from what is no longer the correlative for an inner state but in the full sense of the word: 'Gegenstand'. In the *Gedichte an die Nacht* there is great emphasis on this theme of 'Fremdheit'. But it is already present at the time of the composition of *Sterne hinter Oliven*:

NÄCHTLICHER GANG

Nichts ist vergleichbar. Denn was ist nicht ganz
mit sich allein und was je auszusagen;
wir nennen nichts, wir dürfen nur ertragen
und uns verständigen, daß da ein Glanz
und dort ein Blick vielleicht uns so gestreift
als wäre grade *das* darin gelebt

was unser Leben ist. Wer widerstrebt
dem wird nicht Welt. Und wer zuviel begreift
dem geht das Ewige vorbei... (SW II, 30)

This is an extreme formulation and somewhat against the general
trend of Rilke's understanding of the relation of the human
consciousness to the external world. But it does lead in the
direction of the other aspect of the ambivalence of night. The
poem ends by suggesting that in the experience of night there
may be found some mitigation of this estrangement:

> ...Zuweilen
> in solchen großen Nächten sind wir wie
> außer Gefahr, in gleichen leichten Teilen
> den Sternen ausgeteilt. Wie drängen sie.

What is significant for the present discussion is that the situation of being 'den Sternen ausgeteilt', while seeming to contain
the possibility of overcoming alienation, is still one of 'Gegenüber-sein'. In other words, night as well as representing a state
in which 'Gegenständlichkeit' is overcome, can be an object
itself and thus 'für den Betrachter und Beurteiler...somit
"opaque" und zu'.[17] The self may stand 'vor der Nacht' or
'vor dem Sternenhimmel' in the same way as it may stand 'vor
der Natur'. Night may offer the same resistance to empathy,
to the attempts of the self to achieve contact in the sphere of
transcendent reality, as may any other object in the external world.
As an example of 'Nacht' as a reality which is closed to the
projection of human feeling, one may take the last six lines of the
sonnet *Sonnenuntergang* written in August 1907:

> Und dein Leben, von dem man die lichten Gewichte gehoben,
> stieg, soweit Raum war, über das Alles nach oben,
> füllend die rasch sich verkühlende Leere der Welt.
> Bis es, im Steigen, in kaum zu erfühlender Ferne
> sanft an die Nacht stieß. Da wurden ihm einige Sterne,
> als nächste Wirklichkeit, wehrend entgegengestellt. (SW II, 28f.)

To read these lines side by side with *Sterne hinter Oliven* is to
see the full duality of the 'Nacht'-motif: that it may be *both*
the antithesis of 'Gegenüber-sein' *and* that it may be experienced

in the form of 'Gegenständlichkeit': 'dem Ich "wehrend entgegengestellt"'.

Now that the origins of the ambivalence of night in the *Gedichte an die Nacht* have been shown, its various meanings may be summarised as follows:

(a) 'Nacht' *both* as a state of human consciousness *and* as a phenomenon in the external world.

(b) As a phenomenon in the external world: *both* an element of commonplace experience *and* a manifestation of numinous being.

(c) As the latter: *both* accessible to the human consciousness as 'mögliche Existenz' *and* closed to it as an impenetrable 'Gegenstand'.

Some of the perplexity which such a range of meanings might cause at first sight has been dispersed by showing how it develops out of the situation of the *Stunden-Buch* and how 'Nacht' becomes the focal point of two distinct but related problems which are central to Rilke's work: the relation of the self to the world of objects and the relation of immanence to transcendence. These problems are both emotional and intellectual and Rilke's treatment of them is anything but simple, logical and consistent. The extreme flexibility in his use of 'Nacht' – making it sometimes merely a metaphor for something else, while at others an 'einzige Wirklichkeit' – is entirely characteristic of his poetic logic which is not that of formal argument. Yet these poems can be interpreted and provide us with a key to understanding the *Gedichte an die Nacht* within the perspective of Rilke's earlier work. This understanding involves neither an act of faith on the part of the reader nor reduction of the problem of transcendence to one of 'Künstlersehnsucht'. It remains for us to inquire how the meaning of night in the *Gedichte an die Nacht* is influenced by the problem of 'Gegenständlichkeit'.

At the beginning of this chapter it was said that 'Nacht' may oscillate between representing 'Transzendenz' and 'mögliche

Existenz'. As a result of tracing the development of the 'Nacht'-theme in the years preceding the Spanish journey, we must add to this the fact that night may also alternate between 'Gegenständlichkeit' and the kind of participation in which the barriers between subject and object are absent. We can now tie up some of the loose ends, which the thematic analysis of necessity left, by showing firstly the negative situation, secondly a stage in which positive and negative are unresolved and, thirdly the positive situation.

The state in which night is placed 'steil vor dem Herzen' in the manner of the god of the *Improvisationen aus dem Capreser Winter* is best illustrated by the following fragment:

> Unwissend vor dem Himmel meines Lebens,
> anstaunend steh ich. O die großen Sterne.
> Aufgehendes und Niederstieg. Wie still.
> Als wär ich nicht. Nehm ich denn Teil. Entriet ich
> dem reinen Einfluß? Wechselt Flut und Ebbe
> in meinem Blut nach dieser Ordnung? Abtun
> will ich die Wünsche, jeden andern Anschluß,
> mein Herz gewöhnen an sein Fernstes. Besser
> es lebt im Schrecken seiner Sterne, als
> zum Schein beschützt, von einer Näh beschwichtigt.   (SW II, 53)

The conviction that the self *should* be 'am Nachthimmel beteiligt' is expressed in the phrases 'Himmel meines Lebens' and 'mein Herz gewöhnen an sein Fernstes'. It is thereby implied that the establishing of contact is a task which the poet feels he must perform. But in the meantime the heavens remain 'Gegenstand' and their relatedness to the self is fraught with the same uncertainties as appear in the poem which Rilke begins with the categorical statement: 'Nichts ist vergleichbar', namely:

> ...wir dürfen nur ertragen
> und uns verständigen, daß da ein Glanz
> und dort ein Blick vielleicht uns so gestreift
> als wäre grade *das* darin gelebt
> was unser Leben ist...

The full despair which this 'Gegenständlichkeit' is capable of producing is evidenced in the lines quoted above from the poem *Vor Weihnachten 1914*:

Was willst du fühlen? Ach dein Fühlen reicht
vom Weinenden zum nicht mehr Weinenden.
Doch drüber sind, unfühlbar, Himmel leicht
von zahllos Engeln. Dir unfühlbar. Du
kennst nur den Nicht-Schmerz. Die Sekunde Ruh
zwischen zwei Schmerzen... (SW II, 97)

This, when it is reinforced by the alienation from the world of objects is the furthest negative position. It is virtually impossible to explain why it should appear in one poem and not in another. Alternations between hope and despair in Rilke's emotional life are amply attested by the letters, but whatever may have produced them is precisely what is not accessible through his poetry. It is at this point that a psychological interpretation becomes a tissue of conjectures which may be fascinating in itself but can hardly prove anything about the poetry.

An intermediate stage in which 'Gegenständlichkeit' and 'Beteiligung' co-exist rather confusedly as elements of the experience of night is represented by the poem *So angestrengt wider die starke Nacht*. At the beginning of the poem Rilke sharply criticises those who regard the night as an opposing force and resist it as an object. The poem then goes on to maintain that night is not 'gegenständlich' at all, but rather a medium *in* which humanity exists *a priori*:

> ...Und atmet doch den Raum,
> in dem die Sterne gehen...

So that instead of being opaque and closed, the night:

> ...schlägt sich auf
> uns gegenüber und zerstreut vielleicht
> an uns sein Dasein...

But the doubt implied by the 'veilleicht' is rather apposite for a few lines further down 'Nacht-Raum' appears in an image suggestive once more of 'Gegenständlichkeit':

> Umsonst. Denn wer gewahrts? Und wo es einer
> gewärtig wird: wer darf noch an den Nacht-Raum
> die Stirne lehnen wie ans eigne Fenster?

158

Nevertheless the night reappears as 'dieses eingeborne Element' and the thread of the argument becomes entangled with other themes. In fact, it is the gods at the end of the poem which are uncommunicative and indifferent, and which have attributed to them the otherness implicit in the night as 'Gegenstand'. The dilemma which this poem presents, and does not solve, is an excellent illustration of the difficulty of interpreting the *Gedichte an die Nacht* for the poem does not offer a unity in conceptual terms. Such unity as it may have must be a dynamic one, must consist in the unresolved interaction of two modes of experiencing night which are antithetical to each other. Again one must invoke the lines from the fourth Elegy:

> Uns aber, wo wir Eines meinen, ganz,
> ist schon des andern Aufwand fühlbar...
>
> Da wird für eines Augenblickes Zeichnung
> ein Grund von Gegenteil bereitet, mühsam,
> daß wir sie sähen... (SW I, 697)

for it is this principle which determines the structure of the poem. Of course, this is not the case with every poem in the collection but it does result in a situation where individual poems appear to contradict each other, particularly as far as the nature of night is concerned.

The third stage in which 'Gegenständlichkeit' gives way to 'Beteiligung' is exemplified by the conclusion of *Die große Nacht*. In the beginning of the poem the self confronts the night as something strange and inexplicable. The strangeness of the night at first seems little different from that of the world of objects but the turning point of the poem, and with it a different kind of astonishment, comes when the poet suddenly realises that, no matter how alien the immediate surroundings may be, the apparent strangeness and indifference of the night is not the case at all. It is interesting to note the stages of the union which then takes place. The first stage:

> ...da war es, du Hohe,
> keine Schande für dich, daß du mich kanntest.

does not exclude the possibility that the separation of 'Ich' and 'Nacht' in *emotional* terms may not still exist as before. The second stage then brings them into a quite sensuous contact: 'Dein Atem ging über mich.' And in the final stage the words 'trat in mich ein' show that any previously existing barrier to feeling has quite disappeared:

> Dein auf weite Ernste verteiltes
> Lächeln trat in mich ein.

Die große Nacht shows this union in the process of becoming and sets it apart from the 'hungernde Fremdheit' which still prevails in the immediate environment. But in the poem *Gedanken der Nacht*, written shortly before, the fusion of the 'unendliche Nacht' and the night within the poet is achieved by the poet doing no more than thinking appropriate thoughts. This could lead us to the conclusion that the overcoming of 'Gegenständlichkeit' is largely a matter of the poet being able to adopt a particular 'Bewußtseinshaltung' and that sometimes this is possible and at other times not. The implications of this will be dealt with in the chapter entitled 'The Modes of Transcendence'.

The aspect of this third stage which should be stressed at the moment is that shown in the turning away from the immediate surroundings which accompanies the union with the night and which is implicit in the situation of the poem *Gedanken der Nacht*. Such an exclusive directedness towards the sphere of transcendent existence tends to leave the problem of the relation of the self to the world in which it must continue to exist largely unresolved. This tendency is further illustrated by one of the drafts for the *Gedichte an die Nacht*:

> An das Stillende hinaufgekehrt,
> hab ich mich zur heilen Nacht entschlossen,
> meine Sinne sind mir abgeflossen
> und das Herz ist namenlos vermehrt. (SW II, 407)

These lines stress the inwardness of the 'Nacht'-experience – the words 'meine sind Sinne mir abgeflossen' imply that the poet is no longer in contact with external reality and one would not have to go very much further in this line of interpretation to see the night at this extreme as entirely a 'Richtung des namenlos vermehrten Herzens', in the sense of the letter on the subject of prayer. This must, of course, be seen in the perspective of what we have already shown of night as an intentional object and as an aspect of external reality. Hence it appears at one extreme of the scale of meaning and does not constitute an exhaustive definition in itself. However, this tendency shows something of the limitation of the experiences of union in *Die große Nacht* and *Gedanken der Nacht* and of the way in which these fall short of the ideal totality of experience towards which the *Gedichte an die Nacht* as a whole aspire – but which they do not quite reach.

For, from the completion of the *Stunden-Buch* onwards, Rilke is not only torn between two needs, which are both intellectual and emotional: firstly, to establish a satisfactory 'In-der-Welt-Sein' on the basis of a different experience of and attitude to external reality from that which produced his vision of the 'Künstler-Gott', and secondly, to achieve a new relation of the self to divine or transcendent reality to replace the lost god of the *Stunden-Buch*. But there is a further imperative which he strives to obey and that is to fulfil these needs not separately but as a unity. But even when, as in some of the *Gedichte an die Nacht*, the relation of self to night has been successfully established, there still remains an 'ungelöster Rest' in Fülleborn's sense,[18] namely, the unresolved problems which still surround the self in the world. For just as Rilke's declaration in the letter to von der Heydt that he has 'die Menschen übersprungen' is entirely premature in the light of the rôle which the 'Geliebte' plays in the *Gedichte an die Nacht*, so does any 'Eines meinen, ganz' in these poems either remain extremely precarious or else lead directly into 'des andern Aufwand'. This is reflected by the fact that there is no single consistent experience of 'Nacht' in these poems but rather that its meaning must be seen as a scale which reflects the conflicts of experience within the self.

This does not necessarily mean that these experiences have to be dismissed as 'merely subjective' – if that were grounds for dismissing them anyway – for one such conflict might be the inability of the self to reconcile a genuine experience of transcendence with one of estrangement in his immediate environment or one of alienation from another human being. In this way our inquiry into the meaning of 'Nacht' leads in the direction of a closer examination of the apparent disunity of the self in these poems and this will be our object in the next chapter.

6. THE HUMAN SITUATION

The question that immediately arises is whether or not there is any point in trying to establish a single, definitive human situation in these poems. The inquiry into the meaning of 'Nacht' in the previous chapter has brought to light its shifting and inconstant quality throughout the collection. In some contexts night is encountered as a concrete, external reality, while in others it is used to signify an intensity of feeling which no longer needs any object at all. There is a strong temptation to conclude that attitudes as different as these must proceed from situations which have very little in common with one another. Such a conclusion would also accord with the traditional usage of the term 'lyrisches Ich' which, as an essentially pragmatic critical device, is normally used to describe the persona or 'Aussagesubjekt' of a single poem.[1] The main advantage of 'das lyrische Ich' is that it enables us to discuss the self of a given poem with a view to showing that poem's unique structure and without any obligation to integrate this self with what we know of the poet's biography, his theory of art or any statements he may have made about his intentions in writing the poem. We may certainly go on to relate the 'lyrisches Ich' to the poem's biographical or historical context, as long as we realise that we are dealing with two different kinds of data and that we cannot argue prescriptively from one to the other. But even if we preserve this distinction, another difficulty arises. Since each poem creates its own frame of reference, there is a strong tendency for the reader or critic to react to each 'lyrisches Ich' as to a personality in its own right. On the level of critical analysis this tendency is reinforced by the fact that a seemingly complete self and its whole relation to the world are implied by and must be deduced from the relatively few elements of a single poem. If the poem offers a conceptual unity, then there is no obstacle to making statements about the 'world' of the poem, even though the presentation of the 'lyrisches Ich' may be limited to a very few explicit characteristics.[2] But when we take a number of poems by the same author then we may well find that the implications of each 'lyrisches Ich', while leading in a somewhat similar direction, do not converge in a single, precise structure but, indeed, result in as many discrepancies as consonances.

There are various ways of dealing with this problem in the context of the *Gedichte an die Nacht*. One of them is to postulate a series of 'existential moments', as Wodtke does, and not be overly concerned with establishing connections between them:

Diese subjektive, welt-immanente Transzendenz entsteht von Fall zu Fall im existentiellen Augenblick, indem der Mensch sich selbst 'übersteigt'...[3]

But the use of the word 'existentiell' here creates more problems than it solves. For by and large we simply lack precise knowledge of what correspondences or differences there may be between Rilke's own personal experiences and the experiences presented by the poems. We cannot determine to what extent *Die große Nacht* may be a factual record of a single 'existential moment', whether it is an amalgam of a large number of different personal experiences or to what degree any actual experience may have been modified by the poetic imagination to produce what we encounter in the poem. So Wodtke's referring of the problems back to 'existentielle Augenblicke' can be seen either as an admission of defeat or an invitation to speculate on the unknowable. Also, by emphasising the 'von Fall zu Fall' quality of these poems, Wodtke seems to imply that if one cannot find perfect consistency, then there is little to be gained by painstakingly examining similarities and differences from context to context: each poem is its own 'world', each 'lyrisches Ich' a *sui generis*. The implications of Wodtke's statement seem to be too ambitious in one sense, while too restricting in another. Relating each poem to its 'existentieller Augenblick' will tend to involve the critic in those very difficulties which the use of the concept 'lyrisches Ich' should enable him to avoid. On the other hand, a too ready acceptance of the 'von Fall zu Fall' aspect of the *Gedichte an die Nacht* may well lead to ignoring such connections and developments as can be made visible. We saw in the last chapter that 'Nacht' means different things in different contexts. But it was also possible to show that these differences were not simply a case of 'sometimes this, sometimes that' but rather made sense within a framework of larger issues with which Rilke's poetry is concerned from the period of *Das Stunden-Buch* onwards.

Steering a middle course between these two extremes therefore means preserving the initial distinction between 'lyrisches Ich' and biographical or existential self, while extending the application of the term 'lyrisches Ich' beyond the individual poem. What will result will be a kind of aggregate poetic self, at first sight perhaps no more unified than the meaning of 'Nacht' is free from ambiguity, and such a result is already strongly implied by the interpretations offered in the earlier chapters. Given the strong thematic connections between the individual *Gedichte an die Nacht*, there is every reason for trying to relate the 'lyrisches Ich' of one poem to that of another. If the overall image of the poetic self which results is a disunified one, then it may well be the case that this disunity is what the collection as a whole is about, not merely because the poems were written at different times and in different states of mind, but because they exemplify a theory of the divided self which is of prime importance for an understanding of Rilke's whole work.

Instances of the division of the self within the same poem were seen in the analysis of *Die spanische Trilogie* and *Die große Nacht*, perhaps the two most impressive poems of the collection. At the beginning of the trilogy, the self which confronts the landscape is divided into an active consciousness, which can mirror and record the harmonious organisation of the scene before it, and a less articulate, more emotional residuum which manifests itself as a feeling of exclusion from the very harmony which the other half of the self is depicting. If the active consciousness is to bring about unity, then it must strive to assimilate two different objects at once: 'aus mir und alledem ein einzig Ding/zu machen', it must unite both with what is denoted by the 'mir', the other half of the total self, and with the 'alledem', the whole of the external reality before it. As if to stress this division within the self, Rilke in the second poem of the trilogy sets out to illustrate it by another kind of example. It becomes the alienation of the consciousness from its own memories, captured in the image of the porter obliged to carry around with him the 'fremdlings mehr und mehr gefüllten Marktkorb'. Here the terms of the division within the self are not quite identical with those in the first poem, but in each case we are made aware that a unified self is just as much a goal to be striven for as is the unity between self and world. In *Die große Nacht* the dual nature of the 'lyrisches Ich' is not at first apparent, since at the beginning of the poem the night itself and 'die nächsten Dinge' seem equally inaccessible. What brings the division of the self to light is the differentiation which occurs within the external reality which it confronts. At the turning point of the poem, the self is suddenly able to distinguish the 'erwachsene Nacht' as a force separate from the 'children's game' of the immediate surroundings. The intensified recapitulation of the theme of 'Fremdheit' which then follows shows that union with the night does not extend to union with the immediate surroundings. Although in the ending of the poem the emphasis quite naturally shifts to celebrating the contact which has been established, the restatement of the theme of alienation *after* the turning point of the poem shows that in the crucial moment when this contact occurs, the self is simultaneously aware of 'Fremdheit' on one level and 'Beteiligung' on another. We know from other contexts, such as the first part of *Die spanische Trilogie*, that emotional contact with 'die nächsten Dinge' is an essential element in any complete fulfilment. By stressing in *Die große Nacht* that participation on this level still does not occur, Rilke is implicitly showing in what sense the triumphant conclusion of the poem still falls short of the ultimate and ideal totality of a harmonious self which may serve as the unifying point of immanent and transcendent reality. Such an ideal is given in the figure of the shepherd in *Die spanische Trilogie* who is both at one with the natural surroundings and at the same time quite open to the visitation of transcendent powers. Significantly, the shepherd is introduced into the trilogy as a direct contrast to the figure of the 'Träger' who, as we have seen, stands for a division within the self. Essential to the ideal quality of the shepherd is the fact that he is quite free from any such inner dividedness. The self of *Die große Nacht*, on the other hand, is not endowed from the beginning with any such ideal unity. Rather, its potential for inner conflict is representative of what Rilke sees as the actual human situation in the *Gedichte an die Nacht* and so the poem makes clear that achievement of 'Beteiligung' in one direction, with one half of the self as it were, need not extend to that part of the self which must remain in contact with its immediate environment.

Not every poem in the collection raises the possibility of a divided 'lyrisches Ich'. It was shown, for example, with regard to the poem *Gedanken der Nacht* that the relation of the self to its immediate environment could be simply left out of account. But instances such as these only reinforce the need to compare the 'lyrisches Ich' from poem to poem, to see each example of 'Fremdheit' or 'Beteiligung' within the larger framework of the *Gedichte an die Nacht*. Here we must also remember that the *Gedichte an die Nacht* are a collection and not a clearly organised cycle. They share a common thematic field, but there is no progression from initial doubt and confusion to final clarity. The outlines of an ideal totality may be deduced by putting together the various separate instances of fulfilment and disappointment and drawing the furthest conclusions which they allow, but this process also leads to the conclusion that the factors determining the basic situation of the self in these poems effectively prevent the ideal from being completely realised. In this way the aggregate of all the various situations presented in the *Gedichte an die Nacht* can be seen as a parallel to the point of departure of the *Duineser Elegien*. At the beginning of the first Elegy, it is as if the opening statement of man's exclusion from the transcendent reality of the angels forces the poet to make the complementary and equally negative statement that man is also estranged from the world he lives in. The resultant need to achieve 'Beteiligung' in two directions at once points in the direction of the theme of division within the self which is then given such powerful expression in the fourth Elegy, where, with the image of the 'Puppenbühne', the consciousness sits 'vor seines Herzens Vorhang', the one half of the divided self becomes the distanced spectator of the other. The first two Elegies are from the first months of 1912 and the fourth Elegy from November 1915.[4] Falling chronologically between them, the *Gedichte an die Nacht* present a range of situations which clearly derive from that of the first two Elegies. There is the same overall imperative towards establishing 'Beteiligung', the same awareness that 'Fremdheit' can be a quality of both immanent and transcendent reality, the same inability to arrive at a decision to strive for 'Beteiligung' in one direction at the expense of the other. What the *Gedichte an die Nacht* as a whole show is that partial or temporary fulfilments are indeed possible within the situation defined by the opening of the *Duineser Elegien*. The self of the *Gedichte an die Nacht* seems in a number of instances to gain access to some transcendent reality, thus apparently fulfilling one half of the dual imperative. But, as we have seen, the further conclusion is that this is not enough. Because of the disunity inherent in the self, contact with a transcendent power does not automatically integrate the self with its immediate environment, rather it makes the fact of this disunity all the more plain. So it is not surprising that the statement which sums up the human situation in the fourth Elegy: 'Wir sind nicht einig.' (SW 1, 697) is shown by the rest of the Elegy to refer to two kinds of disunity: that between self and world and that which presents the two opposed halves of the self as puppet-play and spectator. The strong re-emergence of this theme in 1915 confirms what has already been suggested with regard to the *Gedichte an die Nacht*, namely that the overall human situation presented in these poems should be understood as illustrating the problems of the divided self, implying the terms of an ideal resolution of them but essentially going no further than that.

An even more striking proof of this is provided by the essay *Puppen*, written about the beginning of February 1914 and thus at the conclusion of the period of the *Gedichte an die Nacht*.[5] I have published elsewhere a detailed interpretation of this essay,[6] showing its relevance to Rilke's poetry in this period, and so it would be superfluous to repeat the analysis here. However it is necessary to point out that *Puppen* does provide a key to understanding Rilke's own attitudes towards the theme of division within the self. For in the essay Rilke not only shows his awareness of these issues but develops an elaborate and coherent theory of how this predicament might have originated. The conclusion drawn from the discussion of the *Gedichte an die Nacht*, that a state of 'Fremdheit' between self and other will tend to be accompanied by a division within the self, is confirmed by statements in the essay to the effect that both forms of disunity are basic determinants of adult human experience.[7] In *Puppen* Rilke is chiefly concerned with theorising about the genesis of this double disunity and places the blame, perhaps somewhat arbitrarily, on the childhood experience of playing with dolls. An initial, ideal state of childhood is posited – somewhat reminiscent of the Freudian doctrine of infant omnipotence – where the child is unaware of any difference between itself and the world and consequently enjoys an untroubled wholeness of the self. This state assumes for Rilke the connotations of a mythical paradise – admittedly with only one inhabitant – and the inevitable loss of it goes hand in hand with the growth of self-awareness. A certain amount of confusion is created by the fact that Rilke insists that it is *only* the experience of playing with dolls which effects the unhappy transition from wholeness of experience to separation and disunity, thus giving his own version of the perennial myth a very idiosyncratic twist and obliging him to differentiate dolls from all other objects of experience in terms that are more vehement than logical. In fact, Rilke uses the doll as a device to present the enormously complex question of the relatedness of self and world in the drastically simplified form of an either/or. As a reaction to the intricate inconclusiveness of the *Gedichte an die Nacht*, this is quite understandable, but it does mean that within the framework of the essay one single aspect of childhood experience has to bear the brunt of virtually all the ambivalences present in the relation of self to other throughout Rilke's work.

In the main argument of the *Puppen*-essay Rilke seems quite unwilling to admit of any compromise between the lost paradise of earliest childhood and the complete isolation and disunity of adult experience, but such intransigence is clearly not true of his treatment of these issues over the whole of his work, nor indeed of the mixture of partial failure and partial fulfilment present in the *Gedichte an die Nacht* themselves. Such poems as *Die große Nacht*, apparently written less than a month before *Puppen*, show that, given the potential for disunity within the self which *Puppen* establishes, the possibilities are not limited to either total 'Fremdheit' or total 'Beteiligung' but rather that each may be present at the same time with regard to different objects. An implicit awareness of this state of affairs may also be detected in *Puppen* by the very difficulties presented on a conceptual level by Rilke's attempt to justify his differentiation of the child's dolls from all other 'Dinge', whether playthings or not. For this raises the paradox that while, on the one hand, Rilke's statements about the doll are clearly meant to apply to the nature of human experience as such, on the other hand he insists that the negative qualities of the doll are *not* shared by other inanimate objects.[8] The dubious logic of this distinction does, however, point to further ambivalences in Rilke's theory of the division of the self. For while we have been led to conclude from the *Gedichte an die Nacht* that this division of the self is always potentially present in these poems, it is certainly not always developed as an explicit theme. Looking then at Rilke's work as a whole, it is also the case that in some contexts this theme will be not only present but dominant, while in others it will be absent entirely. It seems that the more Rilke is concerned in a particular context with looking beyond the present towards such an ideal totality as he sketches in his myth of earliest childhood, the more likely it is that his awareness of the discrepancy between real and ideal will lead on to further formulations of the theme of the divided self. Where, for example, the need is felt to establish 'Beteiligung' in two different directions at once, as at the beginning of the first Duino Elegy, then the very magnitude of the task creates tensions which in turn produce the theme of the divided self in the fourth Elegy and, more immediately, in the *Gedichte an die Nacht*. But the imperative towards realising an ideal totality is not always present in the same form or the same strength in Rilke's work, just as in the *Gedichte an die Nacht* themselves the basic impulse towards 'Beteiligung' appears in some contexts at its most extreme and ambitious, bringing with it the theme of the conflicts within the self, while in others it is directed towards more limited goals and the tension created in the poem is correspondingly less.

The view of human experience which Rilke develops around the dolls can be seen as a summary of the human situation in the *Gedichte an die Nacht* in its most negative terms. The doll comes to represent not only a world that is intrinsically alien to the self, but, more importantly, it stands for the false and illusory nature of any 'Beteiligung' that may seem possible in such a world. By presenting this view so vehemently, Rilke tends to put himself out on a limb and so, as if to redress the balance, he places excessive emphasis on the distinction between dolls and all other 'Dinge'. What he is in fact distinguishing here are two opposed views of human experience: in the world of the doll, 'Beteiligung' is a grotesque illusion; in the world of 'Dinge' it is genuine and eminently possible. On a conceptual level this would seem to lead to straight-out contradiction, but in the poetry we find the two views mixed in varying proportions according to which of the two emotional states of 'Fremdheit' or 'Beteiligung' happens to be the stronger at the time. The value of such extreme statements as we find in the main argument of *Puppen* or, at the opposite end of the scale, in the series of experiences evoked in the prose-piece *Erlebnis* is in showing clearly what positive and negative elements combine in the human situation of the *Gedichte an die Nacht*. *Erlebnis*, written in Ronda in early February 1913,[9] sets out to record and evoke occasions in the past when a maximum relatedness of self and world was experienced. The main argument of *Puppen*, written exactly a year later, would tend to invalidate what *Erlebnis* affirms. The poems we have examined from this period show that in practice a great degree of merging and interaction between the two views takes place and that it would be wrong to give one primacy over the other. *Erlebnis* clearly foreshadows the concept of 'Weltinnenraum', while the theory of the divided self put forward in *Puppen* reinforces a quite opposite set of themes throughout the middle and later periods of Rilke's work. The intertwining of these two thematic strands in the *Gedichte an die Nacht* effectively prevents them from being a unified cycle but at the same time makes the overall human situation in the poems so complex and interesting.

The theme of the divided self is not confined to the period of the *Gedichte an die Nacht*. Like the 'Nacht'-motif, it first appears quite early in Rilke's poetic production and recurs in variations throughout the work. In a poem of 1898, one of the *Lieder der Mädchen*, it appears in the form of the longing for some firm identity:

> Ich war in ferner Fremde Kind,
> bis ich mich: arm und zart und blind –
> aus meinen Schämen schlich;
> ich warte hinter Wald und Wind
> gewiß schon lang auf mich.
> Ich bin allein und weit vom Haus
> und sinne still: wie seh ich aus? (SW I, 179–80)

This seems innocuous enough: the poem evokes the uncertainty attending the transition from childhood to adult life with all the preciosity of Rilke's early manner. 'Waiting for oneself' seems to mean not much more than being lost and confused in the world. But the last two lines of the poem:

und geh gewiß umsonst umsonnt [*sic*]
und fremd an mir vorbei...

take the metaphor one stage further. The 'Ich' feels that it is composed of two separate entities, but these are alien to one another to the point of being unrecognisable, so that it is hard to see how any unity could ever be achieved. One might be tempted to dismiss this instance as nothing more than a hyperbole, since the image of the self in Rilke's early poetry is on the whole free from any such complications, but there are other instances of the same theme in the early work which should make us wary of doing this. In a poem addressed to Paula Becker and Clara Westhoff in November 1900 Rilke pays them the compliment of saying they are 'wie Schwestern meiner Seele'. From this he goes on to say that he is not yet in possession of his soul, rather it is imprisoned somewhere, like a fairy-tale princess in a tower:

> denn hinter Wänden wohnt sie weit,
> wohnt wie im Turm, noch nicht von mir befreit,
> kaum wissend, daß ich einmal kommen werde. (SW III, 706)

Once more the self has become two distinct entities. The 'Ich' feels its present state to be incomplete and looks forward to eventual union with its complementary 'Seele'. In terms of the imagery this is explicitly seen as a marriage of the two aspects of the same self, for later in the poem the soul is described as 'meine Braut'. But no sooner has Rilke postulated this ideal unity of the self, than he begins to have doubts about it, as the following lines show:

> Ich aber geh durch die Winde der Erde
> auf die wachsende Mauer zu,
> hinter welcher in unbegriffener Trauer
> meine Seele wohnt.... (SW III, 706)

It is interesting here that the 'Wände' of a few lines before have now become a 'wachsende Mauer', indicating that the closer the 'Ich' comes to the object of its quest the more formidable the final obstacle becomes. The soul's expectancy now acquires the negative emotional shading of 'unbegriffene Trauer', so that the final unification of the whole self has become much more equivocal than the image at first suggested. Here again one might well say that Rilke simply lets the image run away with him and that one need not take its implications too seriously. But the use of the words 'Wände' and 'Mauer' here to denote barriers between one part of the self and another does call for serious consideration, for usually they are used to denote the separation between self and world. This can appear either in the form of a splendid isolation, as in a letter of December 1906:

> ...wohl aber muß ich sehen, nach und nach zu einem Kloster anzuwachsen und so dazustehn in der Welt, mit Mauern um mich, aber mit Gott und den Heiligen in mir, mit sehr schönen Bildern und Geräten in mir... (B. 1906–07, 117)

or else in the form of alienation at its worst, as in the fragment of November 1913:

> Ich wurde manchmal im Vorübergehn
> die Wände inne, die uns stumm begleiten,
> und sah erstarrt, wie auf den beiden Seiten
> von Gittern die Gefangenen entstehn... (SW II, 404)

That Rilke in 1900 can already use this imagery to signify the separation of two aspects of the same self suggests strongly that the later idea of the division of the self into 'Teil und Gegenteil' is already present in its essentials, although the main direction of Rilke's work at the time keeps it from being developed or becoming too prominent.

Nevertheless, a fragment of November 1902, written at a time when Rilke was finding Paris 'unendlich fremd und feindlich' and his contact with Rodin aroused acute feelings of personal inadequacy,[10] is very similar in tone and language to the 'confessional' fragments of the period of the *Gedichte an die Nacht*:

> Ein Verleugneter der eignen Hände,
> und vergessen wie ein totes Tier –
> und die vielen fremden Widerstände,
> und der Aufstand gegen mich in mir.
> Ob aus alle diesem etwas Neues,
> Wirkliches und Wietes kommen kann, – (SW III, 764)

The 'fremde Widerstände' presumably refer to the hostile reality of Paris of which Rilke speaks in his letters at this time. But this evocation of 'Fremdheit' between self and world seems immediately to suggest the complementary theme of conflict within the self, thus anticipating the twofold estrangement described much later in the essay *Puppen*. The same pattern is also present in sections of *Die Aufzeichnungen des Malte Laurids Brigge*. The division in Malte's case is that between his 'surface-consciousness' and the 'Inneres von dem ich nicht wußte'.[11] Just as Malte distinguishes in general terms between 'die Ober-fläche des Lebens' and a still unknown reality which he conjectures to lie beneath it, so he also uses the model of a known surface and an unknown core for describing his own personality. Just as he has intimations of unknown forces active behind the façade which Paris presents to him, so he also lives in dread of whatever may be lurking in his unknown 'Inneres'. Malte can never be more specific about it than to call it 'das Große' or 'das Unerhörte', for, though it may come from within himself, it is none the less alien and incomprehensible. So the situation occurs where the active consciousness is not only threatened by the alien quality of *external* reality, but where it also finds itself the victim of another aspect of the self:

...im Kapillaren nimmt es zu, röhrig aufwärts gesaugt in die äußersten Verä-stelungen deines zahlloszweigigen Daseins. Dort hebt es sich, dort übersteigt es dich, kommt höher als dein Atem, auf den du dich hinaufflüchtest wie auf deine letzte Stelle. Ach, und wohin dann, wohin dann? Dein Herz treibt dich aus dir hinaus, dein Herz ist hinter dir her, und du stehst fast schon außer dir und kannst nicht mehr zurück. Wie ein Käfer, auf den man tritt, so quillst du aus dir hinaus, und dein bißchen obere Härte und Anpassung ist ohne Sinn. (SW VI, 777)

Having 'das Unerhörte' as likely to burst forth from within the self as to assault it from outside results in a quite different presentation of the theme of inner conflict from what we find in the *Gedichte an die Nacht*. But the underlying pattern is the same and the obstacles in the way of any final unity are equally effective in both cases. It is worth noting that whatever particular image or model of the divided self Rilke chooses to elaborate in a given context, the theme functions consistently as an intensification of the theme of 'Fremdheit'. It is in no way necessary for the idea of a twofold self to develop in this direction. The two complementary aspects may merge harmoniously into one another, as happens with Novalis' concept of the relation of 'empirisches Ich' to 'höheres Ich'. But in Rilke's case, the idea of the duality of the self becomes related to the theme of 'Gegenüber-sein', of the problematical relation of subject to object, which is presented in the eighth Elegy as another form of alienation.

Once again, it is the essay *Puppen* which makes the relation of the two themes quite explicit. When postulating the ideal state of earliest childhood, Rilke speaks of 'die Welt, die unabgegrenzt in uns überging' (SW VI, 1067), while the result of the experience of the doll is expressed as 'die Welt...vom Leibe zu halten'. The process is seen as follows: the child demands an emotional response from whatever it is in contact with, the doll cannot provide this because it is, in Rilke's terms, totally devoid of any qualities of its own, so the child makes up for the doll's vacuity by projecting into it its own feelings and experiences. In this way the child becomes the spectator of that part of the self which it has projected on to the doll and in addition continually invents feelings to project when there are no real ones at hand. The consequences are threefold: first, by placing itself 'der Puppe gegenüber' the child learns to distinguish subject from object; secondly, by projecting feelings on to the doll it 'objectifies' part of its own self, thus breaking the primal unity; thirdly, by *inventing* a response from something outside the self and mistaking it for a genuine one, it becomes aware of the possibility that any other response from any other external object may be equally an invention of the self, thus bringing a strong degree of doubt and uncertainty into the whole question of the relatedness of self and world. For, despite Rilke's own protestations, the essay raises the possibility that instead of the doll's being an aberrant exception in the world of objects, its vacuity and indifference might rather be representative of 'die Dinge' as such and any imagined 'Beteiligung' might be no more than an invention of the self.

Having seen the way in which the theme of the divided self functions as an intensification of the initial division between self and world, it remains to consider further aspects of the subject-object relationship in the period of the *Gedichte an die Nacht*. Even in those poems of the collection where the poetic self seems to be single rather than double, the question of the limits of the self, of the distance between subject and object and of the barriers which stand in the way of achieving 'Beteiligung' may be posed just as forcefully and appear to be just as difficult to answer. In *Puppen* Rilke evokes:

...jenes überlebensgroße Schweigen..., das uns später immer wieder aus dem Raume anhauchte, wenn wir irgendwo an die Grenze unseres Daseins traten. (SW VI, 1069)

and again and again in the poems we have examined we find him concerned either with establishing the limits of the self or with attempting to push further into 'die schwarzen Sektoren..., die das uns Unerfahrbare bezeichnen'.[12] Furthermore, we have seen that these limits are anything but fixed and stable. They may range from a complete isolation of the self within the 'drinnen irrlichen Bezirk'[13] of its own feelings and perceptions to encompassing various aspects of external reality. But even when the field of experience is stretched to its uttermost, dark segments remain. The ideal totality remains elusive and the region of human consciousness and experience still borders on 'das Namenlose', 'das uns Unerfahrbare'. The ambivalence of 'Nacht' in the collection shows that the limits of the self may advance or recede significantly from poem to poem and the two contrasting views of the subject-object relationship put forward in *Puppen* indicate that the degree of this fluctuation will depend on how far Rilke is prepared to admit the consequences of the more negative view. *Puppen* thus gives an intellectual basis for the uncertainty as to where the self ends and the other begins by pointing to the degree of subjectivity which may be present in any experience of 'Beteiligung' and by underlining the fact that Rilke was by no means always able to accept the full implications of this with the same untroubled enthusiasm with which he, as a young man, recorded his vision of the 'Künstler-Gott' or was able to speak of the act of prayer:

Et si le Dieu qu'elle (la prière) projette hors de soi ne persiste point: tant mieux: on le fera de nouveau, et il sera moins usé dans l'éternité. (AB I, 277)

For in the essay *Puppen* there is too much resentment at the self-deception this may entail and the scepticism of *Puppen* is also clearly present in the human situation of the *Gedichte an die Nacht*.

From a thematic point of view, the most important 'Grenze unseres Daseins' in the poems of the collection is the human visage. So many of the attempts to establish 'Beteiligung' are tied to the visual sense that it is not surprising that the physical location of this sense should come to represent the frontier between self and world. Moreover the ambiguity of the word 'Gesicht', signifying both 'visage' and 'vision' in various senses, makes it extremely suitable for Rilke's purposes. When Rilke is allowing the theories related to the theme of 'Fremdheit' their fullest rein, any kind of limit to the self may acquire over-tones of imprisonment and isolation. This is the case in the frag-ment *Nicht daß uns, da wir plötzlich erwachsen sind...* where even childhood is seen in purely negative terms and Rilke laments 'die Kerker von früh an/die sich aus unserem Atem bilden' (SW II, 444). Virtually all aspects of human experience seem to contribute here towards isolation in the prison of the individuality. The 'prisons' can form themselves 'aus der noch eben rein durchdringlichen Luft, aus jedem Geschauten', and so it seems that the very act of perceiving the external world as something other than the self can intensify this already grossly exaggerated awareness of isolation. Within this context, 'Gesicht' comes to be used as an image of separation:

O der Getrennten sind mehr. Jahrzehnt und Jahrtausend
von Gesicht zu Gesicht. Und zwischen Erkannten
steht vielleicht im Kerker der Kindheit das besser,
das unendlich berechtigte Herz. (SW II, 445)

As the surface which one presents to the world and the point from which the other is perceived as an object, 'Gesicht' can imply awareness of the distance between self and 'Gegenstand'. In this way 'ein Gesicht haben' can be almost synonymous with the use of 'Gegenüber-sein' in the eighth Duino Elegy, for both are used to suggest that the specifically human mode of encountering reality is a distortion of the 'pure' reality of the material world. This idea is already present in the *Improvisationen aus dem Capreser Winter* of 1906:

> Hat der Wald ein Gesicht?
> Steht der Berge Basalt
> gesichtlos nicht da?
> Hebt sich das Meer
> nicht ohne Gesicht
> aus dem Meergrund her?
>
> . . .
>
> Und wir
> Tiere der Seele, verstört
> von allem in uns, noch nicht
> fertig zu nichts; wir weidenden
> Seelen
> flehen wir zu dem Bescheidenden
> nächtens nicht um das Nicht-Gesicht,
> das zu unserem Dunkel gehört?   (SW II, 12)

It is interesting that this poem which reflects the same 'Krise des Anschauens'[14] as do parts of *Malte Laurids Brigge* should connect 'Gesicht' with the confusion and isolation of the self and plead for a 'Nicht-Gesicht' in the same lines as it evokes the 'Dunkel' of the earlier sections of *Das Stunden-Buch*. 'Nicht-Gesicht' would in fact represent a state in which subject and object were no longer separated by the act of perception, no longer 'einander gegenüber'. This is confirmed by the following passage from *Malte Laurids Brigge*, where darkness does mean an absence of barriers between self and other:

Besser vielleicht, du wärest in der Dunkelheit geblieben und dein unabgegrenztes Herz hätte versucht, all des Ununterscheidbaren schweres Herz zu sein. Nun hast du dich zusammengenommen in dich, siehst dich vor dir aufhören in deinen Händen, ziehst von Zeit zu Zeit mit einer ungenauen Bewegung dein Gesicht nach.   (SW VI, 777)

But remaining in the darkness, like having 'das Nicht-Gesicht', is not really offered as a practical way out of the predicament – rather the evocation has something about it of the impossible longing for the secure darkness of the womb. In the poetry of the following years Rilke tends to put the idea of the 'Nicht-Gesicht' aside and concentrates instead on exploring the subject-object relationship with a view to discovering what possibilities of fulfilment it may contain. The initial separation of self and other becomes the accepted point of departure and 'Gesicht' soon loses most of the negative connotations which it has in the *Improvisationen* or the exceptionally pessimistic fragment which speaks of 'die Kerker von früh an'. Rilke indeed goes so far as to use 'Gesicht' or 'gesichthaft' as positive attributes of external reality. It is a way of making whatever he confronts more anthropomorphic and hence accessible to human feeling. This is the case in the following excerpt from *Erlebnis*, where the use of the word 'gesichthaft' instead of pointing to any final separation, seems rather to bring self and other closer together and even to foreshadow a dissolving of the barriers between them:

Auch fiel ihm wieder ein, wie viel er darauf gab, in ähnlicher Haltung an einen Zaun gelehnt, des gestirnten Himmels durch das milde Gezweig eines Ölbaums hindurch gewahr zu werden, wie gesichthaft in dieser Maske der Weltraum ihm gegenüber war, oder wie, wenn er Solches lange genug ertrug, Alles in der klaren Lösung seines Herzens so vollkommen aufging, daß der Geschmack der Schöpfung in seinem Wesen war.   (SW VI, 1040)

So it is that 'Gesicht' figures prominently in the *Gedichte an die Nacht*, often without any negative connotations whatsoever, for example:

und fühlt sich kühn, weil er die ganzen Sterne
in sein Gesicht nimmt, schwer – , o nicht wie einer,
der der Geliebten diese Nacht bereitet
und sie verwöhnt mit den gefühlten Himmeln.   (SW II, 45)

Und nun geruhts und reicht uns ans Gesicht
wie der Geliebten Aufblick; schlägt sich auf
uns gegenüber und zerstreut vielleicht
an uns sein Dasein...   (SW II, 52)

Ist dort nicht Lächeln? Siehe, steht dort nicht
in Feldern, die von Fülle übergingen,
was wir zu einem kleinen Aufblühn bringen,
wenn wirs bemühn in unser Angesicht?   (SW II, 405)

Indeed, it is the poet's face which is more than once offered to the 'Geliebte', the night and the angels as a means of establishing communication:

> Nun erst, Nachtstunde, bin ich ohne Angst
> und darf im aufgeblühten Schauen stehen,
> da du für dein unendliches Geschehen
> mein ungenügendes Gesicht verlangst... (SW II, 408)

> O was ward mir Ausdruck eingesät,
> daß ich, wenn dein Lächeln je gerät,
> Weltraum auf dich überschaue.
> Doch du kommst nicht, oder kommst zu spät.
> Stürzt euch, Engel, über dieses blaue
> Leinfeld, Engel, Engel, mäht. (SW II, 70)

> O von Gesicht zu Gesicht
> welche Erhebung.
> Aus den schuldigen bricht
> Verzicht und Vergebung.

> Wehen die Nächte nicht kühl,
> herrlich entfernte,
> die durch Jahrtausende gehn.
> Hebe das Feld von Gefühl.
> Plötzlich sehn
> Engel die Ernte. (SW II, 73)

One may comment on all of these passages at once by saying that in them Rilke is, in a sense, making a virtue of necessity. The basic structure of the experiences presented in his later poetry is that of 'Gegenüber-sein', 'von Gesicht zu Gesicht', a separation of the subject and object. In these passages Rilke is attempting to establish communication of subject and object within the situation of 'Gegenüber-sein' and hence 'Gesicht' assumes a positive aspect. Contact may still be possible 'von Gesicht zu Gesicht' – hence a mediate position between the isolation of the self within the subjectivity of perception and the merging of self and other 'auf der anderen Seite der Natur'[15] or in the *unio mystica*. Perhaps the best examples of the ambivalence of this mediate position are the two instances where 'Nacht', quite paradoxically, both does and does not present a 'Gesicht':

Atme das Dunkel der Erde und wieder
aufschau! Wieder. Leicht und gesichtlos
lehnt sich von oben Tiefe dir an. Das gelöste
nachtenthaltne Gesicht giebt dem deinigen Raum.   (SW II, 54)

> Nacht. O du in Tiefe gelöstes
> Gesicht an meinem Gesicht.
> Du, meines staunenden Anschauns größtes
> Übergewicht.   (SW II, 178f.)

Fülleborn is quite right to see the first instance, from a poem written in April 1913, as a preliminary version of the second, written in October 1924, and his remarks are extremely pertinent. In terms of our discussion, the quotations represent the point where the highly ambivalent relation of the self to the other is held at finest balance, where the other is both 'Gegenstand' and 'Nicht-Gegenstand' in the same moment, where 'Nacht' appears both as 'Gesicht' and 'Nicht-Gesicht'. That one may pursue this theme from the *Improvisationen* of 1906 through the *Gedichte an die Nacht* of 1913–14 to the last phase of 1922–6, testifies to its importance for an understanding of Rilke's whole work. Our concept of 'Gesicht', and hence of the relation of self and 'other' cannot be simple: it must comprehend the isolation of the self and its division into 'Teil und Gegenteil' in *Puppen*, the point of balance represented by the quotations above, and the *unio mystica* at the conclusion of *Die große Nacht*.[16]

Rilke's preoccupation with the limits of experience in the period of the *Gedichte an die Nacht* means that these limits themselves become the material of his poetry and that they are exceedingly ambivalent. Moreover, wherever they are posited to lie, there is beyond them 'das uns Unerfahrbare', the 'schwarzen Sektoren' of the essay 'Ur-Geräusch' (1919), which reappears later in the concept of the 'Bewußtseinspyramide'.[17] Rilke's determination not to accept the limits of human experience as they present themselves, is for him a significant element of the human situation and produces those poetic techniques which Fülleborn has shown to be expressions of 'die spekulative Phantasie'. In a fragment written towards the end of the period of composition of the *Gedichte an die Nacht* Rilke celebrates the inexplicable and contradictory nature of human experience, and, indirectly, his own determination to make the unknowable known, to make 'das Unkenntliche' part of human experience and hence 'kenntlich':

> O Leben Leben, wunderliche Zeit
> von Widerspruch zu Widerspruche reichend
> im Gange oft so schlecht so schwer so schleichend
> und dann auf einmal, mit unsäglich weit
> entspanntem Flügel, einem Engel gleichend;
> O unerklärlichste, o Lebenszeit.
>
> Von allen großgewagten Existenzen
> kann eine glühender und kühner sein?
> Wir stehn und stemmen uns an unsre Grenzen
> und reißen ein Unkenntliches herein... (SW II, 411)

The theme of 'Kenntlich-/Unkenntlich-Sein' provides a means of summarising this discussion of the human situation. Rilke's use of the word 'unkenntlich' may be shown to express his understanding of the relation between the human situation and 'das uns Unerfahrbare', between immanence and transcendence.

Rilke is concerned in the *Gedichte an die Nacht* with attempting to go beyond 'die Grenzen des Endlichen und Sichtbaren'. The intentional objects towards which this attempt is directed, the night, the angel and the stars clearly represent in part 'ein Unkenntliches', in that the self when confronted with them is ignorant and bewildered, finds the night unyielding and the heavens 'stark wie voller Leuen', doubts the possibility of any contact between man and angel and must ask of the heavens: 'Nehm ich denn Teil?' These intentional objects are images for the furthest limits of human experience – they are entirely problematical in their nature, as is the relation of the self to them, and beyond them lies what is altogether 'unkenntlich'. The night and the angel are ambivalent. They are to represent the beginning of the unknowable, of the completely other, and yet at the same time the self of the poems makes every attempt to know them, to establish a relationship to them, in short, to bring them within the sphere of human experience. The uneasy logic of this is best illustrated by the poem *An den Engel*, most of which is devoted to lamenting the fact that the angel is unreachable, indifferent, unknowable, while at the same time describing the angel's being in great detail and leaving open the possibility that the angel may not be the completely other at all. It is precisely by such ambivalences that Rilke sets about what he terms: 'und reißen ein Unkenntliches herein'. In the case of *An den Engel* this does not come about by Buddeberg's grandiose 'Grenzüberschreitung' but rather by making the limits themselves so ambiguous that they tend to disappear amid the various levels of the imagery and the nuances of the poetic concepts.

One may object to these techniques as 'ungeheure Experimente',[18] or one may praise them as a legitimate approach to the problem of transcendence in a historical situation where transcendence itself is no longer accepted simply but is the object of much doubt and controversy. In Rilke's case this doubt tends to be expressed by what one might term the dialectic of 'Unkenntlichkeit'. For if in a diagram of the ideal totality of experience one includes transcendent reality among the 'schwarzen Sektoren, die das uns Unerfahrbare bezeichnen', then clearly they are for humanity 'unkenntlich'. However, from the standpoint of these transcendent realities, the sphere of human existence may be equally 'unkenntlich'. This thought is explicit in one of the *Gedichte an die Nacht*:

> Ob ich damals war oder bin: du schreitest
> über mich hin, du unendliches Dunkel aus Licht.
> Und das Erhabene, das du im Raume gereitest,
> nehm ich, Unkenntlicher, an mein flüchtig Gesicht. (SW II, 67)

However, the 'Unkenntlichkeit' of the human situation is a different one from that of the night or the angel. For whereas the latter tend to be too intense or splendid for humanity to experience, human existence tends to be too insignificant and confused to be recognised by the transcendent powers. Hence the two kinds of 'Unkenntlichkeit' and the tension between them come to represent the discrepancy of *value* between immanent and transcendent being. This is made clear by the nuances of darkness in the *Gedichte an die Nacht,* most evident in the poem *An den Engel.* There we saw that the darkness in which humanity exists is that of confusion and transience:

> wir ver-geben uns in unerhellter
> Zögerung an deinem Unterbau.   (SW II, 48)

This is emphasised by the juxtaposition of 'unkenntlich' and 'flüchtig' in the lines quoted above and there are many other instances in the poems which we have examined. Human existence is, from the point of view of transcendence, 'unkenntlich' because it lacks those qualities which are imputed to the night and angel in abundance. Outstanding among these are immunity from the destroying processes of time:

> Der Himmel singt in seiner Sicherheit,
> hoch über Zeit die reichen Sterne singen,
> wir treiben mit den abgehärmten Dingen
> zweischweigende Geselligkeit.   (SW II, 398)

and a corresponding 'wholeness' of being, an absolute freedom from the despair and conflicts inherent in the human self:

> Ist uns nicht mehr gegeben, bis dorthin
> des Wesens reine Wallung fortzupflanzen,
> wo einig sich ein Überfluß von Sinn
> beseligt in verständigten Distanzen?   (SW II, 405f.)

> Während uns, die wirs nicht anders wissen,
> eins sich wehrt und eins umsonst geschieht,
> schreiten sie, von Zielen hingerissen,
> durch ihr ausgebildetes Gebiet.   (SW II, 70)

The examples could be multiplied from the poems which have been treated.[19] To put it most concisely, the 'Unkenntlichkeit' of the human situation is, at its most extreme, the complete isolation of the self. This isolation may be both spatial and temporal. The temporal aspect occurs when the self cannot experience its own existence as a meaningful continuity in time. This is a central theme in *Malte*,[20] and is part of the 'Grund von Gegenteil' which underlies the *Gedichte an die Nacht*:

Wir wissen nicht, was wir verbringen: siehe,
Benanntes ist vorbei und jedes Sein
erfindet sich im letzten Augenblick
und will nichts hören/Wink von Zeichen, kaum
ein Blatt verkehrts: wir aber sind schon anders,
verleugnen, lächeln, kennen schon nicht mehr,
was gestern Glück war. Und die Göttin selbst
schwankt über uns. (SW II, 391)

The isolation in spatial terms has already been explored at some length. It is the alien quality of the external world in *Die spanische Trilogie* and *Die große Nacht* and its most extreme expression is the image of the imprisonment of the self within the subjectivity of experience. Such are the elements of which human 'Unkenntlichkeit' is composed and the *Gedichte an die Nacht* represent various attempts to transcend it.

It is here that a form of dialectic is implicit in the poetry. For if human 'Unkenntlichkeit' can be recognised by 'ein Unkenntliches' in the form of transcendent reality, then the darkness of the self, with all the negatives and conflicts which this implies, becomes illumined. The self then becomes 'angeschauter bei den Sternen', becomes 'kenntlicher...Engeln, Unsichtbaren' and by a reciprocal process the other 'Unkenntlichkeit', that of transcendent being, is absorbed into the sphere of human experience and becomes in human terms 'kenntlich'.[21] Hence the tendency to establish *mediate* figures, to effect the transition from immanence to transcendence and *vice versa* by fixing intentional objects which are both immanent and transcendent, which partake of both forms of being. Of course, this makes the otherness of such intentional objects a very doubtful quality. In the process, they may become 'nur eine Übertreibung des Irdischen', images for a heightened form of 'mögliche Existenz'. But this danger is inherent in Rilke's understanding of the nature of human experience as a whole. For what one experiences as an object is, in these terms, a product of the object's pure reality and of the self which is divided into contrary halves. So any intentional object must be in some measure the self as its own object. Within the framework of experience posited by *Puppen*, and in a somewhat different sense by the eighth Elegy, there can be no such thing as a 'pure' object. However, on this issue there is no one doctrine which Rilke holds. Hamburger is perfectly right to emphasise Rilke's apparently unquestioning acceptance of what she terms 'etwas von dieser Selbstverschlingung im "Weltinnenraum" der "universalen Subjektivität"', and to lead her examination of the concept of 'Weltinnenraum' to the following conclusion:

...und er ist zentral, weil sich nicht nur, wie zu zeigen versucht wurde, die schon in der Frühzeit sich ankündigende Problematik der Intentionalitätsspannung in ihm löst, sondern auch, weil er gleichsam in die auf ihn folgende Dichtung ausstrahlt, um sich seinerseits schließlich in *die* 'Transzendentalität' aufzulösen, die der Dichter, des Wesens seines Dichtens bewußt, erreichen kann: eben das Tun des Dichters selbst.[22]

The mode of thought which produces the concept of 'Weltinnenraum', as well as the seventh and ninth Elegies, has been amply demonstrated by Rilke criticism with varying degrees of commitment and hostility, and scarcely requires further comment here. What one can do, however, is to emphasise the 'Grund von Gegenteil' which accompanies this throughout Rilke's work and which is especially evident in the period of the *Gedichte an die Nacht*. In this opposite mode of thought there is an implicit recognition of the role which the subjectivity of perception plays in the experience of the isolation of the self. The ambiguity of the human situation which results from the interaction of these two modes of understanding, appears in the rather tortuous dialectic of 'Kenntlich-/Unkenntlich-Sein'. So it is that on the one hand the self must be *recognised* by the other, must receive a confirmation of the significance and value of its own existence from *outside* the subjectivity, from that which is in this sense 'Unkenntlich', and on the other hand may strive to achieve the same effect by an extreme intensification of subjective experience, most obvious in the theme of 'Strömung'. For side by side with the need to justify the self by the experience of the other in the sense of the conclusion of *Die große Nacht*:

...da war es, du Hohe,
keine Schande für dich, daß du mich kanntest...

where the essence of the proof is that it comes from outside the self, we have present in the theme of 'Strömung' the possibility that the self may be able either to force this response, or else dispense with it entirely, as for example in the lines from the tenth Elegy written during this period:

...Daß mich mein strömendes Antlitz
glänzender mache... (SW 1, 721)

So that 'Kenntlich-Sein' may imply *both* to be recognised by a higher power, in the sense of having the validity of human existence acknowledged, *and* a state of subjective emotion so intense that it provides its own justification. This is made possible by the fact that 'Unkenntlichkeit' implies far more than just the problem of perception. For it absorbs all those negatives such as the despair produced by the transience of human life or by the failure of love, which are only related *by association* with the problem of being 'perceived' by a higher power.

Hence the human situation of the *Gedichte an die Nacht* is determined by opposite attitudes towards the nature of experience. The one, which appears in the poem *Es winkt ʒu Fühlung fast aus allen Dingen*, points in the direction of a transcendental and self-sufficient subjectivity. The other, which emphasises the isolation of the self and the obstacles which stand in the way of an experience of the other in a way not distorted by 'Gegenständlichkeit', expresses a radical and often anguished doubt in the validity of this 'universale Subjektivität'. Both attitudes are in constant conflict with each other in the period of the *Gedichte an die Nacht* and in their conflict is mirrored the ambivalence of the human situation, which we may demonstrate, but not resolve to any single meaning. On the basis of this we may now turn to the problem of transcendence itself.

7. THE MODES OF TRANSCENDENCE

The previous chapters have, to a large extent, summarised the results of the thematic analysis and shown what conclusions may be drawn from them. It remains now to approach directly the problem which has continually intruded into the discussion and there received such partial and provisional treatment as the direction of the argument has allowed. The problem of transcendence may present two aspects: a problem of definition and a problem of interpretation. The problem of definition need not be directly relevant to an understanding of Rilke's poetry, the problem of interpretation is very much so.

The definition of transcendence is essentially a philosophical problem and, since Kant, a somewhat vexed one. To pose it philosophically is to inquire into the nature of human experience as such, and the answers which one gives must be consistent and tenable in terms of philosophical criteria. But just as the methods of literature are different from those of philosophy, so the criteria by which one may approach the 'truth' of literature are different from those by which one may test and establish philosophical truth. Ideas of transcendence which we accept as literature we may reject as philosophy, and so the question of what, in philosophical terms, constitutes transcendence is a different one from how we may interpret an idea, or indeed, *feeling*, of transcendence embodied in a work of literature.

However, this distinction has a tendency to become blurred when we approach literature with philosophical terminology and in the case of Rilke's work, which, as Frau Hamburger says 'so beschaffen ist, um auf philosophische Fragestellungen antworten zu können',[1] this is virtually unavoidable. As far as the problem of transcendence is concerned, the critic is in a sense between Scylla and Charybdis. For on the one side there is the problem of definition – and this means in effect: *whose* definition? – and on the other the problem of interpretation, where he must find ways through the legendary maze of Rilke's poetic thought. If the meaning of transcendence were axiomatic for the modern philosophical tradition, then the student of literature could adopt it as a tool, without necessarily embracing it by an act of faith, and use it in attempting to solve the various problems of interpretation. But it is anything but axiomatic and hence the problem arises: whose definition of transcendence does one apply to the poetry? Within the relatively limited field of those contemporary German philosophers whose works are quoted in relation to Rilke's poetry, there are considerable differences in the manner in which transcendence is understood by Husserl, Jaspers and Heidegger. Furthermore, none of these philosophers can meaningfully be called religious and there is certainly a case to be made out for understanding transcendence as an essentially religious concept. But again, a marriage between Rilke's poetry and the theology of, say, Rudolf Otto is at the very best a sorry misalliance, because of the radically different ways in which the two authors approach the divinity, and moreover religious categories are by nature prescriptive – in other words, set down what the given individual *ought* to experience in terms of the religious tradition.[2] In Rilke's case this means that interpretation may give way to polemics, as for example in Mason's *Der Zopf des Münchhausen*.[3]

In this way the problem of definition arises, and, as I have said, this problem *need* not be directly relevant to Rilke's poetry. For one might write a whole book on conflicting definitions of transcendence put forward in the last hundred years without ever mentioning Rilke at all. However, Rilke-criticism has traditionally made very free with the word and so often confused problems of definition with problems of interpretation, that one must first go to some lengths to elucidate what certain critics understand by transcendence before one can determine whether one agrees with their interpretation or not. This situation becomes aggravated when a critic changes definitions in midstream, as does Buddeberg when discussing the poem *An den Engel*. Buddeberg's vaunted 'Verwandlung innerhalb des Gedichts' can be seen, albeit less emotionally, as a case of sloppy definition. Where, on the other hand, a critic adopts and adheres to the definition found in the works of a single philosopher – as with Frau Hamburger's essay in *Philosophie der Dichter* – a very desirable clarity is gained. However, even among critics who seek and attain a maximum of clarity, the problem of definition can still attain formidable proportions. Is, for example, what Wodtke terms 'diese subjektive, welt-immanente Transzendenz' the same as what Hamburger terms 'transzendentale Subjektivität'?[4] To ask such a question is not hair-splitting if one is dealing with poetry such as Rilke's, where so much meaning may hinge on one's understanding of nuances; and yet questions of this kind – because they often require to be solved by an exegesis of the work of the critic rather than of the poet – cannot help but encumber an interpretation. An understanding of the poetry which attempts to come to terms with previous interpretations can become exaggeratedly complex and tortuous by the problems of definition which this procedure requires; to ignore the problem of definition, however, or to allow imponderables to breed unchecked, is to move in the direction of Buddeberg's *Denken und Dichten des Seins*. Heftrich's comparatively mild critique in *Die Philosophie und Rilke* does not nearly do justice to the amount of linguistic confusion contained in the former work.

To conclude these remarks on the problem of definition, one might consider the following passage by the contemporary American Phenomenologist, Marvin Farber. Farber, in his book *Phenomenology and Existence*,[5] traces something of the history of the concept of transcendence from Kant onwards and comes to the following conclusion:

'Transcendence' means in practice anything you care to make it mean – a divine being, or a whole order of divine beings; a natural order, partly known and partly unknown, a superior spiritual order, or another realm about which nothing can be said except that there must be such a realm. The term is clearly used in numerous senses. The practically universal vote that could be obtained for 'transcendence' might well be the signal for a many-sided dissension.

What is most disturbing about this statement is not what a disciple of Husserl or Heidegger might feel to be its impiety, but that one could produce from Rilke's work, with very little hesitation, poems or excerpts to support each one of these definitions![6] In terms of the philosophic and religious tradition, at least some of these definitions would clash violently with others, but in Rilke's work their untroubled co-existence places a philosophical solution to the problem of definition beyond the reach of the critic who tries to interpret Rilke as literature.

The procedure which I have adopted is also open to criticism. The definition which was put forward in the Introduction, which derives essentially from the angel of the first two *Duineser Elegien* and which posits a transcendent entity as having both splendour and otherness, is a makeshift one. It lays no claim to philosophical validity and is clearly inadequate for a number of instances of 'transcendence' in Rilke's work. It was adopted as an instrument of interpretation, as a means of differentiating one kind of 'transcendence' from another. For interpreting the *Gedichte an die Nacht* has shown that there is no single meaning of transcendence in these poems – any more than there is a single meaning for 'Nacht' – but rather a number of possible modes of thought and feeling and a corresponding number of objects which one might, from one point of view or another, term transcendent. This does not mean that one might as well term *any* aspect of Rilke's poetry transcendence, but it does mean that transcendence in Rilke's work cannot, within the Western tradition at least, be made wholly respectable as philosophy. One may demand of philosophy that it be logically consistent and, in a sense, 'verbindlich' – the same cannot be demanded of poetry.[7]

To turn now to the problems of interpretation which transcendence poses in the *Gedichte an die Nacht*, one must ask why there are so many possible modes of transcendence. As already indicated, this may be partly explained by the fact that Rilke does not, on the whole, differentiate between intellectual and emotional problems. If he were writing philosophy, this would be a grievous fault, but it is surely part of the nature of poetry. Because thought and feeling are rarely discrete from one another, intellectual contradictions may be resolved in emotional terms, and fluctuations of feeling may produce opposed conceptual systems. The clearest instance of this is the radically opposed structures of human experience put forward in the essay *Puppen* and the poem *Es winkt zu Fühlung fast aus allen Dingen* respectively. Both 'Gegenständlichkeit' and 'Weltinnenraum' can be developed in opposite directions as concepts of human experience, the former towards isolation and despair, the latter towards the jubilant affirmation of the seventh and ninth *Duineser Elegien*. On the conceptual level the two are contradictory for the self which laments that it is 'gespalten in Teil und Gegenteil' has a quite different understanding of subjectivity from that which celebrates the joys of 'Weltinnenraum', and yet both are possibilities of human experience and both are part of the thematic field of the *Gedichte an die Nacht*. If one traces these radically opposed concepts back to their origins, one finds, in effect, that they stem from two opposite emotional states which were termed 'Fremdheit' and 'Beteiligung'. A feeling of alienation from the external world becomes elaborated into the theory which advances all the negative aspects of 'Gegenständlichkeit', a feeling of participation and emotional identification with the objects of experience likewise becomes explicit as 'Weltinnenraum'.

That these intellectual structures should have their roots in, and be to a considerable extent determined by emotion, does not make them in the least spurious as far as poetry is concerned, though, strictly speaking, it might disqualify them as philosophy. The phrase of the young Rilke in which he describes the aim of his poetry as: 'Bilder zu finden für meine Verwandlungen'[8] has often been quoted, and here it is important to realise that, in his later work, intellectual structures may function precisely as *images*. What determined the succession of Rilke's 'Verwandlungen' is a psychological question and hence unanswerable within the framework of this book, but we can be sure that it was not the laws of formal logic – although these same laws are very prominent within the images themselves. Hence, in the case of 'Gegenständlichkeit' and 'Weltinnenraum' one meets structures which are susceptible of logical analysis, and which may be deduced logically from the work, but which need not stand in a logical relationship to one another.

As a further example one may take the theme of the 'Geliebte' in the *Gedichte an die Nacht*. In most of these poems the theme of love tends to establish the discrepancy of value between human and angelic being as an idea, not merely as an emotional reaction. And there is a logical structure which one may erect around this idea and the concept of the self which it implies. This structure is intelligible and, while perhaps not very attractive, quite in accord with certain traditional concepts of religious transcendence. However, from 26 January 1914 onwards a 'Verwandlung' occurs within the poet which is documented to some extent in the letters to Magda von Hattingberg. The poems which Rilke subsequently writes present a quite different *concept* of the function and value of human love from that which we found in the *Gedichte an die Nacht*.[9] But in early February another 'Verwandlung' produces the essay *Puppen* which sets forth a predominantly negative view of human experience whose origins one may trace in Rilke's work back to the *Improvisationen aus dem Capreser Winter* of December 1906. In June 1914 the somewhat controversial 'Wendung' occurs, or does not occur, and Rilke once more makes a decision for 'Liebe'. The new command which the poet then gives himself, to love his own 'inneres Mädchen', is disconcertingly reminiscent of the circle of Narcissus and does not go very far towards solving the problem of human love which emerges from the *Gedichte an die Nacht* and the contrasting poems to Benvenuta. There are good reasons for agreeing with those critics who find this 'Wendung' more a matter of wishful thinking than actuality, but it does represent another and somewhat abortive attempt on Rilke's part to solve the problem of love in terms of his own poetry.

Then in August–September of the same year the poem *Es Winkt zu Fühlung fast aus allen Dingen* gives a rather different understanding of the way in which self and world are related, an understanding which it is difficult to reconcile with the essay *Puppen*. In the concept of *Weltinnenraum* a certain amount of the

love which *Wendung* calls for does seem to be present in a somewhat vague way, but it does not really answer or refute any of
the theories put forward in *Puppen*. In this way various concepts
and theories succeed one another, develop themes from earlier
phases of the work and often point forward to phases yet to
come. Their succession is not logical, often only partly explicable
by biographical data, but this should lead neither to a condemnation of these ideas as spurious, nor to an attempt to enforce
logical consistency where it does not exist. Within poetry logical
contradictions may be both accepted and interpreted.

The interpretative problem of transcendence is thus to distinguish and do justice to the various themes or modes of experience
within the work to which the word 'transcendence' can be
applied in terms of one accepted definition or another. In this
way, certain aspects of the broad theme of alienation may evoke
the transcendence of the 'Dinge an sich', or a poem such as *Die
große Nacht* may be very close to the quite different transcendence
of the *unio mystica*. I have tried, by a maximum of differentiation,
to respect the thematic complexity of the *Gedichte an die Nacht*
and to avoid championing one form of transcendence at the
expense of another. This has also meant avoiding the various
reductions, existential and otherwise, by which, at a certain
remove from the poetry, a semblance of 'Eindeutigkeit' may be
achieved. This was partly for methodological reasons. The work
of Mason, Wodtke and above all Fülleborn has amply demonstrated how the complexity which characterises the surface of
Rilke's poetry can be understood more simply in terms of the
single theme of Rilke's own artistry. This view is certainly
tenable and very little remains to be said about it. The present
work is not an attempt to refute it but to offer an understanding
of the poetry which both takes this view into account and avoids
the reductions which it necessarily entails. This has meant
renouncing synthesis in favour of differentiation, but in Rilke's
work there is every justification for doing this.

This is not to say that one must reject or avoid the conclusions
to which Fülleborn comes. His identification and critique of

'die spekulative Phantasie' is beyond doubt a major break-through in Rilke-criticism. It is rather the evaluative judgments which proceed from these conclusions that are open to disgreement. When Fülleborn, for example, censures 'die im Grunde unfromme Haltung eines Experimentators, dem es um Ausweitung seines Erkenntnis- und Herrschaftsbereiches geht',[10] it is the word 'unfromm' which is contestable. One may accept most of Fülleborn's conclusions, among them his distinction of 'symbolisch' from 'symbolistisch', without accepting the various imponderables contained in his definition of 'echte Symbole':

> Im zweiten Fall, in symbolischer Dichtung, ist ein höherer Grad an Objektivierung erreicht: die im Glauben erschaute Welt schenkt sich dem Dichter im Bild, worin Endliches und Unendliches vermählt erscheinen.[11]

Fülleborn may say of this concept of the symbol: 'Es ist wie das Leben selbst'[12] – but one may surely say the same of the mingling of reason and irrationality, of documented experience and speculation, of logical order and of contradiction in Rilke's work. It now remains to characterise, by way of summary, the various modes of transcendence which exist within the thematic field of the *Gedichte an die Nacht*, and, where possible, to indicate how they may be related to one another.

The first mode is that exemplified by the concept of 'prière' in the letter to Mimi Romanelli,[13] and it is characterised by more than a touch of solipsism. It is the state in which a particular 'Richtung des Herzens' becomes so intense as to transcend the limits of the finite self and so self-sufficient that it can dispense with any object. The paradigm for this mode is the figure of 'die Verlassene',[14] but we may find another form of it in the concept of 'Strömung' in the *Gedichte an die Nacht*. The self achieves transcendence not by encountering any transcendent entity, but by the sheer intensity of feeling directed into the cosmos. We have dealt with this in Chapter 4, but it may be helpful to recall two clear examples:

> ...In dir hörte ich auf,
> so aber streng ich mein Herz an, ströme, und immer
> hat der Raum nicht genug. (SW II, 392)

THE MODES OF TRANSCENDENCE

...Faß ich es denn, daß die zweimal genommene Braue
über solche Ströme von Aufblick reicht. (SW II, 66)

Apart from the obvious self-admiration, which one may find
rather odious, the logic of this form of transcendence leaves
much to be desired and indeed would seem to lead quite naturally
towards solipsism. If the self may transcend itself entirely by
itself, then there seems no need for the external world at all. A
tendency towards solipsism is one of the threads which runs
through Rilke's work and becomes quite explicit in the figures of
'Narziß' and the 'Künstler-Gott'.[15] But in this Rilke is not
alone in the lyric tradition from Mallarmé onwards.

What it is important to realise about this mode is that whatever
transcendence it may lay claim to is not one of quality, or otherness, but one of intensity. This becomes clear if we consider the
following lines from the strange phallic cycle, chastely designated
Sieben Gedichte, written in 1915:

> Plötzlich starrt er von Vollendung,
> und ich, Seliger, darf ihn beziehn.
> Ach wie bin ich eng darin.
> Schmeichle mir, zur Kuppel auszutreten:
> um in deine weichen Nächte hin
> mit dem Schwung schooßblendender Raketen
> mehr Gefühl zu schleudern, als ich bin. (SW II, 437)

The last line indicates in what way prayer or 'Strömung' may,
without objects, be considered modes of transcendence. For if the
'Ich' produces 'mehr Gefühl...als ich bin', then it has, in
terms of intensity, passed beyond the limits of the 'ordinary' self.
This is admittedly contradictory, but then so are many accepted
forms of religious transcendence. It is also, like the orgasm, brief
and subjective and clearly one of the problems which beset
Rilke was how to render it less private and ephemeral. The
following poem in the *Sieben Gedichte* moves already in the
direction of a kind of objectification:

> Bist du's bin ich's, den wir so sehr beglücken?
> Wer sagt es, da wir schwinden. Vielleicht steht
> im Zimmer eine Säule aus Entzücken,
> die Wölbung trägt und langsamer vergeht. (SW II, 437)

197

and this passes over into his poetic technique in the phrase: 'Auch noch das Entzücken wie ein Ding/auszusagen'. Wodtke provides an illuminating commentary to this technique, and we may regard it in one sense as an artistic solution to the extreme subjectivity of such transcendence. As became clear when discussing *Puppen*, Rilke was not always indifferent to the dangers of subjectivity. Nevertheless, this mode of transcendence, for all its paradoxical 'Selbsterhebung', passes into the *Duineser Elegien* in the figure of 'die Verlassene' and we may also find an echo of it in the tenth Elegy:

> ...Daß mich mein strömendes Antlitz
> glänzender mache... (SW I, 721)

The second mode of transcendence might bear the motto: *transcendere est percipi* and is exemplified by the theme of 'Kenntlich-Sein/Unkenntlich-Sein'. Unlike the first, this posits a transcendent entity as intentional object and seeks to achieve transcendence by having the validity of human existence recognised by a transcendent power. There are many instances of this in the *Gedichte an die Nacht*: the 'starker Beweis' which confirms the 'Gedanken der Nacht', the lines from *Die große Nacht* 'da war es, du Hohe, keine Schande für dich, daß du mich kanntest...', and above all the last lines of the poem *An den Engel*. To recognise and be recognised by a higher power is posited as dispelling the darkness of the human condition, which, as we have seen, means its limitations and its impermanence. This mode also may rest on a philosophical fallacy, but it produces some very fine poetry.[16]

An aspect of this mode which we have stressed is the turning away from the realm of immediate experience and its problems. In this way it constitutes an attempt to go beyond the human situation, best illustrated by the lines from *Hinhalten will ich mich*:

> o, wie sollte ein Fühlender nicht, der *will*, der sich aufreißt,
> unnachgiebige Nacht, endlich dir ähnlicher sein. (SW II, 75)

Here and elsewhere in the *Gedichte an die Nacht* there is no indication as to how the self, which has become more like the night, is to integrate this into its 'empirisches Dasein'. In fact, this mode contains a disavowal of the value of 'Hiersein' in its exclusive directedness towards 'das Übernächste, das Engelische', and hence its acceptance by the poet of the *Duineser Elegien* can be partial at the very best. It is a mode more characteristic of Novalis' thought than of Rilke's – with its implied transition from an 'empirisches Ich' to a 'höheres Ich' – and its abnegation of fulfilment 'im Hiesigen' is clearly rejected by the time of the completion of the *Duineser Elegien*. A highly ambitious resolution of this mode is offered in the prose piece *Über den Dichter*,[17] but in the *Gedichte an die Nacht* Rilke attempts no such synthesis.

Clearly the nature of the transcendent entities towards which this mode is directed is not simple. They may be balanced between a terrible otherness on the one hand and on the other 'mögliche Existenz'. In this way they provoke the whole dilemma of the definition of transcendence, which Marvin Farber characterises as follows:

> There are two possible views of transcendence to be weighed: (a) that the transcendent entities are merely extensions beyond the field of experience, continuing or developing further from what occurs there; or (b) that the transcendent entities have an entirely different basis and nature, closed to us as knowers. The first type bears the burden of relationship to the limited field of human experience, and is admittedly unsatisfactory when viewed against the aspirations of finite beings. The second type is the more unassailable the less it says, and it would be most impregnable if it said nothing. It stands or falls with the concept of ontological otherness.[18]

When considering the figure of the angel in the *Gedichte an die Nacht*, we saw how it may change from being terrible and unknowable in its radical otherness to being, in certain of the poems, essentially a more intense form of human existence – as Rilke said in another context: 'nur eine Übertreibung des Irdischen'.[19] The logical difficulties of this mode of transcendence are in no way solved in the *Gedichte an die Nacht*. Instead, they are tacitly employed to express in poetry a number of possibilities of human experience.

The third mode of transcendence, which is not fully developed in the *Gedichte an die Nacht*, but pertains rather to the *Duineser*

Elegien and *Die Sonette an Orpheus*, is best characterised by the enigmatic phrase 'die vorausgeschickten Himmel'. This is found in a letter to Ilse Jahr of 22 February 1923:

Erst zu dem, dem auch der Abgrund ein Wohnort war, kehren die vorausgeschickten Himmel um, und alles tief und innig Hiesige, das die Kirche ans Jenseits veruntreut hat, kommt zurück; alle Engel entschließen sich lobsingend zur Erde. (BM, 186)

This constitutes an apparent reversal of the first two modes. For in the first case prayer or 'Strömung' may, as 'un rayonnement de notre être soudain incendié' pour out into space without ever finding an object,[20] and in the second there is, on the whole, no question of a return to the limited sphere of 'das Hiesige'. Hence it might seem to be a renunciation of transcendence.

But it is not. We must distinguish the concept of 'die vorausgeschickten Himmel' from the very definite renunciation of the striving for transcendence expressed in the poems to Benvenuta.[21] For what the return of 'die vorausgeschickten Himmel' means is that immanent experience is imbued with all the intensity and splendour which is initially posited in the transcendent sphere. This is, in effect, what happens in the *Duineser Elegien*. In the first two Elegies, as in the *Gedichte an die Nacht*, human existence is defined by transience and privation, in other words: 'Unerhellt-Sein', and angelic being by fullness and splendour. In the seventh and ninth Elegies the same human situation has acquired an intensity and splendour equal to that of the angels – 'die vorausgeschickten Himmel' have returned – and at this point the angel, rather than being embraced as an equal, is dismissed. Since 'Hiersein' has acquired a splendour equal to that of transcendent otherness, this *initial* transcendence becomes an empty category. The emotional equivalent of 'alle Engel' has been transferred to 'die Erde'. The way in which this is achieved is the poetic triumph of the *Duineser Elegien*. It is not a strictly logical process and the transition from: 'Und dennoch, weh mir, ansing ich euch. . .' to: 'Werbung nicht mehr, nicht Werbung, entwachsene Stimme. . .' would require a complete interpretation of the *Elegien* to demonstrate fully.

The *return* of 'die vorausgeschickten Himmel' does, however, provide a way in which the first two modes of transcendence contribute towards the later imperative: 'Preise dem Engel die Welt.' The desire to leave the earth behind and to find fulfilment in the transcendence of the region 'bei den Sternen', which is so marked in many of the *Gedichte an die Nacht*, can thus be seen as contributing towards the future pronouncement: 'Hiersein ist herrlich.'

In this third mode of transcendence, then, there is a return to the 'hartnäckige Diesseitigkeit', which has been seen as characteristic of Rilke's world-view and which comes out most forcefully in the *Brief des jungen Arbeiters*:

Welcher Wahnsinn, uns nach einem Jenseits abzulenken, wo wir hier von Aufgaben und Erwartungen und Zukünften umstellt sind. Welcher Betrug, Bilder hiesigen Entzückens zu entwenden, um sie hinter unserm Rücken an den Himmel zu verkaufen! (SW VI, 1114)

Rilke seems at this point to have been unmindful of the figure of the angel in the *Gedichte an die Nacht*, as it corresponds precisely to this accusation. However this be, the world which is illumined by the splendour of what one might call 'die zurückgeholten Himmel', is a quite different world from that in which 'Fremdheit' and isolation prevail, and so we may see something of the rôle of the *Gedichte an die Nacht* in the 'Entstehungsgeschichte' of the *Duineser Elegien*. In the *Gedichte an die Nacht* the tension between immanence and transcendence is largely unresolved; with the completion of the Elegies it is resolved, but then one should speak rather of intensity of experience than of transcendence.

To conclude the discussion of this mode, there is one example from the *Gedichte an die Nacht* which, while not quite identical with 'die vorausgeschickten Himmel', has elements of this idea. The poem *Atmete ich nicht aus Mitternächten* speaks of the self as acquiring various attributes from the transcendent sphere so as to communicate them to the 'Geliebte' when the eventual meeting comes about. The self is thereby transformed, the face becomes filled with 'Weltraum', but unfortunately the meeting does not take place:

...doch du kommst nicht, oder kommst zu spät... (SW II, 70)

But the poem does not end in defeat, for, as we have seen, all the attributes which the 'Ich' has acquired, are transformed into the image of 'dieses blaue Leinfeld' and offered to the angels. In the manner in which 'Gesicht' acquires all the accumulated connotations of 'dieses blaue Leinfeld' we may see a first anticipation of the return of 'die vorausgeschickten Himmel'.

The fourth mode of transcendence is art. A great deal has been written about this aspect of Rilke's work, and so very little need be said about it here. Moreover, art is not an explicit theme in the *Gedichte an die Nacht*, except perhaps in the first poem of *Die spanische Trilogie*. The work of art as a transcendent entity is well documented in letters concerning Rodin's sculptures and we have seen some examples in Chapter 1. It became clear that this concept is not altogether appropriate to the 'Ding' of *Die spanische Trilogie*, and the interpretation concentrated instead on the theme of 'Fremdheit', which is much more explicit in the *Gedichte an die Nacht*. Yet there is no doubt that the theme of the poet's own creativity is *one* of the important themes of Rilke's work. There are poems where it is quite explicit, poems where it is close to the surface and poems where violence is done to the meaning of the poetry to impose it when it is absent. It is quite absent from the majority of the *Gedichte an die Nacht*.

Nevertheless, art remains for Rilke a mode of transcendence by its power to transform reality and to overcome transience. The transforming power is clearly stated in the poem *Magie*:

Aus unbeschreiblicher Verwandlung stammen
solche Gebilde – Fühl! und glaub!
wir leidens oft: zu Asche werden Flammen;
doch, in der Kunst: zur Flamme wird der Staub. (SW II, 174)

and one may bring this into relation with the thematic field of the *Gedichte an die Nacht* by quoting an extraordinarily beautiful poem, written during the period but, strangely, not included among them:

Wie der Abendwind
    durch geschulterte Sensen der Schnitter,
geht der Engel lind
    durch die schuldlose Schneide der Leiden.

Hält sich stundenlang
   zur Seite dem finsteren Reiter,
hat denselben Gang
   wie die namenlosen Gefühle.

Steht als Turm am Meer
   zu dauern unendlich gesonnen;
was du fühlst ist Er,
   im Innern der Härte geschmeidig,

daß im Notgestein
   die gedrängte Druse der Tränen,
lange wasserrein,
   sich entschlösse zu Amethysten.   (SW II, 78)

The transformation of 'Tränen' into 'Amethysten' in the final stanza could be equated with that of 'Staub' into 'Flamme' in the poem *Magie*. The angel could be here seen as representing the transforming power of art. But this is only one possible meaning for the figure of the angel. There are a number of others which cannot be equated with this one clear instance.

Transformation alone is not enough to merit the label 'transcendence'. But this poem indicates the way in which art may be seen as transcendent. An essential aspect of Rilke's concept of the 'Kunst-Ding' in the period of his interest in Rodin is that it is: 'der Zeit enthoben...dauernd geworden...fähig zur Ewigkeit'. The work of art, then, is not transient in the same way as the thoughts and feelings which produced it, or indeed as its human creator. In this way it escapes the normal progression of time. This is implicit in the image of tears being transformed into jewels, which are immune to transience, and passes eventually into the idea of 'erfüllte Zeit' which Allemann has shown to be part of Rilke's concept of 'Figur'.[22] One could not say that this concept is very important for the *Gedichte an die Nacht*. Because of the essentially unresolved nature of their themes, the problem of transience does not find any final solution, certainly not in terms of art, and we are left with the words 'Denn ich schwinde hin' as one aspect of the open ending of *An den Engel*. It may be that in the figure of Orpheus Rilke does offer a solution in terms of art, but the *Gedichte an die Nacht* are still a long way from *Die Sonette an Orpheus* – just as they are written some ten years after he formulates the concept of the 'Kunst-Ding' in the Rodin-period. So the poems may be given a wider interpretation in terms of possible modes of human, and not solely artistic experience.

The fifth mode of transcendence is almost entirely the province of 'die spekulative Phantasie'. Its clearest formulation occurs in the lines:

> Wir stehn und stemmen uns an unsre Grenzen
> und reißen ein Unkenntliches herein,
> .... (SW II, 411)

This involves an experimental attitude towards the limits of experience and the nature of poetry. Put in another way, it means the attempt to experience what has hitherto been 'das uns Unerfahrbare' and this, if it is to be possible, clearly requires that one transcend the limits of the human situation. But the limits of the human situation, and indeed the limits of the self, are anything but fixed or constant.[23] At one extreme there is the theme of the imprisonment of the self within its own perceptions. When the theme of alienation emerges *fortissimo*, even 'die nächsten Dinge' or 'die Geliebte' can become 'unerfahrbar' or 'unbegreiflich'. At other times, when the theme of 'Beteiligung' is strongest, the limits of the self can extend as far as 'die großen Sterne' and then 'die schwarzen Sektoren', do not begin until somewhere beyond the constellations.

The elusive nature of this transcendence is further complicated by Rilke's tendency not to distinguish between perception and feeling. Hence a lack of emotional participation with some intentional object often produces, or at least coincides with a concept of otherness, as in the lines from *Vor Weihnachten 1914*:

> Auch dieses Fest laß los, mein Herz. Wo sind
> Beweise, daß es dir gehört? Wie Wind
> aufsteht und etwas biegt und etwas drängt,
> wohin? drängt was? biegt was? Und drüber übersteht,
> unfühlbar, Welt. Was willst du feiern, wenn
> die Festlichkeit der Engel dir entweicht?
> Was willst du fühlen? Ach, dein Fühlen reicht
> vom Weinenden zum Nicht-mehr-Weinenden.

Doch drüber sind, unfühlbar, Himmel leicht
von zahllos Engeln. Dir unfühlbar. Du
kennst nur den Nicht-Schmerz. Die Sekunde Ruh
zwischen zwei Schmerzen... (SW ii, 97)

Often, however, a tension may arise between perception and feeling, as for example in the first two poems of *Die spanische Trilogie*. For the self to proceed on the emotional level from a state of 'Fremdheit' to that denoted by the word 'Weltinnenraum' is thus a kind of emotional transcendence. The self goes beyond a feeling of isolation to one of 'Beteiligung'. Strictly speaking, it is not transcendence in a conceptual sense, for the same intentional objects may be present to a consciousness which feels 'Fremdheit' as to one which experiences 'Beteiligung'. The point at which the matter becomes difficult, however, is where either 'Fremdheit' or 'Beteiligung' become the bases of contrasting *theories* of human experience. Thus, in terms of the most extreme forms of the theory of 'Gegenständlichkeit', the state of unity denoted by 'Weltinnenraum' would be either impossible, or else sheer illusion.

But the limits of the self are often the limits of empathy in a particular situation rather than those of human perception as such. It is characteristic of the blending of thought and feeling in Rilke's poetry that this circumstance is rarely made explicit. The poetry abounds in 'Grenzsituationen' of one sort or another, and certain of these allow themselves to be combined to form intellectual structures which may seem irreconcilable with other ideas within Rilke's work. It is necessary when interpreting these 'contradictions' to take into account the various emotional elements which may also determine the line of thought. Thus, what appears on one level as a conflict of ideas may appear on another as a transition between two states of feeling.

August Stahl, in his chapter on 'Das Bild des Randes', gives a large number of examples of 'Grenzsituationen'.[24] His presentation is comprehensive and accurate, however by not raising the problem of the interaction of intellect and emotion in determining these 'Grenzsituationen', he tends to leave the ambiguity of many of them out of account. For, when confronting the problems posed by this mode of transcendence, one must be aware of the different possibilities present in the lines:

> Wir stehn und stemmen uns an unsre Grenzen
> und reißen ein Unkenntliches herein,
> . . .

One possibility is that of a transcendence of perception – that one of the 'schwarze Sektoren, die das uns Unerfahrbare bezeichnen' suddenly becomes illuminated, or, in terms of the image of the 'Bewußtseinspyramide', that the relatively limited field of 'unser gebräuchliches Bewußtsein' suddenly expands to include a hitherto unperceived tract of 'die Tiefendimension unseres Inneren'.[25] This would be transcendence in the sense that something hitherto unknowable and hence other becomes known and hence 'kenntlich'. Another possibility, which is, in effect, an *emotional* analogy of the first, is that something hitherto alien, although perceived, becomes an object of emotional identification. To take a very clear example:

> Schwächliches Herz. Was soll ein Herz aus Schwäche?
> Heißt Herz-sein nicht Bewältigung?
> Daß aus dem Tier-Kreis mir mit einem Sprung
> der Steinbock auf mein Herzgebirge spränge.   (SW II, 98)

The word 'unkenntlich', then, has elements not only of 'unwißbar' and 'unsichtbar' but also of 'unfühlbar', and the same applies to the various words which may denote the overcoming of 'Unkenntlichkeit'. Hence Fülleborn is quite right to speak of 'die fiktiv-*emotionale* Phantasiekraft' as one of the principal poetic techniques of the late Rilke,[26] for the interplay of reflection and feeling is as constant as it is changing. But one can give no constant rule for determining the portion in which conceptual and emotional elements are mixed in any given instance of this mode of transcendence. To establish it is, in each case, a matter of careful interpretation, and striking syntheses or generalisations may serve only to obscure the issue.

But, complex and elusive as many instances of this mode of transcendence may be, the intention is perfectly clear: to experience 'das uns Unerfahrbare'. And it is characteristic of Rilke's whole work that, no matter how far the limits be expanded, no matter how much 'Unkenntliches' becomes 'kenntlich' within the poetry, the unknown regions remain. The attempt to transcend the limits of 'unser gebräuchliches Bewußtsein' in the direction of the unknowable is always potentially there.

The further question, and one which perhaps cannot be answered in terms of 'Literaturwissenschaft', is whether the transformation of 'Erfundenes' into 'Erlebtes' necessarily makes for poetry which is in any sense bad or spurious. I do not think it does. One may see such poetry as the fall from Grace of the Goethean symbol, or, more dispassionately, as the most natural expression of one aspect of modern experience. Certainly Rilke, in writing such poetry, was not alone. In the work of so radically different a poet as Guillaume Apollinaire, who, for all his surrealistic tendencies, nevertheless saw himself in search of 'un lyrisme neuf et humaniste',[27] we may find the theme of pushing to the furthest limits of experience side by side with that of the divided self. In the opening stanzas of the poem *Cortège* we find the realisation of a *non plus ultra* in an image whose impossibility recalls that of the 'Spiegel' at the beginning of *Die zweite Elegie*, of the apotheosis of the lovers in the fifth Elegy and something of the playfulness of the sonnet: *O dieses ist das Tier, das es nicht gibt.* It is also significant that the second stanza looks forward to the ideal unity of 'l'unique lumière' and that the fourth echoes the theme of the divided self which we have been at pains to point out when discussing Rilke's poetry:

Oiseau tranquille au vol inverse oiseau
Qui nidifie en l'air
A la limite où notre sol brille déjà
Baisse ta deuxième paupière la terre t'éblouit
Quand tu lèves la tête

Et moi aussi de près je suis sombre et terne
Une brume qui vient d'obscurcir les lanternes
Une main qui tout à coup se pose devant les yeux
Une voûte entre vous et toutes les lumières
Et je m'éloignerai m'illuminant au milieu d'ombres
Et d'alignements d'yeux des astres bien-aimés

Oiseau tranquille au vol inverse oiseau
Qui nidifie en l'air
A la limite où brille déjà ma mémoire
Baisse ta deuxième paupière
Ni à cause du soleil ni à cause de la terre
Mais pour ce feu oblong dont l'intensité ira s'augmentant
Au point qu'il deviendra un jour l'unique lumière

Un jour
Un jour je m'attendais moi-même
Je me disais Guillaume il est temps que tu viennes
Pour que je sache enfin celui-là que je suis
Moi qui connais les autres...[28]

These modes of transcendence have been offered without attempting to disguise the various logical anomalies which make them highly questionable as philosophy. There seems also little point in adopting one of them as 'verbindlich' in preference to the others. Their separation into five categories is likewise an interpretative rather than a philosophical one. Rilke's work yields examples of these five modes, but, by the constantly changing nature of the image which the poet finds for his transformations, one might find instances where one mode passes almost imperceptibly into another, or where two or more coexist within the same thematic field. If one wishes to abstract a common denominator, then it cannot be a single specific content but rather the gesture of reaching out beyond the limits of the self, whether in space or time, perception or feeling. This gesture may be directed towards a variety of objects, or, in an extreme instance, may have no object at all. To see transcendence essentially as a gesture or movement seems to accord with what Jaspers says in his *Philosophie*:

Transzendieren *ist* als Bewegung im wirklichen Dasein.[29]

The problem for poetry which such transcendence presents, emerges clearly from another of Jaspers' statements:

Eigentliches Transzendieren heißt jedoch: Hinausgehen über das Gegenständliche ins Ungegenständliche.[30]

Within the context of poetry, this may mean on the one hand that the gesture of transcending ends in that 'leere Transzendenz' which Hugo Friedrich has shown so well in *Die Struktur der modernen Lyrik*.[31] On the other hand, the objects towards which this gesture is directed, forfeit their transcendent otherness as soon as they are described or felt. Hence, the paradox of 'Gegenständlichkeit' arises, and Jaspers formulates it as follows:

Wir können nicht außerhalb der Beziehung von Subjekt und Objekt treten. Was wir auch von dieser Beziehung denken, immer müssen wir wieder ein Gegenständliches denken und haben damit dieselbe Beziehung, die wir begreifen möchten, vorausgesetzt und sogleich vollzogen.[32]

In the case of Rilke's poetry, the word 'überwinden' would be more appropriate than 'begreifen', but the vicious circle remains. So it is that his transcendent objects alternate between standing for a noumenal otherness – 'about which nothing can be said except that there must be such a realm' – and for 'eine Übertreibung des Irdischen', some preternaturally intense form of human existence. So it is that images of transcendence at one extreme manifest the 'leere Transzendenz' of what Hamburger terms 'diese Selbstverschlingung im "Weltinnenraum" der "universalen Subjektivität"',[33] or, at the other extreme, the impossibility of certain of the products of 'die spekulative Phantasie'. Similarly, the overcoming of 'Gegenständlichkeit' must, when taken to its logical conclusion, either be projected into a speculative image or be experienced as a momentary ecstasy:

Sie müssen den Begriff des 'Offenen', den ich in dieser Elegie vorzuschlagen versucht habe, *so* auffassen, daß der Bewußtseinsgrad des Tieres es in die Welt einsetzt, ohne daß es sie sich (wie wir es tun) jeden Moment gegenüber stellt; das Tier ist *in* der Welt; wir stehen *vor ihr* durch die eigentümliche Wendung und Steigerung, die unser Bewußtsein genommen hat...Mit dem 'Offenen' ist also nicht Himmel, Luft und Raum gemeint, auch *die* sind, für den Betrachter und Beurteiler, 'Gegenstand' und somit 'opaque' und zu. Das Tier, die Blume, vermutlich, *ist* alles das, ohne sich Rechenschaft zu geben und hat so vor sich und über sich jene unbeschreiblich offene Freiheit, die vielleicht nur in den ersten Liebesaugenblicken wo ein Mensch im anderen, im Geliebten, seine eigene Weite sieht, und in der Hingehobenheit zu Gott bei uns (höchst momentane) Aequivalente hat.[34]

As I have said when previously discussing this letter, much of what Rilke says here does not apply in the period of the *Gedichte an die Nacht.* There the 'Gegenständlichkeit' of 'die nächsten Dinge' and 'die Menschen' does trouble him, but that of 'Himmel, Luft und Raum' on the whole does not. Hence, the problematical nature of his experience of the night and the angel.

Jaspers makes the point that the objects towards which 'die Bewegung des Transzendierens' is directed, thereby cease to be transcendent and this leads him to the conclusion that transcendence:

...bleibt nicht gegenständlich, sondern ist im Verschwinden des Gegenstandes.[35]

Such a transcendent object which dissolves in the moment of transcendence recalls strongly the following passage from *Malte*:

Ziemlich in Ruhe gelassen, machte ich frühzeitig eine Reihe von Entwicklungen durch, die ich erst viel später in einer Zeit der Verzweiflung auf Gott bezog, und zwar mit solcher Heftigkeit, daß er sich bildete und zersprang, fast in demselben Augenblick.   (SW VI, 810)

This does not appear to be characteristic of the transcendent objects in the *Gedichte an die Nacht*. Yet, if we take the various modes of transcendence collectively, the variety and mutability of the objects *does* bring about a 'Verschwinden des Gegenstandes' in the sense that no one object may stand for very long as *the* transcendent reality, but rather, as Rilke says in *An Hölderlin*:

...aus den erfüllten
Bildern stürzt der Geist zu plötzlich zu füllenden; Seeen
sind erst im Ewigen.   (SW II, 93)

At a certain level of abstraction from these images, the individual objects do tend to disappear and what remains is the gesture, the movement. Again the intention is not to claim that Rilke offers the same concept of transcendence as Jaspers. Jaspers' aims and methods have very little to do with the achievements and techniques of poetry. What this shows is that one may, by drastically abstracting from Rilke's poetry, find one common denominator which may be usefully described in terms of Jaspers' definitions. One might go further and say that transcendence as a 'Bewegung im wirklichen Dasein' is the form most appropriate to modern experience. In conclusion we may briefly return to the *Gedichte an die Nacht* to look at the two poems of the collection which were not analysed in the first part. This was not because their themes were in any way uncharacteristic. Rather, they show the tendencies which have been emphasised throughout and may serve here as a summary of what the discussion has been about. The first one presents a vision of harmony which is remarkable for the lack of disturbing tensions and for the modesty of the claims to transcendence:

> Hebend die Blicke vom Buch, von den nahen zählbaren Zeilen,
> in die vollendete Nacht hinaus:
> O wie sich sternegemäß die gedrängten Gefühle verteilen,
> so als bände man auf
> einen Bauernstrauß:
>
> Jugend der leichten und neigendes Schwanken der schweren
> und der zärtlichen zögernder Bug –.
> Überall Lust zu Bezug und nirgends Begehren;
> Welt zu viel und Erde genug.   (SW II, 77)

The visual image of this poem points in the direction of the concept of 'Figur' which is so important for the poetry of Rilke's last years. The last line, where the phrase 'Welt zu viel' perhaps anticipates the 'überzähliges Dasein' of the end of the ninth Elegy, indicates a momentary resting-point and even a renunciation of the gesture of transcendence as it appears in other poems. The poet does not demand that he be acknowledged by the stars, but is content with the 'as if' quality of the image. 'Bezug', which in many other contexts is scarcely to be taken at face value because it seems to be just another form of 'Besitz', is here quite free from suspicion because it is merely potential: 'Lust zu Bezug.' Although the initial situation is entirely familiar from the other poems, this one seems almost too serene and relaxed to be one of the *Gedichte an die Nacht*.

The second poem shows more awareness of the division of the self and insists on the complementarity of 'Leid' and 'Seligkeit'. As August Stahl has pointed out, 'Leid' tends to be what is actual in Rilke's poetry and the ideal of 'Seligkeit' more a matter of wishful thinking. So one could accuse Rilke of making here a virtue of necessity. But after the very real suffering which is in the *Gedichte an die Nacht*, this is surely understandable:

> Ist Schmerz, sobald an eine neue Schicht
> die Pflugschar reicht, die sicher eingesetzte,
> ist Schmerz nicht gut? Und welches ist der letzte
> der uns in allen Schmerzen unterbricht?
>
> Wieviel ist aufzuleiden. Wann war Zeit,
> das andre, leichtere Gefühl zu leisten?
> Und doch versteh ich, besser als die meisten
> einst Auferstehenden, die Seligkeit. (SW ii, 66)

neyed, but which is certainly justified by the course which the literature on both authors has taken, the world of Rilke's poetry is much closer to that of Kafka than it is to that of, say, Stefan George. With Kafka, the labyrinthine and ultimately inscrutable character of the world he is describing is made clear at the beginning and the epic genre enables Kafka to explore it through a large number of figures and guises, few of which we are obliged to identify with Kafka himself. Rilke's world, on the other hand, is explored and presented through 'das lyrische Ich' and, as Käte Hamburger points out, there is often no telling when the self of the poem is a direct expression of the poet as a person and when it is merely a way of assembling a number of statements into a given poetic form. This difference aside, both Rilke and Kafka present worlds in which perspectives of the only-just-knowable recede into others where complete mystery or 'Unkenntlichkeit' prevail, and both offer the wealth of alternative 'solutions' which has caused confusion among their critics ever since. One word which Rilke was fond of using all through his career is 'Vorwand'. Undoubtedly many things in Rilke's thought are a disguise or pretext for something else; the difficulty is in telling when something has ceased to be a 'Vorwand' and is the 'real thing'. The conclusion I draw with Rilke is that one cannot tell with any final certainty and that this is, in one sense, what the poetry is about. This view does not leave Rilke stranded in autistic confusion, for his poetry is clearly meaningful to a lot of people, it does however leave the nuances and intricacies of his thought as something to be respected, contradictions and all, and not pruned back to one coherent body of statement.

In this chapter, I shall attempt to sketch an approach to Rilke, which emerges from the interpretations which have gone before but which lays no claim to being the only approach to his work. It is, of necessity, somewhat personal and does not adopt the pose of objectivity, behind which so much 'Literaturwissenschaft' shelters its prejudices. If it seems like an attempt to simplify Rilke, then this is only because it complements the main part of the study where no attempt is made to reduce the difficulty of the *Gedichte an die Nacht*. Indeed, it is only if one takes the complexity of these poems seriously that the overall approach can be justified.

To begin with what is certainly a truism, the creation of the individual poem is always the most important thing for Rilke. One does not need to have recourse to his own statements on the matter, such as the letter to Lou Andreas-Salomé of August 8th 1903, for the whole deliberate specialisation of his personal life towards artistic creation is proof enough. In fact, there may even be something deliberate about Rilke's largely abandoning critical writing after the monograph and lecture on Rodin. Both from his early lectures and essays on modern poetry and from such a document as *Puppen* it is clear that he had a great talent for analytical thought and writing, yet the mature Rilke seems almost to have suppressed this as something likely to inhibit his poetic creation. There are signs of this also in his highly ambivalent attitude to both psychoanalysis and criticism of his own works, as Simenauer has shown.[1] He was both repelled and fascinated by the critical, as opposed to the creative approach to literature – denied vehemently on the one hand that criticism could have any access to his works, yet dutifully filled out questionnaires for Hulewicz and contemplated writing his own commentary to the *Sonette an Orpheus*. But ultimately, just as Rilke was always ready to sacrifice his emotional attachments for what he conceived to be his poetic vocation, so his critical talent tended to be pushed aside to allow freer reign to his creativity.

While poetic creation may always be foremost with Rilke, however, this does not mean that he is immediately to be ranked with Mallarmé as an advocate and creator of 'absolute Dichtung'. True, one may find in Rilke ample evidences of the doctrine that the artistic products of the human consciousness have a higher reality than that of common experience, but one also finds many traces of a contrary doctrine, indeed of so many doctrines, that the Mallarméan trend often appears rather insignificant among them. What sets Rilke apart from Mallarmé, Valéry, Stefan George and other writers who place the poetic word on an altar and offer it for worship, is his lack of single-mindedness both in doctrine and in practice. Creating the poem may have come first for Rilke, but what moved him to creation and what went into the poem was not simply admiration for his own achievement. One must distinguish between primary and secondary intentions when comparing Rilke's work with that of the late Mallarmé. In both cases the creation of the poem may be seen as the primary intention. With Mallarmé, the secondary intention is to justify the first by making the higher reality of the poem the subject of the poem itself: the quality of *absence* or *pureté* which the poem sets out to realise is at the same time the justification for the poem's being written in the first place. With Rilke, however, there is a wealth of secondary intentions and it is these which are most interesting. For one may say of almost any poet that the creation of the poem is primary – this does not get one very far. It is only with those poets who consistently adapted and applied the doctrines of Aestheticism that the secondary intention is so made to coincide with the first that the well-known extremism of *l'art pour l'art* is the result. Rilke, too, was writing in this tradition, but not exclusively and not consistently. It is necessary to state the primary intention of his work, but, once stated, there is very little more to say about it that is not evident to anyone who enjoys reading Rilke's poetry. It is when we turn to the secondary intentions of Rilke's work that the position becomes far less clear and that there is need of further differentiation.

The first aspect to be considered here is what one might term the 'message' of Rilke's poetry. There is, of course, no one message, but rather a plurality of messages, some of which accord rather oddly with others and many of which take up ideas and doctrines which are well-known from other sources. So one has the seemingly inexhaustible series of 'Rilke and...' titles, beginning on firm ground with 'Rilke and Nietzsche' or 'Rilke and Kassner' and extending to such fields as 'Rilke and Bachofen' and 'Rilke and Zen Buddhism', the last, incidentally, a contribution of Kassner himself. The message or messages to be derived from Rilke's work raise the primal and most vexed problem of all Rilke-criticism: what did Rilke *really* mean? And it is doubtful whether there is any better answer than that given by E. C. Mason in 1939: '"Alle möglichen, nur keine sicheren Schlüsse" – mit diesem einen Satz läßt sich die ganze Weltanschauung Rilkes erschöpfend zusammenfassen.' Many critics have since pleaded eloquently against treating Rilke's poetry as philosophy and I concur heartily with them. K. A. J. Batterby, in the introduction to his *Rilke and France*, argues very convincingly against the confusion of poetry with philosophy, but in his final conclusion he seems to me to be in danger of throwing the baby out with the bath-water. Batterby writes: 'Lyric poetry may be described as the poetry of mood and emotion...The content, as compared with other literary forms, is slight, the force and the appeal deriving from the wording.'[2] He then uses this argument to dismiss the problem of content altogether in favour of that of language. I am not entirely in agreement with this. For one thing, while it is quite true that Rilke was fascinated by language, it is equally evident that he was fascinated by ideas. The fascination may be more like that of a sculptor for his medium than that of a Marxist thinker for Dialectical Materialism and the element of play and the demands of aesthetic unity may well take ascendancy over the development of the thought, but the fact remains that Rilke works with ideas, just as he works with language, mood and 'emotional fundamentals'. The eighth Elegy, for example, is not just an expression of a particular mood in compelling language; it is also an exploration of certain ideas of human experience. That this exploration is by a poet and not by a psychologist or philosopher, goes without saying, but, on the other hand, it is not quite fair to imply that the content of Rilke's poetry is slight and the language all that is worth discussing. For not only does the content of Rilke's poetry often demand a fair amount of thought before it can be understood, but one usually finds, when analysing his poems, that all the apparent obscurities add up in the end to a logical whole. Rilke was clearly able to manage complex ideas and discursive thought-patterns within the individual poem – the trouble arises when one attempts to combine all the statements into one cohesive body of doctrine. Batterby's insistence on language and mood at the expense of ideas applies perfectly well to a poet such as Brentano, whose poems often work on the level of feeling, connotations and mood evoked, but can appear thoroughly confused once one begins extracting concepts and attempting to weld a logical whole out of them. Rilke's poetic thought is very rarely inconsistent or muddled in the individual poem, it is only when the critic is faced with a number of poems, such as the *Gedichte an die Nacht*, that it is difficult to get the results to agree with one another. So that while Rilke is not writing 'Gedankenlyrik', in the sense of using verse as a more or less convenient vehicle for expressing something which could as well be expressed in prose, he is a poet working in ideas, sometimes absorbed by the ideas themselves, sometimes using them in the same way as he uses alliteration, a rhetorical device or a neologism, to secure a particular poetic effect. What makes the deriving of doctrines from Rilke's work dangerous is not that, because he was a lyric poet, the content is, supposedly, slight, but that Rilke himself did not differentiate between the various guises in which an idea may occur in poetry, nor was he concerned with the critical problems raised by the relation of ideas to feelings. For Rilke they were all the one poetic medium. While excluding one aspect may make the others easier to handle, is declaring the thought-content of a poem to be trivial, and concentrating only on language, much different from declaring the content of a poem to be philosophy and neglecting the aesthetic and emotional aspects of it?

To deal with this dilemma, which seems to have become chronic in Rilke-criticism, one may have recourse to that admirable German invention, 'das lyrische Ich'. The voice which speaks in a given poem may be very close to or distant from the poet's personal self. It may be an elaborately drawn or barely sketched personality, thrusting itself into the foreground or discernible only as a kind of lens through which the subject matter of the poem is viewed. It may address the reader as an individual, or it may assume some pose, such as prophet or seer, and make categorical assertions about the nature of the Universe. Being a personality, it expresses itself partly through the attributes of an actual personality and these may be equally feelings, perceptions, memories, moods, ideas or poses. Being initially confined to a single poem, or, at most, a cycle of poems, it is far less complete than any actual personality and, being embodied in a work of art, its shaping is also subject to aesthetic laws, which should prevent us from confusing it with the person of its creator or with a psychological case-history. If we take 'das lyrische Ich', rather than 'language' or 'emotional fundamentals' or 'Dichtungstheorie' or 'mood' or 'das Sein des Seienden', as our prime object when interpreting Rilke, then we are not so much restricted by preconceptions of what we should find in the poetry. We may then find the language in which the self of the poem speaks more interesting than the content of what is said, or we may find that there is rather little to be said about the language, but that the juxtaposition of ideas is arresting, or we may try and show the close interrelation of both – all these things may be included in an inquiry into 'das lyrische Ich'. What emerges then from considering a large number of poems is a kind of aggregate lyrical personality. There will be discrepancies and unexplained gaps, dominant trends and trends in opposition to them, but here they need not occasion the same strictures as inconsistencies in a philosophical system. The antipathy of Mason and others to Rilke's thought is based on the implicit assumption that Rilke is trying to expound a consistent doctrine and doing it badly or dishonestly. Batterby's injunction to disregard the 'logical, philosophical, metaphysical or religious concepts' tends to ignore Rilke as a poet working with ideas as well as with language.[3] By making our object 'das lyrische Ich', we can do justice to both aspects and this is what the best Rilke-criticism, whether explicitly or not, has done from the beginning.

Remains the problem of what attitude one takes to the various 'messages' contained in Rilke's poetry, and a good proportion of poems do appear to have some message to impart. Here I can see no possibility of an objective criterion, and suggest that it must be a function of the reader's own personality. Kassner, in 1938, did Rilke-criticism a great service by saying that Rilke had succumbed to a number of 'falsche Ideen'. While few serious Rilke-scholars would disagree with this, dissension might very well arise as to which ideas were wrong and which right. Nor does it help much to abstain from taking any personal attitude on the grounds that, if one considers literature historically, one idea is just as historically determined as the next and therefore it is wrong to have preferences among them. Rilke's poetry survives by moving and by fascinating people, not by being historically determined, and to refrain from taking a personal attitude ultimately begs the question. What personal attitude we take to doctrines and ideas in Rilke's works is itself likely to be a rather inconstant thing because of the diversity of belief available. We may take Rilke's message at its broadest, the attitude of universal acceptance which permeates the *Sonette an Orpheus*, where all contraries have a tendency to blur and melt into one another, or we may take some very specific concept, such as 'Weltinnenraum', and find the essence of Rilke in that. Whatever we do, the further we penetrate into Rilke's work the more apparent it becomes that there is no single message, any more than there is a single meaning for 'Nacht' in the poems to the night or any single mode of transcendence. One's personal attitude thus becomes an interaction between reader and work, necessarily fluid and changing and there should be no need to codify it into a canon of fixed acceptances and rejections. When considering the modes of transcendence in the previous chapter, we saw that they could not be unified at a conceptual level and that the only unity one could impose upon them was that of the very generalised and abstract gesture of reaching out beyond a given state of the self. Similarly, with the 'message' of Rilke's poetry, one might eventually reduce all specific instances to the equally abstract and generalised state of the reader's being-told-something. If we take it to this extreme, then it obviously appears rather empty and uninteresting, but as I have stressed before, piece *Wie, für die Jungfrau, dem, der vor ihr kniet*, where the pattern of the shawl around the unpatterned centre is likewise made into just such a dance of forces as we find in *Der Panther*. The shawl represents for the late Rilke a *Figur*, which, as Allemann has shown, represents a 'higher reality': '...jener gesteigerte Raum, in welchem nicht mehr das zufällige Nebeneinander, sondern der reine Bezug herrscht.'[4] In the period of the *Neue Gedichte*, Rilke makes equally exalted claims for the reality of the 'Kunst-Ding' and the logical conclusion of both doctrines is to see the poem as a charmed circle, inside which feelings, objects and images are immune to those destructive forces which prevail outside. I have elsewhere tried to show the significance of the image of the circle in Rilke's late poetry, relating it both to the earlier concept of the 'Kunst-Ding' and to the idea of poetry as magic.[5] Implicit in this tendency is the familiar doctrine of the superiority of art over life and here Rilke's allegiance to Aestheticism and his closeness to poets such as Mallarmé is only too clear. Many influences combine to produce this aspect of Rilke's thought and practice – there are ample literary antecedents both in French and German, the idea was certainly current in all fields of art during Rilke's lifetime and it is difficult to assign it to any one source. The immediate stimulus to begin theorising about the 'Kunst-Ding' came, of course, from the encounter with Rodin's sculpture, but here again it is quite possible that Rilke is adapting literary ideas to give expression to his enthusiasm for something non-literary. One may, in fact, explain this tendency in a number of possible ways: as the natural conclusion of the exaltation of the poetic word which begins in German with Klopstock and continues through Romanticism into Symbolism or one may prefer to explain it in terms of Rilke's own psychopathology. When Rilke, in the letter to Lou Andreas-Salomé where he formulates the doctrine of the 'Kunst-Ding', freely admits: 'O Lou, in einem Gedicht, das mir gelingt, ist viel mehr Wirklichkeit als in jeder Beziehung oder Zuneigung, die ich fühle...',[6] then a psychological explanation of this aspect of his work is certainly justified. But explaining it is not really necessary

– the tendency is there and it is more interesting to observe the various forms it takes throughout his work.

The poem as a closed system is best exemplified by such poems as *Römische Fontäne* and *Blaue Hortensie* from the *Neue Gedichte* and *Die Frucht* in the later poetry. In each case, the movement of water or the relationship of the two colours or the process of the fruit's ripening is taken for itself and one does violence to the meaning of the poem if one tries to impose any allegorical or philosophical meaning on to it. The poems represent what Rilke elsewhere terms 'ein Spielen von reinen/Kräften' – a pattern is perceived in the subject matter and this is then translated into the movement of the poem. One may contrast poems such as these with other of the *Neue Gedichte*, such as *Todeserfahrung*, where the subject matter of the poem becomes the starting point for metaphysical speculation, or with most of the *Gedichte an die Nacht*, where no such completeness and organisation of the material is achieved. An interesting case in point is *Die spanische Trilogie*, where, as we have seen, the content of the first two poems remains unresolved, because each poem states problems which the poems themselves do not answer. In the third poem, on the other hand, a quasi-solution is reached in the identification with the figure of the shepherd which does provide a resting point, but also circumscribes the scope of the poem considerably. As became apparent when examining the poem, the identification with the shepherd is a provisional solution which does not really fulfil the need in the first poem for the creation of the 'Ding', but nevertheless gives the trilogy an emotionally adequate ending. Taking the three poems together, then, we may see two contrary tendencies at work. In the first poem there is the absolute demand for the ideal solution, the unity of self and world denoted by the 'Ding', in the second poem more questions are asked and further possibilities sketched in, in the third poem a kind of compromise is arrived at: the ideal unity cannot be attained, but the self of the poem, by using the figure of the shepherd as a mediation, is able to achieve a measure of calm and confidence entirely lacking from the first poem: 'Ein Schein wird ruhig. Der Tod/fände sich reiner zurecht' (SW II, 46). The attitude which enables the third poem of the trilogy to reach a resting point is indeed very similar to that which creates the magic circle of the poem as a refuge from chance and transience and which, in another form, celebrates the closed circle which Narcissus achieves on seeing his own reflection. The 'Kunst-Ding' or 'Figur' is likewise a refuge. Rilke's interpretation of Rodin states that Rodin, seeing that 'alle Schönheit an Menschen und Thieren und Dingen gefährdet ist durch Verhältnisse und Zeit', set about making 'Kunst-Dinge' in which beauty could be preserved in the higher and permanent reality of the work of art.[7] Similarly, when presenting the Kashmir shawl in 1924 as an example of a 'Figur', Rilke exclaims:

> Geweb in das das Leben überging.
> O wieviel Regung rettet sich ins reine
> Bestehn und Überstehn von einem Ding. (SW II, 489)

Whether it is Narcissus saving himself by closing the circle with his reflection, or the artist saving the beauty of something he sees by preserving it in a poem or sculpture, or even the self of *Die spanische Trilogie* taking refuge in the serene image of the shepherd going about his daily work, the tendency is essentially the same and runs through the whole of Rilke's work. It has not been very evident in our analysis of the *Gedichte an die Nacht*, because these, for the most part, embody the opposite tendency, that of reaching out beyond what is given towards something unknown and wonderful. This second tendency has been discussed in great detail in the preceding chapters and provides the substance of the theme of transcendence in Rilke's work. I should like to suggest, by way of conclusion, that the interaction of these two opposing tendencies, or attitudes, or techniques, offers a way of seeing the development of Rilke's work as a whole. In the late poetry, Rilke's preoccupation with the 'Figur' or the magic circle is matched by an equally strong desire to go beyond these and explore the regions of 'das Unkenntliche' which lie outside them. The two possibilities, the poem as a closed system and the poem as a reaching out beyond the limits of given experience, are taken up again and again by Rilke throughout his career and also are prominent in his theoretical statements. The theory of the 'Kunst-Ding', which he develops around 1903, clearly corresponds to the idea of the poem as a model of harmony; the emphasis he lays in *Ur-Geräusch* on the desire to experience what is initially 'das uns Unerfahrbare' provides a theoretical basis for the second possibility. In terms of the Western lyric tradition, the first possibility brings Rilke very close to Mallarmé, the second shows a strong similarity with Rimbaud. In the *Lettre du Voyant*, Rimbaud declares the new poetry to be essentially an exploration of new regions of experience and the justification for this is contained in the phrase: 'car il arrive à l'inconnu'.[8] Rilke does not seem to have known Rimbaud's work well, but the difficulties which are implicit in Rimbaud's theory are very similar to those which 'das lyrische Ich' encounters in Rilke's poetry when it sets out to experience a totality of existence which includes both the immanent and transcendent spheres.

Rilke did not choose the way of hallucination, the 'immense et raisonné *dérèglement* de tous les sens',[9] and in his own poetic development he was a long time in catching up on what Rimbaud achieved in the space of a few years. But the later Rilke's own stubborn attempts to extend the limits of experience, his insistence on the makeshift and provisional quality of even those solutions which he himself proposes:

> Auch die sternische Verbindung trügt.
> Doch uns freue eine Weile nun
> der Figur zu glauben. Das genügt.   (SW 1, 738)

and his never ceasing fascination for what lies just beyond the resources of language – all of this places him securely in the line of development leading from Rimbaud.

If one accepts these two tendencies as the systole and diastole of Rilke's creative activity, then the multiplicity of doctrines which may be extracted from his work becomes easier to accept and to understand. For the alternation of these attitudes in a kind of 'Wechselspiel'[10] throughout his work, like the alternation of the emotional states of 'Fremdheit' and 'Beteiligung', produces very different statements as the emphasis shifts from the creation of the poem as something august and self-sufficient to the use of the poem as a means of exploring new states of consciousness or effecting the ideal unity of immanence and transcendence. In the former case, the emphasis is on art as an end in itself, requiring no justification beyond its own existence; in the second instance, the poem often becomes an expression of the discrepancy between the limitations of the human self and the perfection of the ideal unity towards which it is directed. The contrast between the two modes can be seen immediately in the difference of tone and attitude between two poems such as *Römische Fontäne* and *Hinhalten will ich mich*, from the *Gedichte an die Nacht*. In other poems and phases of the work it is less obvious, but if one looks for it, the alternation is certainly there.

To see something of the genesis of this 'Wechselspiel' in Rilke's work, we may look briefly at the lecture *Moderne Lyrik*, written in 1898, but not published until 1965. At the beginning of the lecture, Rilke characterises modern poetry as follows:

Sehen Sie: seit den ersten Versuchen des Einzelnen, unter der Flut flüchtiger Ereignisse *sich selbst zu finden*, seit dem ersten Bestreben, mitten im Gelärm des Tages hineinzuhorchen bis in die tiefsten Einsamkeiten des eigenen Wesens, – giebt es eine *Moderne Lyrik*. (SW v, 360)

Rilke is here emphasising the exploratory character of artistic creation. The specifically modern impulse is, he says, to penetrate to the furthest regions of the self and express the result in poetry. He says later in the speech:

Daß darin die große, vielleicht mächtigste Bedeutung der Lyrik besteht, daß sie dem Schaffenden ermöglicht, unbegrenzte Geständnisse über sich und sein Verhältnis zur Welt abzulegen, kann nur von einer Zeit erkannt werden, welche fühlt, daß sie etwas eingestehen will. (SW v, 368)

The chief purpose of art is, then, to make 'unbegrenzte Geständnisse' about oneself and one's relation to the world. Reading the two quotations together, it is clear that this does not simply mean confession for its own sake, but rather that the content of the 'Geständnis' must be sought by an exploration of the self and its relation to the world. The emphasis is here on what is

When Rilke says of them: 'sie stehen nicht auf der Erde, sie kreisen um sie', then he is clearly using poetic licence.[11] But Rilke was also very prone to take himself literally and the 'Kunst-Ding' survives in his thinking as something preternatural, as an aesthetic doctrine which may have helped him write some outstanding poetry, but which none the less represented a grossly distorted view of what poetry is. Rilke was by no means alone in his deification of art and the artist, but it nevertheless remains one of the severest limits on his stature as a writer. It may be that these exaggerations were necessary as a context in which he produced his best work, but they are the least impressive aspects of his work in retrospect. However, it is important to realise that they are exaggerations of tendencies which in themselves remain interesting. The desire to subject the self to an intense scrutiny, to push forward to the limits of experience and language and to make poetry of it is a perfectly legitimate artistic intention. It is only when this becomes magnified into the vision of the 'Künstler-Gott', or the doctrine of the power of Orpheus as an antidote to everything unpleasant in the world, that the exaggeration becomes grotesque. Similarly, poets have always held their art to be superior to ordinary language and to confer some measure of immortality on what they celebrate. This is so, and few people would have it otherwise. It is only when art becomes a substitute religion and the work of art is assigned all kinds of absolute values, that the quality of the art itself is diminished. Both these myths are present in German Romanticism and in the French poets from Baudelaire onwards, often in forms or contexts which keep them under control. Rilke, coming at the end of a tradition, imbibed them in a particularly strong form, obviously because they accorded with certain tendencies in himself. The myths were useful to him, supporting the extremism both in thought and feeling, which helps to raise his mature work above his rather mediocre beginnings as a poet. At the same time they also date his writing, and are largely responsible for the disapproval with which he is regarded in Germany today. What one must stress, however, is that while these myths are present in his work, they are not his whole work, nor are they the essence of his work. They are exaggerated forms of the two major tendencies of his work, but his work remains that of a great poet.

Throughout the preceding chapters, I have laid great stress on the poem *An Hölderlin* as a key to understanding Rilke's attitudes to poetry in the period of the *Gedichte an die Nacht*. When assessing direct influences on Rilke, the French poets and Rodin and Cézanne tend to come first. Batterby and others are in all probability right in seeing France as the decisive influence. But there is also a strong German contribution and this is most marked by what one might term the idealist imperative. Rilke's interest in Hölderlin and Klopstock was not only limited to the contribution they made to his poetic language. The attempt to reconcile in poetry the human and the divine, to create a vision of the world in which the immanent and transcendent are related through poetry is also present in Rilke and produces the striving towards an ideal unity of self, world and transcendent reality which marks the *Gedichte an die Nacht*. Rilke sought to fulfil the idealist imperative in his writing and failed to do so, if only because he was writing at the end of Romanticism rather than at the beginning. Rilke may have felt the idealist imperative in a way somewhat similar to Hölderlin, but to compare *Hyperion* with *Malte Laurids Brigge* is to see from what vastly different bases the two poets were writing. But this situation did not make of Rilke merely a failed Romantic writing a century after his time. The attempt to fulfil the idealist imperative in a historical situation which denies most of the values of Idealism, produces in Rilke's poetry the phenomenon of the divided self. Because 'das lyrische Ich' cannot realise the ideal unity within the poem and because the imperative to do so cannot be laid aside, the self divides into contraries and becomes, over the whole of the work, a disunified and contradictory figure. But it is this fact, I think, which, together with Rilke's enormous power of language, makes of his poetry something unique and accounts for its lasting fascination.

NOTES

INTRODUCTION

1 In SW II, 755 Ernst Zinn lists the poems included in the *Gedichte an die Nacht* and mentions their presentation to Kassner. On pages 887–90 and 916–18 of the same edition, dates are given for the poems and for fragments written during the same period.

2 Käte Hamburger, *Philosophie der Dichter*, Stuttgart 1966, p. 180.

3 So Else Buddeberg, *Rainer Maria Rilke – Eine innere Biographie*, Stuttgart 1960, when interpreting *An den Engel* points out with proper indignation that there is nothing subjective about what the 'Ich' is doing: 'Man würde den Charakter dieser Wirklichkeit völlig verkennen, wenn man annähme, daß hiermit ein "Antworten" des Engels im Sinne der Herstellung einer subjektiv-individuellen Bezogenheit eingeschlossen wäre.' The ironical thing about this is that the situation of the 'Ich' in the *Gedichte an die Nacht* is so much one of isolation that the poet is hardly in a position to seek anything else!

4 For a discussion of the metaphysics of 'absolute Kunst' see E. Heftrich, *Die Philosophie und Rilke*, Freiburg/München 1962, pp. 13–23, which is concerned mainly with Fritz Kaufmann's essay and U. Fülleborn, *Das Strukturproblem der späten Lyrik Rilkes*, Heidelberg 1960, pp. 25–6, for a summation of W. Günther's equally metaphysical doctrine of 'absolute Poesie'.

5 For example H. W. Belmore, *Rilke's Craftsmanship*, Oxford 1954, K. Batterby, *Rilke and France*, London 1966, F. W. Wodtke, *Das Problem der Sprache beim späten Rilke* and the sections on the style of the late poetry in Fülleborn's *Strukturproblem*.

6 Käte Hamburger, when speaking of *Die spanische Trilogie* says: 'Es ist dann anderthalb Jahre später in den großen Gedichten *Waldteich* und *Wendung*... die Möglichkeit erwogen, Anschauen durch die Liebe ersetzen zu können... In unserem Zusammenhang ist hier nur relevant, daß diese Krisis nicht zugunsten der Liebe entschieden werden konnte (und das Werk des letzten Lebensjahrzehnts Rilkes wahrscheinlich eine andere Gestalt angenommen hätte, wäre es so gewesen), Herzwerk als Kraft der Seinsbewältigung "Werk des Gesichts" nicht ersetzen konnte.' (*Philosophie der Dichter*, p. 239f.) Fülleborn, from a different point of view, is equally sceptical of the reality of the 'Wendung'. He sees the poem as 'nicht Zeugnis einer gesamtmenschlichen Wandlung' and says that it 'faßt...nur eine Möglichkeit ins Auge'. There may still be room for controversy here, but I tend very much to accept the views of these two critics.

7 Cf. TF, 206: 'Alles war zunächst darauf angelegt...' and 'Hast du noch nie bemerkt...'

8 In *The Owl and the Nightingale*, London 1960, pp. 239–56.

1 . *Die spanische Trilogie*

1 For a list of the *Gedichte an die Nacht* see SW II, 755f. and for the date of composition of the Trilogy SW II, 887.

2 Cf. W. Günther, *Weltinnenraum*, 2. Auflage 1952, p. 118, also Fülleborn, *Strukturproblem*, p. 76 note 8 and Käte Hamburger, *Philosophie der Dichter*, p. 237.

3 Käte Hamburger, op. cit., p. 238f.: 'Es ist mit Hinblick auf die folgende Entwicklung erlaubt, den Begriff des Dinges, als Zeichen für ein solches Werk, gewissermaßen als Hindernis zu verstehen, diesen Gedanken schon zu vollenden...Und horcht man tiefer in diese Verse hinein, so erscheint das wiederkehrende Wort Ding als ein hart aufklingender, stumpfer Laut, der aufgelöst werden will.'

4 P. Washburn Shaw in her chapters entitled 'The Self' and 'The Self in the World' in *Rilke, Valéry and Yeats*, New Jersey 1964, does not really treat this theme, although there is a certain similarity of terminology between her work and this. She says a great deal about 'the self' in Rilke's poetry, but does not take up the line of thought indicated by the words from the fourth Elegy: 'Wir sind nicht einig...'. So it is that she says of the first poem of *Die spanische Trilogie*: '...at the end of the poem, in the rapidity of the alternation and repetition, we have a kind of dramatic equivalent of the fusion...' (p. 77), but does not go on to say what prevents the fusion from becoming real and what makes it remain merely a 'dramatic equivalent'.

5 BLA-S, 96f. It is remarkable that the despair and disorientation of August 1903 should reappear in a poem written in January 1913 in such similar terms. This is undoubtedly related to the similarity between the 'Kunst-Ding' of the letters of 1903 and the 'Ding' of the first part of *Die spanische Trilogie*. It is as if Rilke, when faced with a similar crisis, at first considers solving it by similar means. That he does not do so and that the 'Ding' does not occur again in the *Gedichte an die Nacht* points to the fact that other developments within the poet do not allow this regression.

6 Cf. Fülleborn, op. cit., pp. 51-4.

7 E. C. Mason, *Lebenshaltung und Symbolik*, 2nd ed. Oxford 1964, chapter on 'Das Weltbild der Nuance' (pp. 3-25).

8 See below, pp. 97ff. and p. 109.

9 Cf. SW II, 92f. *Es winkt zu Fühlung fast aus allen Dingen.* The concept of 'Weltinnenraum' is based on a feeling of the homogeneity of inner and outer worlds and on the absence of any barriers to emotional identification. It represents a strand of Rilke's thought which, as W. Günther and others have shown, may be traced throughout Rilke's poetic development. It is often at variance with other modes of thought or feeling in the work and in the period of *Die Gedichte an die Nacht* appears as one theme among many others.

10 As a result of Martin Heidegger's views on Rilke's and Hölderlin's poetry, much has been said of the figure of the poet as 'Hirt des Seins', usually with reference to the poems *Nicht Geist, nicht Inbrunst wollen wir entbehren* (SW II, 277f.) and *Da schwang die Schaukel durch den Schmerz* (SW II, 176). In these

poems from 1926 and 1924 respectively, the equation of 'Hirt' with poet is clear enough. Not much attention has been paid, however, to what seems the origin of this image in a poem written not in Ronda, but in February 1907 as part of the *Improvisationen aus dem Capreser Winter* (SW 11, 17ff.). There what differentiates the shepherd from the ordinary run of mortals, the poet included, is his total openness to experience, one which makes him virtually devoid of self:

> (Sahst du den Hirten heut? Der geht nicht zu.
> Wie sollte er's? Dem fließt
> der Tag hinein und fließt ihm wieder aus
> wie einer Maske, hinter der es schwarz ist...)   (SW 11, 18f.)

Here there is as yet no concept of the shepherd as 'Hirt des Seins' or as poet. What it does show is the way in which the shepherd is particularly suited to being a *mediate* figure, precisely because of this 'emptiness'. The shepherd in the third poem of *Die spanische Trilogie* is clearly a development of this earlier figure, but whether he is also Heidegger's 'Hirt des Seins' is another question.

11 Cf. J. Gebser, *Rilke und Spanien*, 2. Auflage 1945 and E. Buddeberg, *Rainer Maria Rilke*, Stuttgart 1955, pp. 229–53. See also F. W. Wodtke, *Rilke und Klopstock*, Kiel 1951, pp. 94–111.

12 B. 1907–14, 264.

13 Fülleborn, op. cit., p. 82.

14 That Rilke should have seen the vision of 'ein ganzes Leben' as a quality of Hölderlin's poetry is interesting in view of the importance of the concept of 'die intellektuelle Anschauung' for Hölderlin's poetic theory. Lawrence Ryan in his book *Hölderlins Lehre vom Wechsel der Töne*, Stuttgart 1960, analyses this concept in some detail (pp. 22–5) and says of it: 'Sie wird... definiert als jene "Einigkeit mit allem, was lebt, die... vom Geiste erkannt werden kann" – das heißt auch, als Erkenntnis der Einigkeit *von* allem, was lebt, von allem Seienden – die als absolute Einigkeit die "Unmöglichkeit einer absoluten Trennung und Vereinzelung impliziert"...' (p. 23). As the poem *An Hölderlin* and the *Gedichte an die Nacht* make clear, such a confident vision is just what Rilke lacks in this period.

15 One might argue that in the *Fünf Gesänge* of August 1914 Rilke makes a quite uncharacteristic attempt to write 'hymnische Dichtung' in the Hölderlinic mode. But these poems are anything but successful and it is obvious that the intention behind *Die spanische Trilogie* is different from that which produces the *Fünf Gesänge* some twenty months later. The words in the third part of the Trilogy: 'Sei er wer immer für euch...' are in complete opposition to the attempt to speak in terms of 'das gemeinsame Herz' in *Fünf Gesänge*.

2 . THE ENCOUNTER WITH THE NIGHT

1 This order is given in SW 11, 755f.

2 In answer to inquiries concerning the possible significance of the order in which the poems were copied into the book presented to Kassner, Professor

Ernst Zinn wrote a reply which reads in part: 'Wenn Rilke also bei der Aufnahme der einzelnen Gedichte in das Schreibbuch von der chronologischen Entstehungsfolge abwich, die ihm durch die Eintragung der entsprechenden Entwürfe und ersten Niederschriften in sein damaliges Taschenbuch ohne weiteres zur Hand war, so muß man zugeben, daß die im Schreibbuch anzutreffende Reihenfolge eine "ausdrücklich von Rilke gewählte" ist... Nun aber weiß man gar nichts Näheres über die Entstehung dieser kleinen Sammelhandschrift und über die Absicht, die Rilke etwa bei der Schenkung dieses Manuscriptes an Rudolf Kassner hegte.'

3 Cf. Wodtke, *Rilke und Klopstock*, Kiel 1948, p. 63 and Fülleborn, *Strukturproblem*, p. 80.

4 Holthusen, 'Rilkes mythische Wendung', in *Hochland*, 1939–40, p. 307. Cf. also 'Rilkes letzte Jahre' in *Der unbehauste Mensch*, 3. Auflage, München 1955.

5 Cf. SW ii, 31:

...Wer widerstrebt,
dem wird nicht Welt. Und wer zuviel begreift,
dem geht das Ewige vorbei...

Cf. also B. 1907–14, 253: *An NN am 17. November 1912.*

6 SW ii, 68.

7 Cf. Fülleborn, op. cit., passim and especially pp. 80, 243, 276.

8 SW i, 690.

9 Wodtke, op. cit., p. 63.

10 Fülleborn, op. cit., p. 82.

11 O. F. Bollnow, *Rilke*, zweite erweiterte Ausgabe, Stuttgart 1956, p. 101.

12 Ibid., p. 99.

13 Fülleborn, op. cit., p. 27.

14 F. J. Brecht, *Schicksal und Auftrag des Menschen*, München 1949, p. 19.

15 See below, pp. 84ff.

16 Wodtke, op. cit., p. 114.

17 Fülleborn, op. cit., p. 27. Fülleborn is here speaking of Bollnow's interpretation.

18 Cf. Fülleborn, *Form und Sinn der Aufzeichnungen des MLB*, in *Unterscheidung und Bewahrung*, Berlin 1961, p. 163. The threat to his identity which Malte feels so acutely may well be 'weil er durchaus noch an den alten Benennungen der Dinge hängt', but the theme of the breakdown of the 'Grenzen des Ich', which is also partly that of an excessive sensitivity to impressions, is an important part of the threat as well.

19 Cf. SW i, 691: 'Doch wer wagte darum schon zu *sein?*' See also the Sonnet, SW i, 753, *O dieses ist das Tier, das es nicht gibt*, where Rilke plays on different qualities of 'sein'.

20 SW ii, 356:

'man zeigt uns dies; man hält uns nicht wie Gäste
die man nur nimmt, erheitert und erfrischt.'

21 In the prose-piece *Ur-Geräusch* these are referred to as 'die schwarzen Sektoren, die das uns Unerfahrbare bezeichnen' (SW vi, 1091). A similar

indication of the regions beyond the limits of experience is given in the late poem *Da schwang die Schaukel durch den Schmerz* (SW II, 176), where 'die Göttersitze' are placed beyond our furthest conjecture. A similar line of thought is also present in the concept of the 'Bewußtseinspyramide' (AB II, 453). Cf. also Anthony Stephens, 'The Problem of Completeness in Rilke's Poetry 1922–1926', *Oxford German Studies*, vol. 4.

22 Cf. Fülleborn, op. cit., p. 80.

23 Ibid., p. 74.

24 Ibid., p. 78.

25 Bollnow, op. cit., p. 56.

26 Ibid.

27 August Stahl, '*Vokabeln der Not*' und '*Früchte der Tröstung*', Heidelberg 1967, treats this poem very briefly and lays most emphasis on the act of 'Stehen' in the overcoming of 'Trennung' (p. 122). He does not, however, emphasise the other acts which seem to me to be much more important, namely: 'wegschauen' and 'begreifen'. The image of 'Stehen' need bear no causal relation to the subsequent 'begreifen', which *does*, however, proceed directly from 'wegschauen'.

28 Bollnow, op. cit., p. 57: 'Aber etwas hat sich schon geändert – wenn es auch objektiv kaum angebbar ist – nämlich im Tonfall dieser Schilderung. Er ist voller, dunkler, im ganzen auch gefaßter geworden, ins Kosmische ausgeweitet und nicht mehr so im Kleinlichen unserer Umgebung verzettelt...' and further: 'Und darin drückt sich schon ein verändertes Verhältnis des Menschen zu dieser Unheimlichkeit aus: Indem er nicht mehr davor auszuweichen versucht, sondern ihr klar ins Gesicht sieht:

> .... da war es, du Hohe,
> keine Schande für mich, daß du mich kanntest.

Da also hat sich der Mensch des Anspruchs der Nacht als würdig erwiesen.'

29 Fülleborn, op. cit., p. 75.

30 BT 1899–1902, 203: 'Ich fürchte in mir nur diejenigen Widersprüche, die Neigung haben zur Versöhnlichkeit...'

31 Fülleborn, op. cit., p. 80, note 96.

32 Ibid.

33 Cf. B. Allemann, *Zeit und Figur*, Pfullingen 1961, pp. 25ff. and Bollnow, op. cit., pp. 315ff.

34 K. Hamburger, *Philosophie der Dichter*, Stuttgart 1966, p. 215.

35 Ibid., p. 220.

36 Ibid., p. 217.

37 SW VI, 1035.

38 Cf. Hamburger, op. cit., pp. 242ff.

39 See the letter to Ilse Blumenthal-Weiß, AB II, 286.

3 . THE NIGHT AND THE LOVERS

1 Wodtke, *Rilke und Klopstock*, pp. 15ff. and Fülleborn, *Strukturproblem*, pp. 90ff.
2 Wodtke, op. cit., p. 159.
3 Fülleborn, op. cit., pp. 102ff.
4 Ibid., p. 103.
5 Mason, *Lebenshaltung und Symbolik*, Oxford 1964, p. 129.
6 Wodtke, op. cit., p. 159.
7 Ibid., p. 154.
8 As indicated above, the resurrection of the Last Judgment can no longer be called the human situation of the *Gedichte an die Nacht*. The solution is far too drastic for the thematic field of the poems. Rather, the poem points in the direction of the ninth and tenth Elegies. In his edition of the Elegies (Oxford 1965), Ernst Stahl interprets the words 'in uns erstehn' at the end of the ninth Elegy as positing a resurrection in death. This is different from the traditionally mythical resurrection in the poem *Die Geschwister II*, but one may see the thought developing towards the much later concept of the Elegies.
9 Cf. Rilke's letter to Lou Andreas-Salomé of August 8 1903, where he praises Rodin's relationship to 'die Dinge' and makes the famous declaration: '...und was sind mir die nahen Menschen als ein Besuch, der nicht gehen will'. In the poem we are considering there is perhaps an echo of 'Ding' as *Herzwort* (cf. H. Kunisch, *Rilke und die Dinge*, Köln 1946). That Rilke often prefers objects to people is an aspect of his 'Versagen am Menschlichen' and has provided the exponents of psychological criticism with much ammunition. All one can really say is that in the *Gedichte an die Nacht* Rilke does try to deal with the problems of love in his own terms, whereas the result would have been neater had he avoided them altogether. In a number of places he does try to 'solve' these problems by one kind of poetic sophistry or another, but it is, I think, to his credit that he does not attempt to conceal his failure to do so.
10 SW VI, 1035: *Über den Dichter*.
11 Wodtke, op. cit., p. 66.
12 Cf. SW II, 366: Daß aus Aufsteigendem und Wiederfall
auch ganz in mir so Seiendes entstände:
o Heben und Empfangen ohne Hände,
geistiges Weilen; Ballspiel ohne Ball.
13 Cf. SW II, 73: 'O von Gesicht zu Gesicht/welche Erhebung...'
14 In *Hinweg die ich bat* the poet is trying to achieve a break with all his previous experience, so the 'Geliebte' becomes plural in much the same way as the 'Pein der Liebesmöglichkeiten' (SW II, 400).
15 In contexts such as the second poem of *Die spanische Trilogie* and the fragment *An die Erwartete* (SW II, 388), there is a tendency to see the self, for good or ill, as the sum of its conscious memories. By banishing the memories of previous 'Geliebte' from the consciousness, Rilke is clearly trying to

bring about 'la nouvelle opération' by disassociating his present self from his previous existence.

16 SW II, 216f. and especially SW II, 955–8.
17 Cf. Wodtke, op. cit., pp. 32–51.
18 Fülleborn, op. cit., p. 99.
19 B. 1907–14, 264.

4 . THE NIGHT AND THE ANGEL

1 E. Buddeberg, *R. M. Rilke*, Stuttgart 1954, p. 258.
2 Wodtke, *Rilke und Klopstock*, p. 107.
3 Buddeberg, op. cit., pp. 260ff.
4 Wodtke, op. cit., p. 105.
5 Buddeberg, op. cit., p. 259.
6 Ibid., pp. 254, 255, 257.
7 Ibid., p. 260f.
8 Karl Jaspers, *Philosophie I – Philosophische Weltorientierung*, Heidelberg 1956, p. 50.
9 Buddeberg, op. cit., p. 255.
10 Ibid., p. 258.
11 Ibid.
12 Jaspers, op. cit., p. 50. I do not suggest that Jaspers is the final authority on matters of transcendence, or even that his definition comes particularly close to more than one of the various modes of transcendence to be encountered in Rilke's work. His definition is quoted here because of the agreeable contrast which its clarity makes with the confusion attending Buddeberg's use of the word.
13 Buddeberg, op. cit., p. 260.
14 Ibid., p. 258.
15 See below, p. 153 f.
16 Wodtke, op. cit., p. 107.
17 Still unpublished. Quoted by Wodtke, op. cit., p. 96f.
18 Fülleborn, *Strukturproblem*, p. 276 and passim.
19 Mason, *Lebenshaltung und Symbolik*, p. 11.
20 Hamburger, op. cit., p. 179.
21 Cf. SW II, p. 756.
22 Fülleborn, op. cit., p. 77.
23 B. 1907–14, 264.
24 See especially SW II, 392.
25 Cf. Hamburger, op. cit., passim, e.g.: 'Denn der Engel ist...der letzte große intentionale Gegenstand, den Rilkes erkenntnishafter Impuls geschaffen hat... (p. 226).
26 Wodtke, op. cit., p. 63.
27 Fülleborn, op. cit., p. 70.
28 M. Betz, *Rilke in Frankreich*, trans. W. Reich, Wien 1938, p. 291. Cf. M. Heidegger, *Holzwege*, Frankfurt 1957, pp. 263ff. It is rather surprising that this extremely important letter has not been included in the *Ausgewählte Briefe*.

5 . THE MEANING OF 'NACHT'

1 The principle that entities should not be allowed to multiply beyond necessity, or, in the case of Rilke's poetry, that they should be drastically reduced in the course of the interpretation, is best shown by the first systematic use to be made of it, namely in E. C. Mason's *Lebenshaltung und Symbolik*, first published in 1939. There Mason maintains: 'Das Werk aber als Ganzes bleibt vollkommen unbegreiflich, vollkommen undurchdringlich, ein Knäuel von unlösbaren Widersprüchen, wenn man von der Persönlichkeit des Dichters absieht, wenn man es in irgendeinem anderen Sinne zu ergründen versucht, als eben in dem eines persönlichen Dokuments...' (p. 68). Faced with this *Knäuel*, Mason resolves it by reducing all the apparent complexities and contradictions to the single theme of Rilke's own understanding of himself as an artist (pp. ix, 45, 155 etc.). The same tendency in Fülleborn's work has been shown in the beginning of Chapter 3 above. While the scepticism which produces these methods has had a very salutary effect on Rilke-criticism, there is the danger that the baby sometimes gets thrown out with the bath-water.

2 *Goethes Werke*, Hamburger Ausgabe, Bd. 1, ed. E. Trunz, p. 358.

3 BT, 339:
Alles Gefühl, in Gestalten und Handlungen
wird es unendlich groß und leicht.
Ich ruhe nicht, bis ich das eine erreicht:
Bilder zu finden für meine Verwandlungen.

4 Cf. K. Jaspers, *Philosophie*, Bd. 1, p. 50f.: 'Dieser Begriff des Transzendenten meint nicht etwa, was über meine gegenwärtige Erfahrung hinausgeht, aber prinzipiell der Möglichkeit nach von mir erfahren werden könnte, sondern transzendent ist, was schlechthin nie Gegenstand werden kann wie Dasein, und nie als es selbst bewußtseinsgegenwärtig wird wie mögliche Existenz.' This is not to overlook the fact that Rilke would never agree that transcendence 'nie Gegenstand werden kann wie Dasein' – Jaspers' distinctions, however, while they do not cover the whole of the field of transcendence in Rilke's work, do serve to make two contrary aspects of it clear.

5 Cf. Mason, *Exzentrische Bahnen*, p. 189: 'Die wahre Quelle von Rilkes Inspiration ist, so ungern er es auch gewöhnlich zugibt, sein eigenes Unterbewußtsein...'

6 SW 1, 402. Cf. K. Hamburger, *Philosophie der Dichter*, Stuttgart 1966, p. 232f.

7 Cf. SW 1, 856.

8 Cf. SW 1, 268:
Ich liebe dich, du sanftestes Gesetz,
an dem wir reiften, da wir mit ihm rangen;
du großes Heimweh, das wir nicht bezwangen,
du Wald, aus dem wir nie hinausgegangen,
du Lied, das wir mit jedem Schweigen sangen,
du dunkles Netz,
darin sich flüchtend die Gefühle fangen.

9 August Stahl in '*Vokabeln der Not*' usw. goes into the question of 'Gesicht' in some detail (pp. 92ff.) and for the most part quite accurately. I am not entirely convinced that 'Gesicht' is always as negative as Stahl would have it. See the further discussion of 'Gesicht' in the following chapter.

10 SW II, 323, *Der Anfänger*. Compare Malte's statement: 'Ich bin ein Anfänger in meinen eigenen Verhältnissen' (SW VI, 775). The crisis which forces this 'new beginning' is both a 'Krise des Anschauens' and one of the relation of 'Ich' and 'Gott'.

11 Malte's loss of any stable feeling or concept of his own identity is, in a sense, his inability to effect the transition between an understanding of the world which is no longer valid for him and 'Ein neues Leben voll neuer Bedeutungen' (SW VI, 775). In this new life, God has become both distant and enigmatic, as in the story of the Prodigal Son at the end of the book. Fülleborn, in his essay 'Form und Sinn der Aufzeichnungen des Malte Laurids Brigge' in *Unterscheidung und Bewahrung*, Berlin 1961, shows the connexion between Malte's disorientation and his inability to be more than an 'Anfänger' in his own circumstances: 'Es handelt sich also in den Aufzeichnungen um einen Prozeß, in dessen Verlauf die Grenzen des Ich von zwei Seiten durchbrochen werden, von den Tiefen der Außenwelt her und aus den Tiefen des eigenen Innern heraus... Diese fluktuierende Wirklichkeit, die Malte unter Schmerzen erfährt, weil er durch aus noch an den alten Benennungen und Unterscheidungen der Dinge hängt, bezeichnet Rilke im Spätwerk mit dem Namen "Welt".' The god of the *Stunden-Buch* being both 'innen' and 'außen', the loss of contact with him coincides with this assault on the 'Grenzen des Ich' from two directions.

12 SW II, 354. Compare this 'daß wir nicht sind' with the passage in the second Elegy:

> Seht, mir geschiehts, daß meine Hände einander
> inne werden oder daß mein gebrauchtes
> Gesicht in ihnen sich schont. Das giebt mir ein wenig
> Empfindung. Doch wer wagte darum schon zu *sein*? (SW I, 691)

where a similar non-existence appears, and also see the somewhat mannered fourteenth poem of the *Gedichte für Lou Albert-Lazard* (SW II, 224ff.): 'Sieh, ich bin nicht, aber wenn ich wäre...'

13 Malte hopes that his 'tiefes Elend' might of its own accord become 'Seligkeit' (SW VI, 756) but the necessary 'Umschlag' fails to occur within the novel.

14 SW II, 26. Cf. also the prose-description of the same 'Nacht der Frühlingswende' in B. 1906–7, 232f.

15 The same image occurs in the poem from the *Neue Gedichte*, *Der Ölbaumgarten* (SW I, 492f.):

> Warum ein Engel? Ach es kam die Nacht
> und blätterte gleichgültig in den Bäumen.
> Die Jünger rührten sich in ihren Träumen.
> Warum ein Engel? Ach es kam die Nacht.

Die Nacht, die kam, war keine ungemeine;
so gehen hunderte vorbei.
Da schlafen Hunde und da liegen Steine.
Ach eine traurige, ach irgendeine,
die wartet, bis es wieder morgen sei.

16 Hamburger, op. cit., p. 218: 'Aber es war hinzuweisen auf die Dominanz der dinglichen Kategorie..., weil sie zuletzt zusammenhängt mit der Problematik der Intentionalität als der Grundhaltung Rilkes'. Frau Hamburger tends to emphasise the conceptual structure of 'Intentionalität' at the expense of the emotional aspect, for a *feeling* of relatedness or separation may determine what aspects of the conceptual structure of 'Gegenüber-Sein' Rilke develops or excludes in a given context.

17 M. Betz, *Rilke in Frankreich*, trans. W. Reich, Wien 1938, p. 292.

18 Fülleborn, *Strukturproblem*, p. 63 and passim.

6 . THE HUMAN SITUATION

1 For a discussion of the term 'lyrisches Ich', see Käte Hamburger, *Die Logik der Dichtung*, 2nd ed., Stuttgart 1968, pp. 217–32.

2 Cf. H. O. Burger, 'Von der Struktureinheit klassischer und moderner deutscher Lyrik' in *Festschrift für Franz Rolf Schröder*, Heidelberg 1959, esp. pp. 230–3.

3 Wodtke, *Rilke und Klopstock*, p. 63.

4 Cf. SW I, 872f.

5 Cf. SW VI, 1624.

6 'Rilke's Essay *Puppen* and the Problem of the Divided Self', *German Life and Letters* vol. XXII, no. 4, July 1969 (reprinted in *Rilke in neuer Sicht*, ed. K. Hamburger, Stuttgart 1971) and 'Puppenseele and Weltinnenraum', *Seminar* vol. VI, no. 1, March 1970.

7 Cf. SW VI, 1067, passage beginning: 'Der Puppe gegenüber waren wir gezwungen, uns zu behaupten...'.

8 Ibid., 1069f., passage beginning: 'Es könnte ein Dichter unter die Herrschaft einer Marionette geraten...'.

9 Cf. ibid., 1624.

10 The poems entitled *Rodin* which come immediately before and after the fragment quoted in SW III make of the sculptor an almost divine manifestation in his aloofness, certainty and creative power. For all Rilke's pride in contact with his 'Meister', the immediate effect seems to have been more crushing than inspiring, as the whole of the fragment *Ein Verleugneter der eignen Hände...* shows.

11 SW VI, 710: 'Ich lerne sehen. Ich weiß nicht, woran es liegt, es geht alles tiefer in mich ein und bleibt nicht an der Stelle stehen, wo es sonst immer zu Ende war. Ich habe ein Inneres, von dem ich nicht wußte. Alles geht jetzt dorthin. Ich weiß nicht, was dort geschieht.'

12 Cf. *Ur-Geräusch*, SW VI, 1091, passage beginning: 'Indem ich mich so ausdrücke...

13 Cf. *An den Engel*, SW II, 48.

14 K. Hamburger, *Philosophie der Dichter*, p. 253.

15 SW VI, 1038: '...fragte er sich dringend, was ihm da geschehe, und fand fast gleich einen Ausdruck, der ihn befriedigte, vor sich hinsagend: er sei auf die andere Seite der Natur geraten.'

16 Cf. Fülleborn, op. cit., p. 73.

17 AB II, 453. Letter of 11 August 1924 to Nora Purtscher-Wydenbruck: 'Mir stellt es sich immer so dar, als ob unser gebräuchliches Bewußtsein die Spitze einer Pyramide bewohne, deren Basis in uns (und gewissermaßen unter uns) so völlig in die Breite geht, daß wir, je weiter wir in sie nieder-zulassen uns befähigt sehen, desto allgemeiner einbezogen erscheinen in die von Zeit und Raum unabhängigen Gegebenheiten des irdischen, des, im weitesten Begriffe, *weltischen* Daseins.'

18 Cf. Fülleborn, op. cit., p. 104.

19 Note especially the lines from *Verständigt mit abnehmender Natur*, SW II, 398:

> Den Engel stellt Gott vor wie eine Uhr,
> er mag im Herbst künftigen Herbst empfinden.
> Wir aber schlürfen mit den Winden
> und ziehen Spur und wischen Spur.

20 Malte's problematical relationship to his own past, both immediate and distant, appears in a number of ways:
'Ich will auch keinen Brief mehr schreiben. Wozu soll ich jemandem sagen, daß ich mich verändere? Wenn ich mich verändere, bleibe ich ja doch nicht der, der ich war, und bin ich etwas anderes als bisher, so ist klar, daß ich keine Bekannten habe. Und an fremde Leute, an Leute die mich nicht kennen, kann ich unmöglich schreiben.' (SW VI, 711)
'Hätte man wenigstens seine Erinnerungen. Aber wer hat die? Wäre die Kindheit da, sie ist wie vergraben. Vielleicht muß man alt sein, um an das alles heranreichen zu können.' (721)
'Ist es möglich, daß alle diese Menschen eine Vergangenheit, die nie gewesen ist, ganz genau kennen? Ist es möglich, daß alle Wirklichkeiten nichts sind für sie; daß ihr Leben abläuft, mit nichts verknüpft, wie eine Uhr in einem leeren Zimmer –? Ja, es ist möglich.' (727)

21 See Wodtke's remarks on 'der absolute Komparativ', op. cit., p. 108, especi-ally note 17. Just as the absolute comparative does not demand a specific object to be compared with, so the concept of 'Kenntlich-Sein' can take on an absolute sense. In a fragment of 1909 the overcoming of 'Unkenntlichkeit' through the sheer intensity of pain seems to be absolute and in no need of any observer to confirm it:

> Wehtag, der wie eine Wunde klafft,
> hohler wird das Haus von ihrem Heulen,
> und sie drängt an alle Porphyrsäulen
> aufgerissen ihre Schwangerschaft.
> Und sie wirft sich wie ein Innenbrand
> aufwärtsschlagend in die Fensternischen
> und sie möchte sich mit Haar vermischen
> überhängt und unerkannt.

> Aber löschte sie sich durch ein Wunder
> wirklich unter Haar und Händen aus,
> stünde nicht ihr treibender und runder
> Leib aus der Unkenntlichkeit hinaus –?   (SW II, 371)

22 Cf. K. Hamburger, op. cit., p. 250f.

7 . THE MODES OF TRANSCENDENCE

1 K. Hamburger, *Philosophie der Dichter*, p. 179.

2 When Fülleborn criticises the 'Ratio' active in Rilke's poetry he says: 'Sie muß subjektiver Willkür und Unverbindlichkeit verfallen oder Richte und Maß von außen empfangen, z. B. eben von der Theologie in Form einer "Synthesis a priori"' (*Strukturproblem*, p. 51). Such a 'Synthesis a priori', when applied to the practice of literary criticism, is similar to the basic assumptions of Freudian criticism. In each case a relationship – of the rational to the irrational or the conscious to the subconscious – is assumed *a priori*. If the work conforms explicitly to these preconceptions, well and good. If however for want of information within the work these conditions do not appear to pertain, then the 'Synthesis a priori' supplies them in terms of what *ought* to be there if the presuppositions are correct. Such an approach to poetry is disturbingly prescriptive.

3 While there is no doubt that Mason has written some of the best Rilke-criticism, the message of *Der Zopf des Münchhausen* seems to be that Rilke's soul and those of his readers would be less endangered had he not written poetry at all.

4 Wodtke, op. cit., p. 63, Hamburger, op. cit., p. 220f.

5 Marvin Farber, *Phenomenology and Existence*, New York 1967, p. 154.

6 For the first one might take the god of the *Stunden-Buch*, the god of the story of the Prodigal Son in *Malte* or the god of the *Brief des Jungen Arbeiters*. For the second, one could have 'der Engel Ordnungen' or any of the instances where Rilke invokes 'Götter', as in *So angestrengt wider die starke Nacht*. The third possibility is given in *Ur-Geräusch* and elsewhere. 'A superior spiritual order' might be found 'im mythischen Raum des Geistes' (Wodtke, op. cit., p. 154). Farber's final possibility is also represented in Rilke's work – sometimes in the region 'hinter den Sternen', sometimes simply as 'das uns Unerfahrbare'.

7 'Verbindlichkeit' is certainly desirable in many contexts outside of art. But the aesthetic element, by which the beautiful or fascinating is not necessarily the same as the verifiably true, the logically correct or the socially acceptable, is only incidental to philosophy while it is essential to poetry. One may of course treat the contents of poetry as philosophy within certain limits, but just as it would be unfair to attack Fichte's or Hegel's thought on the grounds of the undeniable ugliness of their language, so it is equally silly to demand that poetry forfeit that element of play and decorativeness which makes it often 'unverbindlich' if one wishes to treat it as something else.

8 BT, 339.

9 Cf. SW II, 955ff. See also the *Briefwechsel mit Benvenuta*, Esslingen 1954,

where Rilke takes back most of the doctrines of love which the *Gedichte an die Nacht* put forward.

10 Fülleborn, op. cit., p. 272.

11 Ibid., p. 82.

12 Ibid., p. 235.

13 AB I, 276f.

14 Cf. B. 1907–14, 176ff., where Rilke speaks of Gaspara Stampa, Louise Labé and Marianna Alcoforado, and the recapitulation of these themes in the first *Duineser Elegie*.

15 Rilke's two *Narziß* poems are from the period of the *Gedichte an die Nacht* (SW II, 56f.) and the concept of the 'Künstler-Gott' provides a resounding conclusion to the *Florenzer Tagebuch* of 1899 (TF, 139f.). Rilke's Narziß is very much in the same tradition as Mallarmé's Hérodiade and Valéry's Narcisse. It is interesting to note that Karin Wais, *Studien zu Rilkes Valéry-Übertragungen*, Tübingen 1967, places Rilke's first encounter with Valéry's work in the year 1921, eight years after the Narziß-poems were written.

16 M. Farber, op. cit., says on this point: 'There is a time-honoured illusion to the effect that one who views the eternal is eternal. Descartes illustrated this interesting type of wishful thinking in his own way, in connection with the idea of a perfect being. Unfortunately, there is no such convenient shortcut to perceptual felicity, unless it were also true that the proposition "The Empire State Building is tall" is therefore a tall proposition.' Fallacious or not, this is essentially the idea behind the dialectic of 'Kenntlich-/Unkenntlich-Sein'. By being directed towards a transcendent object, the self overcomes its own 'Unkenntlichkeit'. When this process is complete, 'die vorausgeschickten Himmel' have, as it were, been overtaken.

17 *Über den Dichter* is ambitious because Rilke there attempts a synthesis which is not borne out by the poetry of the next years, notably the *Gedichte an die Nacht*. *Über den Dichter*, written in Duino in February 1912 (SW VI, 1473f.) presents 'das Verhältnis des Dichters im Bestehenden' in the form of an 'Ausgleich': 'Während seine Umgebung sich immer wieder mit dem greifbaren Nächsten einließ und es überwand, unterhielt seine Stimme die Beziehung zum Weitesten, knüpfte uns daran an, bis es uns zog' (1035). The poet then, although unconcerned about the boat and those in it, nevertheless succeeds – almost unintentionally, it seems – in pulling the boat along. The conflict between 'das Menschliche' and 'das Engelische', which is prominent in the *Gedichte an die Nacht* is thus neatly solved *avant la lettre*. The poet's isolation from his surroundings is not a limitation, because, apparently without meaning to, he enables the ship to keep moving and his song, without being directed to the crew, is meaningful to them and speaks, in a sense, for all.

18 M. Farber, op. cit., p. 154.

19 Cf. Wodtke, op. cit., p. 96.

20 AB I, 277.

21 SW II, 957:   Schau ich aber leise auf, so heilt
mir die Welt am milderen Gesichte –
oh so war ja doch, daß ich verzichte,
allen Engeln noch nicht mitgeteilt.

22 B. Allemann, *Zeit und Figur*, Pfullingen 1961, pp. 9ff., 25ff., and passim.
23 As the power of empathy fluctuates and 'Verwandlungen' succeed one another, so the images by which Rilke represents the limits of the self are in constant change. P. Washburn Shaw, *Rilke, Valéry and Yeats*, New Jersey 1964, gives some extraordinarily sensitive interpretations of the interaction of the various physical senses in the self of a number of Rilke's poems. As she does not abstract to such problems as 'Gegenständlichkeit' or take up the division of the self into 'Teil und Gegenteil' her results have little to do with the issues raised in this book. Her two chapters on Rilke do represent, however, a fruitful and quite different way of approaching the problem of the self in Rilke's poetry.
24 A. Stahl, '*Vokabeln der Not*' usw., pp. 73–104.
25 BM, 280.
26 Fülleborn, op. cit., pp. 290ff.
27 Quoted by Marie-Jeanne Durry, *Guillaume Apollinaire, Alcools 1*, Paris 1956, p. 47.
28 Apollinaire, *Œuvres poétiques*, Pléiade Paris 1956, p. 74f.
29 K. Jaspers, *Philosophie I*, Berlin 1956, p. 39.
30 Ibid., p. 38.
31 *Die Struktur der modernen Lyrik*, rowohlts deutsche enzyklopädie, Hamburg 1956, see especially pp. 46ff.
32 Jaspers, op. cit., p. 40.
33 Hamburger, op. cit., p. 250.
34 M. Betz, *Rilke in Franreich*, Wien 1938, p. 291.
35 Jaspers, op. cit., p. 51.

8 . AN APPROACH TO RILKE

1 E. Simenauer, *Rainer Maria Rilke – Legende und Mythos*, Frankfurt a.M. 1956, pp. 108–13.
2 K. A. J. Batterby, *Rilke and France*, Oxford 1966, pp. 20–1.
3 Ibid., p. 21.
4 B. Allemann, *Zeit und Figur*, p. 100.
5 A. Stephens, *The Problem of Completeness in Rilke's Poetry 1922–1926*, Oxford German Studies IV, 1969.
6 BLA-S, p. 88.
7 BLA-S, p. 85.
8 Rimbaud, *Œuvres Complètes*, Pléiade, Paris 1963, p. 270.
9 Ibid.
10 Cf. SW II, 490: 'Ist es nicht wie Atmen, dieses stete/Wechselspiel von Zauber und Verzicht...' Here one should note that the temporary renunciation of the magic circle means firstly that the 'lyrisches Ich' is exposed and unprotected, but secondly that this may be the starting point for another attempt at transcendence.
11 BLA-S, p. 86.

BIBLIOGRAPHY

A. WORKS AND LETTERS OF RAINER MARIA RILKE

Sämtliche Werke, ed. Ernst Zinn, 6 vols. 1955–1967, Wiesbaden/Frankfurt am Main.

Werke, Insel Verlag, Frankfurt am Main, 1966.

Tagebücher aus der Frühzeit, ed. Ruth Sieber-Rilke and C. Sieber, Leipzig 1942.

Gesammelte Briefe, ed. Ruth Sieber-Rilke and C. Sieber, Leipzig 1936–1939.

Briefe, 2 vols., ed. K. Altheim, Wiesbaden 1950.

Briefe und Tagebücher aus der Frühzeit 1899–1902, Leipzig 1931.

Briefe aus den Jahren 1902–1906
1906–1907
1907–1914
1914–1921
Briefe aus Muzot   1921–1926, all ed. Ruth Sieber-Rilke and C. Sieber, Leipzig 1930–1937.

Briefe an seinen Verleger 1996–1926, ed. Ruth Sieber-Rilke and C. Sieber, Leipzig 1934.

Lettres à Rodin, Paris 1931.

Briefe an einen jungen Dichter, Insel Bücherei 406, Leipzig 1944.

R. M. Rilke, Lou Andreas-Salomé – Briefwechsel, ed. Ernst Pfeiffer, 1 vol., Zürich/Wiesbaden 1952.

R. M. Rilke und Marie von Thurn und Taxis – Breifwechsel, ed. Ernst Zinn, 2 vols., Zürich/Wiesbaden 1951.

R. M. Rilke, Katharina Kippenberg – Briefwechsel, ed. B. von Bomhard, Wiesbaden 1954.

Rainer Maria Rilke et Merline – Correspondance 1920–1926, ed. D. Bassermann, Zürich 1954.

R. M. Rilke, Briefwechsel mit Benvenuta, ed. Magda von Hattingberg, Esslingen 1954.

Lettres milanaises 1921–1926, intr. René Lang, Paris 1956.

Freundschaft mit Rainer Maria Rilke, Begegnungen – Gespräche – Briefe und Aufzeichnungen, mitgeteilt durch Elya Maria Nevar, Bern-Bümpliz 1946.

B. GENERAL STUDIES ON RILKE

For a fuller bibliography of Rilke-criticism the reader is referred to:

Ritzer, W., *Rainer Maria Rilke. Bibliographie,* Wien 1951.

Insel Almanach auf das Jahr 1967, Rainer Maria Rilke zum vierzigsten Todestag –
'*Die Rilke-Kritik 1950–1966*' von Klaus W. Jonas, pp. 94–117.

Andreas-Salomé, Lou, *Rainer Maria Rilke,* Leipzig 1928.

Angelloz, J.-F., *R. M. Rilke – L'évolution spirituelle du poète*, Paris 1936.

Betz, M., *Rilke vivant – souvenirs, lettres, entretiens*. Paris 1936.

Bollnow, O. F., *Rilke*, 2nd augmented ed., Stuttgart 1956.

Buddeberg, Else, *Rainer Maria Rilke – Eine innere Biographie*. Stuttgart 1950.

Butler, E. M., *R. M. Rilke*, 2nd ed., Cambridge 1946.

Carlsson, Anni, *Gesang ist Dasein – Rilkes geistiger Weg nach Muȥot*, Hamburg 1949.

Dehn, F., *Rainer Maria Rilke und sein Werk*, Leipzig, n/d.

Günther, W., *Weltinnenraum – Die Dichtung Rainer Maria Rilkes, ȥweite durchgesehene und stark vermehrte Auflage*, Berlin 1952.

Heerikhuizen, F. W. van, *R. M. Rilke – His Life and Work*, trans. F. G. Renier and Ann Cliff, London 1951.

Holthusen, H.-E., *Rainer Maria Rilke in Selbstȥeugnissen und Bilddokumenten*, rowohlts monographien, Hamburg 1962.

Kippenberg, Katharina, *Rainer Maria Rilke – Ein Beitrag*, 4th ed., Wiesbaden 1948.

Krämer, R., *Der sensitive Mensch. Versuch einer Darstellung am Bilde des Dichters R. M. Rilke*, Mainz/Wiesbaden 1954.

Mandel, S., *Rainer Maria Rilke – The Poetic Instinct*. Carbondale 1965.

Mason, E. C., *Lebenshaltung und Symbolik bei Rainer Maria Rilke*, Oxford 1964.

Mason, E. C., *Rilke*, Edinburgh and London 1963, in series 'Writers and Critics'.

Peters, H. F., *Rainer Maria Rilke: Masks and the Man*. Seattle 1960.

C. SPECIFIC STUDIES

Allemann, B., *Zeit und Figur beim späten Rilke*, Pfullingen 1961.

Bassermann, D., *Der andere Rilke*, ed. H. Mörchen, Bad Homburg 1961.

Bassermann, D., *Der späte Rilke*, 2nd ed., Essen/Freiburg i. Br. 1948.

Batterby, K., *Rilke and France*, London 1966.

Belmore, H. W., *Rilke's Craftsmanship*, Oxford 1954.

Berendt, H., *Rainer Maria Rilkes 'Neue Gedichte'*, Bonn 1957.

Betz, M., *Rilke in Frankreich*, trans. W. Reich, Wien/Leipzig/Zürich 1938.

Blume, B., 'Ding und Ich in Rilkes *Neue Gedichte*', *MLN* 1967, April 1952.

Bollnow, O. F., *Unruhe und Geborgenheit*, Stuttgart 1953.

Bowra, C. M., *The Heritage of Symbolism*, London 1943.

Bradley, B. L., *Rainer Maria Rilkes 'Neue Gedichte'*, Bern/München 1967.

Brecht, F. J., *Schicksal und Auftrag des Menschen*, München 1949.

Buddeberg, E., *Denken und Dichten des Seins*, Stuttgart 1956.

Buddeberg, E., *Die 'Duineser Elegien' R. M. Rilkes*, Karlsruhe 1948.

Buddeberg, E., *Kunst und Existenȥ im Spätwerk Rilkes*, Karlsruhe 1948.

Demetz, P., 'In Sachen Rilke', *Insel-Almanach auf das Jahr 1967*.

Emde, U., *Rilke und Rodin*, Marburg/Lahn 1949.

Friedrich, H., *Die Struktur der modernen Lyrik*, Hamburg 1956.

Fülleborn, U., 'Form und Sinn der *Aufzeichnungen des Malte Laurids Brigge*', in *Unterscheidung und Bewahrung*, Berlin 1961.

Fülleborn, U., 'Zur magischen Gebärdensprache des späten Rilke', *Euphorion Sonderheft* 1955.

Fülleborn, U., *Das Strukturproblem der späten Lyrik Rilkes*, Heidelberg 1960.

Gebser, J., *Rilke und Spanien*, 2nd ed., Zürich 1946.

Goertz, H., *Frankreich und das Erlebnis der Form im Werke Rainer Maria Rilkes*, Stuttgart 1932.

Goth, M., *The Myth of Narcissus in the Works of Rilke and Valéry*, Wisconsin Studies in Contemporary Literature 7, 1966.

Gray, R., 'Rilke', in *The German Tradition in Literature 1871–1945*, Cambridge 1965.

Guardini, R., *R. M. Rilkes Deutung des Daseins*, München 1953.

Hamburger, K., 'Die phänomenologische Struktur der Dichtung Rilkes', in *Philosophie der Dichter*, Stuttgart 1966.

Heftrich, E., *Die Philosophie und Rilke*, Freiburg/München 1962.

Heidegger, M., 'Wozu Dichter?', in *Holzwege*, Frankfurt a.M. 1957.

Heller, E., 'Rilke and Nietzsche', in *The Disinherited Mind*, New York 1957.

Hermann, A., *Rilkes ägyptische Gesichte*, Darmstadt 1966.

Holthusen, H. E., *Der späte Rilke*, Zürich 1949.

Holthusen, H. E., 'Der späte Rilke', *Merkur* Hft 8, 1948.

Holthusen, H. E., 'Rilkes mythische Wendung', *Hochland* 37, 1939.

Holthusen, H. E., *Rilkes 'Sonette an Orpheus'*, Munchen 1937.

Holthusen, H. E., 'Rainer Maria Rilkes letzte Jahre', in *Der unbehauste Mensch*, München 1951.

Huder, W., 'Umkehr der Räume', *Welt und Wort* 13, 1958.

Jonas, K. W. and Schnack, I., 'R. M. Rilke's Manuscripts in German and Austrian collections', *Monatshefte* LVI 1964.

Kanzog, K., 'Wortbildwahl und phallisches Motiv bei R. M. Rilke', *ZDPh*. 76, 1957.

Kayser, W., 'Eine unbekannte Prosaskizze von R. M. Rilke', in *Trivium* 1947.

Kaufmann, F., 'Sprache als Schöpfung', *Zeitschrift für Asthetik* 28, 1934.

Kaufmann, W., *The Owl and the Nightingale*, London 1960.

Kohlschmidt, W., *Rilke-Interpretationen*, Lahr 1948.

Kuhn, H., 'Rilke und Rilke-Literatur', in *Dvjs*. Hft. 1, 1939.

Kunisch, H., *Rainer Maria Rilke und die Dinge*, Köln 1946.

Liedler, L., Das Rilke-Problem, *Plan 2*, Wien 1947.

Mason, E. C., 'Zur Entstehung und Deutung von Rilkes "Stunden-Buch"', in *Exzentrische Bahnen*, Göttingen 1963.

Mason, E. C., 'Rilkes magischer Existentialismus', *Orbis Litterarum 2*, 1956.

Mason, E. C., *Der Zopf des Münchhausen*, Einsiedeln 1949.

Mason, E. C., *Rilke, Europe and the English-speaking World*, Cambridge 1961.

Mayer, G., *Rilke und Kassner*, Bonn 1960.

Meyer, H., 'Die Verwandlung des Sichtbaren', in *Zarte Empirie*, Stuttgart 1963.

Meyer, H., 'Rilkes Cézanne-Erlebnis', in *Zarte Empirie*, Stuttgart 1963.

Mövius, R., *Rainer Maria Rilkes 'Stunden-Buch'*, Leipzig 1937.

Peters, H. F., 'The Space-Metaphors in Rilke's Poetry', *GR* 24, 1949.

Rehm, W., *Orpheus – Der Dichter und die Toten*, Düsseldorf 1950.

SanLazzaro, C. di, 'Die Nacht in der Persönlichkeit und Dichtung Rilkes', *ZDPh.* 65, 1940.

Schoolfield, G. C., 'Late Rilke and a late Rilke Poem', *Festschrift für B. Blume*, Göttingen 1967.

Shaw, P. W., *Rilke, Valéry and Yeats*, New Jersey 1964.

Singer, H., *Rilke und Hölderlin*, Köln/Graz 1957.

Stahl, A., '*Vokabeln der Not' und 'Früchte der Tröstung'*, Heidelberg 1967.

Stahl, E. L., *Creativity. A Theme from 'Faust' and the 'Duineser Elegien'*, Oxford 1961.

Stahl, E. L., *Rainer Maria Rilkes 'Duineser Elegien'*, B.G.T. Oxford 1965.

Steiner, J., 'Gegenwind', *Insel-Almanach auf das Jahr 1967*.

Steiner, J., *R. M. Rilkes 'Duineser Elegien'*, Bern/München 1962.

Steiner, J., 'Das Motiv der Puppe bei Rilke', in *Kleists Aufsatz über das Marionettentheater*, Berlin 1967.

Stephens, A., 'Rilke's Essay "Puppen" and the Problem of the Divided Self', *GLL* July 1969.

Stephens, A., 'The Problem of Completeness in Rilke's Poetry 1922–1926', *Oxford German Studies* vol. 4.

Storck, J. W., 'Wortkerne und Dinge', *Akzente* 4, 1957.

Wais, K., *Studien zu Rilkes Valéry-Übertragungen*, Tübingen 1967.

Weigand, H. D., 'Rilkes "*Archaischer Torso Apollos*"', *Monatshefte* 51, 1959.

Wodtke, F. W., *Rilke und Klopstock*, Kiel 1948.

Wodtke, F. W., 'Das Problem der Sprache beim späten Rilke', *Orbis Litterarum* 2, 1956.

Wolfram, J., 'Essai sur le silence dans les poèmes français de R. M. Rilke', *Revue des lettres modernes* 6, 1959.

INDEX

INDEX

INDEX